ID0422390

Advance Praise

"How successful we are in educating the next generation of Americans will determine our nation's future. This collection of essays from leading conservative minds is the conversation-starter we need. *How to Educate an American* is a welcome contribution to our understanding of what ails our schools and how to fix them."

—**Jeb Bush,** 43rd Governor of Florida

"It is a commonplace to observe that our national success depends in large part on the effectiveness of our K-12 education system. There the agreement ends, and we have sharp differences about how to reshape and improve that system. Regardless of point of view, those who want to enter this debate owe it to themselves to absorb the facts and reflect on the insights of this remarkable collection of thought leaders."

—**Mitchell E. Daniels, Jr.,** president of Purdue University and Indiana's 49th Governor

"A thorough, thoughtful, and critical attempt to bring conservative thought into a central and productive relationship with American schools. It begs for an equally deep response."

—**Richard Elmore**, research professor, Harvard Graduate School of Education

"For many years, conservatives have struggled to explain just what we're 'for' when it comes to education. In this invaluable volume, Petrilli and Finn have assembled a dazzling array of conservative thought leaders to answer that question. Whether a reader is seeking conservative counsel or simply trying to understand how conservatives think about schooling, this collection of lucid, challenging, and immensely readable essays is just the ticket."

—**Frederick M. Hess,** director of Education Policy Studies at the American Enterprise Institute

"These essays seek to grapple with a set of important topics, and they do so in a variety of interesting and challenging ways. The contributors don't seek to peddle a new orthodoxy; they challenge us to think about a fundamental civic challenge."

—**William Kristol**, director, Defending Democracy Together

"This volume presents an opportunity to access in one source a plethora of views on a conservative vision and its rationale for American education. Some permit a provocative contrast with politically liberal views; some would leave education to the school and economic marketplace and others to the needs of particular groups of students with educational needs. This provides considerable diversity of perspectives for a single volume on *How to Educate an American*."

—**Henry M. Levin**, David Jacks Professor, Emeritus, of Higher Education and Economics, Stanford University and William H. Kilpatrick Professor, Emeritus, of Economics and Education, Teachers College, Columbia University

"Many of the most important policy debates for the future of America are getting no oxygen right now. In *How to Educate an American* we get access to a dozen and a half big arguments, and you should hear every one of them."

—**Ben Sasse**, United States Senator from Nebraska

HOW TO EDUCATE AN AMERICAN

HOW TO EDUCATE AN AMERICAN

THE CONSERVATIVE VISION FOR TOMORROW'S SCHOOLS

Edited by

Michael J. Petrilli and
Chester E. Finn, Jr.

TEMPLETON PRESS

Templeton Press
300 Conshohocken State Road, Suite 500
West Conshohocken, PA 19428
www.templetonpress.org

Set in Arnhem Blond by Gopa & Ted2, Inc.

Library of Congress Control Number: 2019954886

ISBN-13: 978-1-59947-569-1 (cloth: alk. paper)
ISBN-13: 978-1-59947-570-7 (ebook)

This paper meets the requirements of ANSI/NISO Z39.48-1992
(Permanence of Paper).
A catalogue record for this book is available from the Library of Congress.

20 21 22 23 24 10 9 8 7 6 5 4 3 2 1

Printed in the United States of America.

Contents

Preface

by Senator Lamar Alexander

I WAS PARTICIPATING in a humdrum educators' roundtable in Buffalo, New York, in 1988 when "Monk" Malloy, president of the University of Notre Dame, asked this question: "What is the purpose of a *public* school?"

There was a long silence until finally Albert Shanker, president of the American Federation of Teachers, proposed this answer: "The public school was created for the purpose of teaching immigrant children reading, writing, and arithmetic and what it means to be an American with the hope that they would then go home and teach their parents."

The reason to read this book is to judge for yourself whether the twenty-two conservative luminaries who wrote its chapters have produced a better answer today to Malloy's question than Albert Shanker did thirty years ago.

Shanker was a patriot—an old-fashioned, anticommunist, Hubert Humphrey–liberal Democrat union organizer whose parents had immigrated from Poland. So he and this book's conservative writers agreed on one thing: In coeditor Chester Finn's words, "Schools should inculcate a solid understanding of and appreciation for why America exists and what it stands for, to transmit history and civics and, yes, a positive attitude toward its strengths as well as a reasoned commitment to addressing its weakness." Or, in Shanker's words, "Public schools played a big role in holding our nation together. They brought together children of different races, languages, religions, and cultures and gave them a common language and a sense of common purpose. We have not outgrown our need for this; far from it."

Today, there is elite disdain for such Americanism. But this is not a popular attitude. Most audiences applaud and some come to their feet when I say, "We should teach more United States history in our schools so our children can grow up knowing what it means to be an American." There is bipartisan support for this sentiment. After September 11, 2001, George W. Bush and Al Gore both reminded the nation that principles create the American character—not considerations of race, religion, or national origin. In my first address to the US Senate, I introduced a bill to create summer academies for outstanding students and teachers of US history. Within a day, Senator Ted Kennedy had rounded up nearly twenty Democratic cosponsors without my asking. Especially in today's internet democracy, an era Peggy Noonan calls "The Great Estrangement," Americans are hungry for institutions that unite. I suspect that most would agree that it would be a good idea to begin each school day with a student leading the Pledge of Allegiance and then giving his or her version of what it means to be an American.

According to education historian Patricia Graham, "Schools in America have danced to different drummers through their long history"— and schools have a very long history. Hunter-gatherer "play schools" helped children learn to survive. Sumerian schools taught scribes to help a culture survive. During the Agricultural and Industrial Revolutions, schools taught youngsters to work and got them out from under their parents' feet. Sociologist James Coleman said that in early America, schools helped parents do what parents could not do as well. That was especially true for teaching literacy. Graham says, "Now the drumbeat demands that all children achieve academically at a high level and the measure of that achievement is tests."

This book's conservative writers would temper that drumbeat with a second great conservative goal—in the coeditors' words, "to restore character, virtue, and morality to the head of the education table where they belong." This is no new thought. Plato said schools should create good men who act nobly. Thomas Jefferson believed that a democracy granting broad liberties needed institutions instilling moral restraint. But Yuval Levin's essay suggests why character education does not rise so easily on a liberal list of priorities: progressive education wants to liberate the student to be himself or herself, Levin writes, while conservative education wants to form the student to be better suited to the responsibilities of citizenship.

After embracing citizenship and character, the book's authors diverge in their emphases. Several show a healthy respect for school choice but also for its limits. There is a shout-out for career and technical education. To me, Bill Bennett's chapter is the most persuasive. He argues that content must be at the center of any conservative consensus on education. He reminds us that in the 1980s and 1990s, conservatives were leading a content crusade with E. D. Hirsch and Governors John Engler, Tommy Thompson, and Jeb Bush as well as Bennett himself as chief architects. This movement was called (shall we whisper it?) "Common Core." This state-by-state reformation of school standards and curricula was well underway when the Obama administration tried to push it faster by making Common Core a quasi-federal mandate. Republicans imagined black helicopters flying. What conservatives had invented, many Republican legislators had voted into state law, and hundreds of thousands of classroom teachers in forty-five states expected they'd be teaching was suddenly condemned and abandoned . . . by conservatives.

This abandonment was less complete than it would appear. Last year, our daughter's family lived with us in Tennessee while her home was being remodeled. She placed two sons in a nearby mountain elementary school. When the boys returned home to their Westchester County, New York, public school, I asked, "Did they have trouble adjusting?" "Nope," she said. "Common Core here. Common Core there." Many states simply renamed Common Core to avoid political flak and charged ahead. One advocate told me, "We won. But we're not allowed to say so."

The backlash to Common Core brings me to the most obvious mission missing from this volume's conservative agenda: local control of schools. America was created community by community. The initiative for American public schools was entirely at the local level, Marc Tucker has written. He termed this an "accident of localism."

I have spent much of my public life trying to preserve this localism. To begin with, federalism—the dispersal of central authority—is a crucial tenet of American liberty. Our revolution, after all, was mostly about distaste for a king. As a practical matter, my experience is that those governing education from a distance have good intentions but limited capacity and that schools can be only as good as parents, teachers, and citizens in a community want them to be. The saga of Common Core is the greatest proof of this pudding. Here was a conservative crusade—new rigor in what students needed to know—blown up by conservatives' fear that Washington, DC, was forcing them to do it. The Common Core federal directive was piled on top of other dictates from Presidents Bill Clinton, George W. Bush, and Barack Obama on how to define standards, teaching, tests, curricula, and remedies for low-performing schools. Almost everyone in public schools became sick of Washington telling them what to do. So, in 2015, teacher unions and governors united to help Congress enact the "Every Student Succeeds Act," which the *Wall Street Journal* said was "the largest devolution of federal control to the states in a quarter century."

Now, after the rise and fall of a national school board, our one hundred thousand public schools have about the same balance between federal leadership and state and local autonomy that existed during the George H. W. Bush administration. Once again, we have it about right. Thirty years ago, President Bush and the governors set the nation's first national education goals and then launched an "America 2000" initiative to help states meet those goals by creating voluntary standards, voluntary tests, and start-from-scratch schools. This was done the hard way, state by state and community by community—not by federal mandates. Today's environment is ripe for a revival of a content-based conservative consensus, or in Bill Bennett's words "a great relearning," as the best way for our public schools to help our country get where we want it to go. But this time, let's avoid the lure of federal mandates and do the job the American Way: state by state, community by community.

Acknowledgments

THIS BOOK IS the work of many hands and brains, beginning with the fantastic authors (and in a couple of cases coauthors) who contributed thoughtful, wide-ranging, and insightful essays as well as participating in a yearlong series of live-audience and online events that included much provocative discussion. (They also endured our pushy editing!) Deep and sincere thanks to Michael Barone, William J. Bennett, Arthur C. Brooks (and Nathan Thompson), Mona Charen, Eliot Cohen, William Damon, Nicholas Eberstadt, Robert P. George, Jonah Goldberg, Kay S. Hymowitz, Yuval Levin, Heather Mac Donald, Adam Meyerson (and Adam Kissel), Rod Paige (also a Fordham Institute trustee), Ramesh Ponnuru, Naomi Schaefer Riley, Ian Rowe, and Peter Wehner. Old friend, mentor, and leading education policymaker Senator Lamar Alexander supplied encouragement, constructive back-and-forth, and—as is obvious in these pages—a wise and provocative preface.

Also aiding us were more individuals than we can name, but allow us at least to recognize the contributions of Evan Abramsky, Jack Butler, Abigail Guidera, and Cecilia Joy Perez at the American Enterprise Institute; Jane Hale at Princeton University; Vita Dougherty; Laura Brownlee and Laura Davis at the Philanthropy Roundtable; Christopher Mohrman and Karen Nussle at Conservative Leaders for Education; and David Cleary and Liz Wolgemuth from Senator Alexander's team.

A massive thank-you to our friends, colleagues, and partners on this endeavor at the DC outpost of the Hoover Institution, particularly

Mike Franc, Paige Mathes, and Erin Nichols, who graciously opened their doors to host ten important and often riveting events.

At our home base, the Thomas B. Fordham Institute, this project was enhanced and supported in a thousand ways by Rachel Holterback, Gary LaBelle, Jessie McBirney, Victoria McDougald, Caryn Morgan, Jeff Murray, Olivia Piontek, Alyssa Schwenk, Brandon Wright, and many others, including a host of extraordinary interns.

We couldn't have done it without the financial assistance of the Kern Family Foundation (special thanks to Beth Purvis, Jim Rahn, Jordan Ryder, Kirstin Werner, and Stasia Zwisler), who swiftly saw the importance of this project and have supported it in so many ways, as well as that of our sister organization, the Thomas B. Fordham Foundation.

We also owe deep appreciation to the entire team at Templeton Press, including ace publisher Susan Arellano, who recognized the venture's value and potential impact, improved it along the way, and meticulously ushered it into production with the help of a first-rate team including (but certainly not limited to) Angelina Horst, Dan Reilly, and Trish Vergilio.

Indebted as we are to so many others, we—and the authors—are responsible for all that follows.

How to Educate an American

Introduction

TIME TO RENGAGE

by Michael J. Petrilli and Chester E. Finn, Jr.

W E CANNOT BE sure whether the national education reform movement that roared across America from *A Nation at Risk* (1983) until recently has halted or simply paused. Reform, however, is definitely at a low ebb—and most student scores and other outcome measures remain flatter at lower levels than the country needs. While reform efforts still inch along in some states and communities, they appear to inch backward almost as often. This deceleration creates a discouraging yet valuable moment for everyone, conservatives included, to contemplate the future of American education while considering past successes and earlier mistakes.

We applaud the successes. Schools today are far more often judged by their results and the gains made by their pupils than by the money spent on them or the programmatic bells and whistles that they offer. Standards and expectations are higher almost everywhere. Achievement has risen a bit, at least in the earlier grades, and especially for the lowest performers. Some learning gaps are narrower, and many opportunities are wider. Career and technical education is enjoying something of a revival. Millions more families have options for their children's education, as it's no longer taken for granted that students will attend the district-operated public schools closest to their homes.

As we celebrate these accomplishments, we should also reflect on how they came about. Many of their driving ideas were conservative in origin, although making them happen typically entailed bipartisanship and compromise, as Democrats and Republicans, left and right (but mostly center-left and center-right), found common ground on behalf of big changes in a deeply entrenched system that was not successfully serving many of their children or the society in which they live. Among the conservative leaders who championed such reforms, the majority were governors and legislators, but key roles were also played by presidents from Ronald Reagan through the Bushes 41 and 43, teaming up with equity-minded progressives, and often with business and civil rights groups that found it possible to link arms. The shared goal was to help more young Americans find opportunity and success, thus addressing conservatives' desire for better outcomes and more choices along with progressives' desire to make the system fairer and close long-standing learning gaps.

Bipartisanship is in tatters today in many realms of our national life, and that's a big problem on countless fronts. Yet it's also an opportunity for conservatives to recognize that the gains made with bipartisanship's help meant suppressing some important differences and neglecting some vital elements of schooling in particular and education in general. As Yuval Levin argues in this volume, it's time to unmask those differences, understand what's been neglected or distorted, address some troubling education voids, and see if we can renegotiate terms before the next wave of reform. Even if we cannot immediately renegotiate, we should at least be able to get our own goals and priorities straight. We suspect that others, including people who don't generally call themselves conservative, will nod in agreement with many of those goals, such as the strengthening of children's knowledge, character, motivation, and civic readiness for which many of the following essays call. But conservatives themselves may benefit from thoughtful engagement with others on the goals that are not fully shared.

That's essential because, as Robby George argues in an essay that follows, "viewpoint diversity" leads to better understanding of the truth. Conservatives have important truths to speak that often aren't heard (or heeded) in discussions of public education—sometimes because conservatives have circumscribed their own truth-seeking behind a wall labeled "school choice" and have withdrawn their own children into schools that suit them without paying great heed to the education of others or the broader needs of the country we all inhabit. Today's reform hiatus creates a space in which conservatives can refresh their own thinking about schooling's proper role and the contents of a first-rate education.

For America to have the prosperous, secure, and vibrant future that we all want, and for our children and grandchildren to enjoy their full measure of that future while contributing their very best to it, we need a primary-secondary education system that delivers the goods—and delivers them for everyone, not just those with the means to procure something special for their own daughters and sons.

For conservatives to absent themselves from the conversation about how to bring about that future, and retreat into enclaves and echo chambers of their own while mouthing (or earnestly insisting on) the policy nostrums of the 1990s, is not just irresponsible. It also yields the shaping of that future to those who now term themselves "progressives." Is there a conservative alive today who actually welcomes that prospect?

We do not. And so, with the help of the Kern Family Foundation, which supported this venture; the Hoover Institution, which cohosted the lively and provocative speaker events that launched it; and the Templeton Press, which saw the value of publishing the speakers' analyses and ideas, we invited eighteen prominent, right-thinking leaders to join with us in a major act of refreshment. (Two of them invited colleagues to join us as coauthors.)

For this endeavor, we did not turn to our usual friends in the small universe of right-of-center education-policy wonkdom (though we were honored to include two prominent former education secretaries, both friends of ours, plus a third—also a friend—who graced this volume with its wise preface). For the most part, we already know what our fellow wonks think—and we weren't looking for the nuts and bolts of detailed policy proposals. We sought instead for big thinkers—public intellectuals and scholars whose work includes education but doesn't focus on policy prescriptions.

Those who answered our call are a most impressive lot, if we say so ourselves. (The reader will likely recognize many names, and short bios of all contributors appear beginning on page 261.)

We didn't tell our authors what to focus on, simply to help us "address the big questions about where America finds itself at this moment in history, where we're going (or should go), and the role of primary-secondary education in taking us there." As should be expected from this cadre of creative thinkers, they set off in many directions—but as the reader will discover, their separate musings turned out to revolve around several key themes.

In part 1, Eliot Cohen and Jonah Goldberg make a powerful case for rekindling students' understanding of American history, civics, and citizenship, including the kind that inculcates an informed love of country even as it acknowledges past failings and present challenges. Adam Meyerson (joined by his colleague Adam Kissel) unpacks some ways that private philanthropy can advance this kind of education. And Robby George explains why that education must be delivered in ways that invite young people to grapple with competing views and conflicting ideas and neither be indoctrinated into groupthink nor shielded from things they may find unexpected or disagreeable.

In part 2, we turn to vital elements of education that often transcend the cognitive and curricular. Pete Wehner examines the decline of character education and the urgency of revitalizing it, while Bill Damon explains the crucial role that having "purpose" in one's life plays in the formation of young people and how that quest connects to citizenship education and love of country. Rod Paige links purpose to striving, the motivation to learn and make something of oneself, and suggests that attention to student effort has been sorely missing from yesterday's education-reform efforts. Michael Barone tackles the education of highly able students who are keen to learn more—a key example of striving. Heather Mac Donald shows how none of this can happen in disorderly classrooms and violent schools, arguing that fashionable but squishy discipline practices cause the greatest harm to the very children whom advocates of such practices think they're helping. And Arthur Brooks (joined by Nathan Thompson) explains why everyone needs to "be needed" in order to enjoy the dignity that gives purpose to life and grounds for striving—and how many of today's popular policy nostrums (e.g., "college for all") actually widen the "dignity gap" for many Americans.

We reconnect education to family and community in part 3, again illustrating some of the limits of voguish policies and practices. Nick Eberstadt shows how many men entirely outside the labor force (i.e., neither working nor seeking work) are there for reasons largely (though not entirely) beyond the reach of K–12 education. Naomi Schaefer Riley explains how children in foster care and otherwise lacking effective parental mentors and navigators need schooling (and other services) that choice alone cannot furnish. Ian Rowe and Mona Charen both take up the "success sequence"—finishing school, getting a job, getting married, then having children, in that order, or else success in life is far less likely to come their way. Charen shows how educators ill-serve disadvantaged youngsters when they shy away from teaching hard truths about the consequences of deviating from that sequence, while Rowe contends that having two parents in one's life is so important to one's education that family structure must become one of the key variables when achievement is analyzed.

Also in part 3, Kay Hymowitz points to child-centric parenting practices, reinforced by schools' endless celebration of individuality, and explains how these habits, all but uniquely American, are harmful to young people's acquisition of a proper work ethic and capacity for collaboration, while Ramesh Ponnuru eloquently depicts the harm done to many youngsters' actual futures by the assumption among educators (and others) that all must attend college.

In part 4, we wrap up with a renewed and revitalized conservative education agenda for America, featuring Yuval Levin, Bill Bennett, and ourselves.

We encourage you to read, enjoy, learn from, and act upon the many keen insights and perceptive suggestions that follow. We'll catch up with you again at the end.

PART I

History, Civics, and Citizenship

CHAPTER 1

Irradiating the Past

by Jonah Goldberg

When the past no longer illuminates the future,
the spirit walks in darkness.
—ALEXIS DE TOCQUEVILLE

FEW STUDENTS TODAY—OR their parents—saw the 1964 James Bond movie *Goldfinger* when it premiered. Like many old Bond films, it violates some modern norms, particularly of the #MeToo variety. But in one respect, it remains very relevant. Its eponymous villain, Auric Goldfinger, loves only gold. The story climaxes at Fort Knox, the famous gold depository, though Goldfinger's plan is not to steal the treasure there but to irradiate it, making it unusable. This will increase the value of Goldfinger's own hoard of gold.

Naturally, because it's a James Bond movie and Goldfinger is the villain, he fails. But his plot is akin to something happening in modern education and our culture, where the largely well-intentioned villains are mostly succeeding in irradiating the historical gold reserve of our civic tradition and national narrative. They seek to make vast swaths of the American story unusable, leaving only their narrative as acceptable currency in the marketplace of ideas. They want to make their stories the only usable past.[1]

This is not new. Radical historians, primarily in the 1910s, the 1930s, and the 1960s, rewrote or revised the standard American story (necessarily, in some cases). It was a mixed effort.[2] But this is how things go. The intergenerational construction of an American narrative must be conversational, to borrow Michael Oakeshott's metaphor for politics. This is how we understand our past, present, and future selves.[3] No historical school monopolizes our national narrative; only competition/conversation of narratives and interpretations deepens our appreciation of our national identity. But today's efforts are not voices in this conversation; they are attempts to shut up everyone else.

These efforts both are helped by and contribute to a crisis of American ignorance. We shouldn't expect the average American to know who Oakeshott was, though would that more did. But every American should know what the Constitution's First Amendment says. Yet more than a third of Americans surveyed by the Annenberg Center for Public Policy in September 2017 failed to name a single First Amendment freedom. Only 26 percent could name all three branches of government; 33 percent couldn't name any branch.[4] Similar results appear elsewhere. Only one respondent out of more than a thousand in a Freedom Forum survey could name all five First Amendment freedoms, but 9 percent said they believed it protected the right to bear arms.[5] Just 36 percent of Americans passed (i.e., scored above 60) a multiple-choice series of questions derived from the US citizenship test, according to a Woodrow Wilson National Fellowship Foundation survey. More than two-thirds couldn't identify the thirteen states that ratified the Constitution. Less than a quarter knew why we fought the British. More than one in ten Americans (12 percent) thought Dwight Eisenhower was a Civil War general (6 percent thought he was a Vietnam general). Only a quarter (24 percent) could name a single thing Benjamin Franklin was famous for, and more than a third believed he invented the lightbulb. At least only 2 percent of Americans said the Cold War was caused by climate change. Most striking: This survey's results differed vastly by age. 74 percent of people sixty-five and older passed but only 19 percent of those forty-five and younger passed.[6]

This might help explain the shocking attitudes of today's young. A generation after global communism's collapse, and during history's greatest poverty alleviation (thanks to spreading market-based economies),[7] more Americans ages eighteen to twenty-nine view socialism positively (51 percent) than do capitalism (45 percent).[8] A movement of campus agitation that started a half-century ago, purportedly inspired by free speech, has culminated in a generation in which 40 percent of Americans ages eighteen to thirty-four think the government should ban "hateful" speech.[9] And 30 percent of Millennials born in a country established as a democratic republic more than two hundred years ago no longer prioritize living in a democracy.[10]

Our educational institutions are failing our students in at least this respect (if not also in many others, as other essays in this volume demonstrate). But children attend school for years, and ever more attend postsecondary institutions. What are they actually learning? The distressing answer is that American students are increasingly being taught that they can learn nothing valuable from America's past except the evil of our constitutional order and our most basic civic institutions.

Now, most teachers do not set out to do this, particularly in K–12 education. I have met too many patriotic and professional teachers who think otherwise. Indeed, they often fight against larger cultural and educational forces. But they are either unwilling or unable to overcome those forces—namely, a cultural movement that began to reject America's past, capitalism's propensity to create an intellectual class hostile to the moral underpinnings of the society, the changes in the way young people think, and the regnant self-loathing elite ideology.

Let us examine these in turn.

First, there is the progressive rejection of America's past. For most of our history, America's future-focused attitude was a boon, and an essential part of American exceptionalism; its citizens self-consciously envisioned themselves as leaving behind the feudal and aristocratic prejudices of the Old World. This attitude is a healthy part of our culture, but only when restrained by civic pride, patriotism, and local institutions. Starting in the Progressive Era, however, when America's own tradition was just barely old enough to be thought archaic, intellectuals declared war on it, believing that scientific tools wielded by "disinterested" experts could liberate citizens in ways that the outdated system of "negative liberty" could not. The Constitution, for the progressives, was a "Newtonian" relic in need of replacement by a more "Darwinian" conception of guided evolution.[11]

Progressive educators, who relished the idea of creating a new citizenry, embraced this. John Dewey mixed a patriotic desire for assimilation with a progressive lust for social engineering. As Thomas Sowell writes, "John Dewey saw the role of the teacher not as a transmitter of a society's culture to the young, but as an agent of change—someone strategically placed with an opportunity to condition students to want a different kind of society."[12] While president of Princeton University, Woodrow Wilson tasked educators with producing men "as unlike their fathers as possible."[13] From kindergarten to college, educators would reshape students as they saw fit.

The second force is capitalism's self-destructive nature. The great economist Joseph Schumpeter predicted capitalism's doom in *Capitalism, Socialism, and Democracy*, arguing that capitalism tends to burn through the social capital needed to sustain itself. Its relentless efficiency destroys not just bad institutions and customs, but also indispensable ones. For Schumpeter, writes economist and historian Deirdre McCloskey, "capitalism was raising up its own grave diggers—not in the proletariat, as Marx had expected, but in the sons and daughters of the bourgeoisie itself."[14]

Schumpeter argued that mass prosperity produced intellectuals: artists, writers, bureaucrats, and, most importantly, educators. Historically, intellectuals served throne and altar. But when society protects the market and free expression, and a mass audience can support intellectuals, little constrains their work. According to Schumpeter, these intellectuals would inevitably then argue that they as a class should rule. "For such an atmosphere to develop," Schumpeter writes, "it is necessary that there be groups whose interest it is to work up and organize resentment, to nurse it, to voice it and to lead it."[15] Schumpeter called this group the "new class."

He wrote this just before the G.I. Bill, but he predicted its effects. The mass affluence of the post–World War II period created a mass market for discontent that exploded in the 1960s. The baby-boom children of the "Greatest Generation," imbued with both generational obligation and guilt, sought social transformation. Unwilling or unable to see Vietnam as their "good war," they turned inward to remake society. Some of their work, such as the civil rights movement, was good, embodying—despite some radical excesses—the highest American ideals. Other work was less beneficial. These well-intentioned acolytes of a secular faith imbued with a desire to transform American institutions conquered large swaths of the universities, journalism, Hollywood, and government bureaucracies, and sought to change America's story. In the Schumpeterian view, this was not only an ideological takeover but also an exertion of class interest.

This dynamic has always been a byproduct of capitalism, or the prosperity it creates. The task, therefore, isn't to eradicate it, but to acknowledge its existence and work to maintain and replenish the social and cultural underpinnings of society—the family and other Burkean "little platoons"—that serve as a check on the ambitions of national elites by fostering a sense of rootedness and belonging and an attachment to traditional notions of civility, citizenship, and patriotism. The founders, Adam Smith, and public choice theorists alike all understood that the danger to a healthy republic lay in factions using the government to impose a singular vision from above on the diverse moral ecosystem of a continental nation.

Such homogenization was central to the progressive project. Wilson, Dewey, and other progressives sought to use the state to forge society into a singular, undifferentiated body politic. The "Newtonian" architecture of the founding, Wilson insisted, needed to be replaced with new "Darwinian" approach that placed national unity, directed by technocrats, at the center of the political project.

Progressive historians like Frederick Jackson Turner argued that history was a series of chapters that led to the present. The closing of the

American frontier ended one chapter. Many progressives demanded new chapters to be opened, devoted to conquering various metaphorical frontiers, including the backward notion of distinct communities and individuals.[16] But at least for many of the early progressives, the earlier chapters of America's story were something to be proud of, even if the old, classically liberal ways had outlived their utility. The later generations of new class intellectuals were different. They took out their red pens and rewrote the early chapters, creating a new story.

This is their Goldfinger project and the late Howard Zinn is its exemplar. Zinn started his widely used textbook, *A People's History of the United States*, thusly:

> In that inevitable taking of sides which comes from selection and emphasis in history, I prefer to try to tell the story of the discovery of America from the viewpoint of the Arawaks, of the Constitution from the standpoint of the slaves, of Andrew Jackson as seen by the Cherokees, of the Civil War as seen by the New York Irish, of the Mexican war as seen by the deserting soldiers of Scott's army, of the rise of industrialism as seen by the young women in the Lowell textile mills, of the Spanish-American war as seen by the Cubans, the conquest of the Philippines as seen by black soldiers on Luzon, the Gilded Age as seen by southern farmers, the First World War as seen by socialists, the Second World War as seen by pacifists, the New Deal as seen by blacks in Harlem, the postwar American empire as seen by peons in Latin America.[17]

Zinn's story of America is the story of victims. The heroes of previous ages become villains, their ideals villainous. James Burnham (a Schumpeter devotee) identified the psychological driver of the transformation of American liberalism from a confident, fundamentally patriotic, and nationalist ideology into an enterprise of collective guilt. He wrote in his *Suicide of the West*:

> For Western civilization in the present condition of the world, the most important practical consequence of the guilt encysted in the liberal ideology and psyche is this: that the liberal, and the group, nation, or civilization infected by liberal doctrine and values, are morally disarmed before those whom the liberal regards as less well off than himself.[18]

This guilt, left untended, festers. Liberals like Reinhold Niebuhr once warned of American liberalism's hubristic overconfidence. Now, guilt and doubt have replaced confidence utterly.

The Zinnian project could be part of the great conversation of American history. The problem is that his perspective, though important, is only one among many, yet is increasingly seen as the only one. It is fine to argue that Christopher Columbus was terrible, but is that all there is to him?

Why is this view now so dominant? Blame the third force: today's young people. In *The Coddling of the American Mind* and at Heterodox Academy, Jonathan Haidt and Greg Lukianoff explain that we are raising children—particularly elites—who can't confront unsettling ideas. Thanks to certain social obsessions—physical safety, college admittance, antibullying, self-esteem, and so on—middle-class and affluent children grow up without resolving peer conflicts absent adult interference, and embrace their racial or gender "identity" as a sort of totem: a toxic combination. Until the Millennial and post-Millennial generations, political correctness was not a "lifestyle." Today's youth are the young minds that new-class college professors and administrators have long awaited. Controversies over "intersectionality," identity, and free speech are familiar to observers of modern campus politics. They are mainstream because this generation has been taught a different language—call it social justice, wokeness, PC, or multiculturalism, it doesn't really matter—that is now institutionalized. Colleges might once have wanted some students "fluent" in left-wing social commitment, for diversity's sake. Now this fluency has gone from an elective to a requirement.

The fourth force is that the new class now controls American education. In 1990, according to one measure, professors were only slightly more liberal than the general population. But according to political scientist Samuel Abrams, "Between 1995 and 2010, members of the academy went from leaning left to being almost entirely on the left. Moderates declined by nearly a quarter and conservatives decreased by nearly a third." Now, by the same measure Abrams used for 1990, the differential in political temper between professors and the general population has tripled (as of 2013).[19]

Hostility toward opposing views is now virtually indistinguishable from bigotry. Sociologist George Yancey reports that

- Thirty percent of his fellow sociologists admitted they were less likely to hire a Republican applicant.
- Fifteen percent of political scientists and 25 percent of philosophy professors would discriminate against Republican applicants.
- A third of all professors surveyed would discriminate against members of the NRA.
- Sixty percent of anthropologists, half of literature professors, 39 percent of political scientists and sociologists, 34 percent of philosophy professors, and 29 percent of historians confessed reluctance to hire evangelical Christians.[20]

This is but a sip of an ocean of data that attests not simply to the academy's ideological turn to the left but also to its sociological turn. Higher education as a profession is a distinct social milieu that sees itself on one side of the culture war.

This transformation has many causes. I've focused on four: America's future-oriented culture, how mass affluence empowers intellectuals to attack tradition, how we raise children, and the regnant elite ideology.

To fix it, educators must discover how to tell a story of America that includes Zinn's focus on victims *and* our failures to embody our ideals.

Consider the most egregious American sin: slavery. Only fools and bigots could belittle its evil. Yet slavery's resonance in America comes not from its evil but from the founders' hypocrisy. Since the Agricultural Revolution, nearly every civilization practiced slavery, but none also claimed to believe that "all men are created equal" and that they are "endowed by their Creator with certain unalienable Rights."

The Zinnian approach takes America's sin of slavery and makes it an eternal blemish that never shrinks in the rearview mirror no matter how much progress we make. But that is not the moral of the story. The staggering hypocrisy of slavery is regrettable in one sense, but glorious in another. Hypocrisy is only possible when you have ideals. The ideal of equality is the arc of America's story. The remarkable thing about America—and Western civilization generally—is not that we had slavery, but that we ended it.[21]

Consider Frederick Douglass, the famous slave-turned-abolitionist. He maintained no illusions about America. How could he? On July 5 (note the date), 1852, while slavery still dominated, Douglass asked, "What to the Slave Is the Fourth of July?" His answer? It is

> a day that reveals to him . . . the gross injustice and cruelty to which he is the constant victim. To him, your celebration is a sham; your boasted liberty, an unholy license; your national greatness, swelling vanity; your sounds of rejoicing are empty and heartless; your denunciations of tyrants, brass fronted impudence; your shouts of liberty and equality, hollow mockery; your prayers and hymns, your sermons and thanksgivings, with all your religious parade, and solemnity, are, to him, mere bombast, fraud, deception, impiety, and hypocrisy.[22]

On an occasion expected to be celebratory, Douglass claimed his fellow citizens were hypocrites "guilty of practices . . . more shocking and bloody" than anyone else on earth.

Students could learn much from Douglass's righteous anger. But his anger is not what is most instructive. Its righteousness matters more. For despite America's sins, Frederick Douglass did not seek its destruction. He focused on America's "hypocrisy,"[23] demanding that we live up to our ideals, not abandon them.

A century later, Martin Luther King Jr. spoke similarly. Like Douglass, King's anger was righteous: "We have waited for more than three hundred and forty years for our constitutional and God-given rights. Meanwhile, the nations of Asia and Africa are moving with jet-like speed toward gaining political independence, but we still creep at horse and buggy pace toward gaining a cup of coffee at a lunch counter," he wrote in his "Letter from a Birmingham Jail."[24]

Like Douglass, King denounced the evils he confronted. But like Douglass, King also recommitted to the ideals. "When the architects of our republic wrote the magnificent words of the Constitution and the Declaration of Independence, they were signing a promissory note to which every American was to fall heir," he proclaimed in his "I Have a Dream" speech. And though black Americans had not yet received it, he maintained hope they someday would. "We refuse to believe that the bank of justice is bankrupt," he insisted. Which is why King maintained hope for his dream, which was "deeply rooted in the American Dream," that "one day this nation will rise up and live out the true meaning of its creed: 'We hold these truths to be self-evident, that all men are created equal.'"[25]

It would have been better if the founders had never been hypocrites. But we should feel deeply grateful for that hypocrisy, because it was the irritant that creates the pearl. This is how we should teach the story of America. But we're not. Instead of telling how we have struggled to embody our principles, we now teach the illegitimacy of the principles themselves. No person, institution, or society can fully embody its ideals; *that's why we call them "ideals."* But rather than accept this, we are toppling those very ideals.

These arguments resonate not only from their undergirding ideology, but also from their self-reinforcing incentives. Belief in diversity may be a sincerely held conviction, but it also conveniently empowers administrators, consultants, and other new-class professionals, as well as students themselves.

This is why the classically liberal tenets of the liberal arts—and of society itself—threaten the new class. It is why America's story cannot be one of hard-won improvement. The idea of progress threatens the business model. Gratitude is heresy in a faith that cannot defeat original sin.

A decent, patriotic, and most important, *honest* education system would not belittle past sins. It would teach these sins to students—future citizens—to show that, while there is always more work to do toward our ideals, those ideals generate our progress and prosperity. Instead, our Goldfingers seek to discredit the ideals from our past, in favor of a stunted future that they can control.

NOTES

1. To borrow a phrase from Van Wyck Brooks.
2. Some overturned or clarified some cherished American myths; some helped mint new myths. Charles Beard's *An Economic Interpretation of the Constitution of the United States* (1913) is a classic example. Beard argued that the Constitution was a grift to protect the personal financial interests of its founders. Matthew Josephson took a similar approach to the industrialists of the nineteenth century in his (far shoddier) *The Robber Barons: The Great American Capitalists, 1861–1901* (1934). Richard Hofstadter's *Social Darwinism in American Thought, 1860–1915* (1944) is well written and occasionally illuminating, but Hofstadter's claims far exceeded his often-attenuated evidence.
3. Beard begins the first chapter of *An Economic Interpretation* with a clear assertion that he is correcting the mistakes of previous historians. Beard then inspired historians, most notably Forrest McDonald, to correct *his* mistakes.

4. "Americans Are Poorly Informed about Basic Constitutional Provisions," Annenberg Public Policy Center of the University of Pennsylvania, September 12, 2017, https://www.annenbergpublicpolicycenter.org/americans-are-poorly-informed-about-basic-constitutional-provisions/.

5. *The 2019 State of the First Amendment Survey* (Washington, DC: Freedom Forum Institute, 2019), https://www.freedomforuminstitute.org/first-amendment-center/state-of-the-first-amendment/.

6. "National Survey Finds Just 1 in 3 Americans Would Pass Citizenship Test," press release, Woodrow Wilson National Fellowship Foundation, October 3, 2018, https://woodrow.org/news/national-survey-finds-just-1-in-3-americans-would-pass-citizenship-test/.

7. Max Roser and Esteban Ortiz-Ospina, "Global Extreme Poverty," *Our World in Data* (blog), March 27, 2017, https://ourworldindata.org/extreme-poverty.

8. Frank Newport, "Democrats More Positive about Socialism Than Capitalism," *Gallup News*, August 13, 2018, https://news.gallup.com/poll/240725/democrats-positive-socialism-capitalism.aspx.

9. Jacob Poushter, "40% of Millennials OK with Limiting Speech Offensive to Minorities," *FactTank, Pew Research Center* (blog), November 20, 2015, https://www.pewresearch.org/fact-tank/2015/11/20/40-of-millennials-ok-with-limiting-speech-offensive-to-minorities/.

10. Roberto Stefan Foa and Yascha Mounk, "The Democratic Disconnect," *Journal of Democracy* 27, no. 3 (2016): 8.

11. Woodrow Wilson, "What Is Progress?" in *American Progressivism: A Reader*, ed. Ronald J. Pestritto and William J. Atto (Lanham, MD: Lexington Books, 2008), 50–51.

12. Thomas Sowell, "The Role of Educators," *National Review*, January 8, 2013, https://www.nationalreview.com/2013/01/role-educators-thomas-sowell/. Even the liberal Richard Hofstader agreed: "The effect of Dewey's philosophy on the design of curricular systems was devastating," he wrote in his Pulitzer Prize–winning book *Anti-Intellectualism in American Life* (1963).

13. Woodrow Wilson, in *Vindicating the Founders*, "The New Freedom: A Call for the Emancipation of the Generous Energies of a People," accessed August 15, 2019, http://www.vindicatingthefounders.com/library/new-freedom.html.

14. Deirdre Nansen McCloskey, "Creative Destruction vs. the New Industrial State," *Reason*, October 2007, https://reason.com/archives/2007/09/18/creative-destruction-vs-the-ne.

15. Joseph A. Schumpeter, *Capitalism, Socialism, and Democracy*, 3rd ed. (New York: Harper Perennial Modern Thought, 2008), 145.

16. Such as William James's call for a new "moral equivalent of war."

17. Howard Zinn, *A People's History of the United States*, 2nd ed. (New York: HarperCollins Publishers, 2005), 10.

18. Quoted in Matthew Continetti, "The Seer," *National Review*, March 23, 2015, https://www.nationalreview.com/nrd/articles/414923/seer.

19. Sam Abrams, "Professors Moved Left since 1990s, Rest of Country Did Not," *Heterodox Academy*, January 9, 2016, https://heterodoxacademy.org /professors-moved-left-but-country-did-not/.

20. Jon A. Shields, "The Disappearing Conservative Professor," *National Affairs*, no. 37 (2018): 139, 145–146, https://www.nationalaffairs.com/publications/ detail/the-disappearing-conservative-professor.

21. MIT economists Daren Acemoglu and Alexander Wolitzky write, "Standard economic models of the labor market, regardless of whether they incorporate imperfections, assume that transactions in the labor market are 'free.' For most of human history, however, the bulk of labor transactions have been 'coercive,' meaning that the threat of force was essential in convincing workers to take part in the employment relationship, and thus in determining compensation. Slavery and forced labor were the most common forms of labor transactions in most ancient civilizations, including Greece, Egypt, Rome, several Islamic and Asian Empires, and most known pre-Columbian civilizations (Daron Acemoglu and Alexander Wolitzky, "The Economics of Labor Coercion," *Econometrica* 79, no. 2 [2011]: 555, http://economics.mit .edu/files/8975).

22. Frederick Douglass, "What to the Slave Is the Fourth of July?" Teaching American History, accessed August 15, 2019, http://teachingamericanhistory .org/library/document/what-to-the-slave-is-the-fourth-of-july/.

23. Ibid.

24. Martin Luther King Jr., "Letter from a Birmingham Jail," African Studies Center at the University of Pennsylvania, accessed August 15, 2019, https: //www.africa.upenn.edu/Articles_Gen/Letter_Birmingham.html.

25. Martin Luther King Jr., "'I Have a Dream,' Address Delivered at the March on Washington for Jobs and Freedom," Stanford University Martin Luther King Jr. Research and Education Institute, accessed August 15, 2019, https: //kinginstitute.stanford.edu/king-papers/documents/i-have-dream -address-delivered-march-washington-jobs-and-freedom/.

CHAPTER 2

History: Critical and Patriotic

by Eliot A. Cohen

W HEN MY mother passed away several years ago at the ripe old age of ninety, my brothers and I had the bittersweet task of emptying out the home she and our father had lived in for well over half a century, and where we grew up. We took various keepsakes and mementoes. Unsurprisingly, I made a beeline for the books and magazines. On leafing through them, I realized how much my picture of America had been formed by them, and by the culture of tempered but patriotic history they conveyed. They reflected the middlebrow culture of mid-twentieth-century America, which carried many of my generation through the turmoil of social change, war, and political crisis.

The first collection—from when I was quite young—was the Landmark series of histories for young people, conceived by Bennett Cerf of Random House and launched in 1948, with books by topnotch novelists like Dorothy Canfield Fisher, C. S. Forester, and Robert Penn Warren, and war correspondents like William Shirer, Quentin Reynolds, and Richard Tregaskis.[1] It eventually ran to some 180 volumes, covering not just American history but everything from the pharaohs of ancient Egypt to the United Nations in war and peace. Although mainly out of print, they retain some appeal for homeschooling parents, and, having sold very well indeed, are easy to find in used bookstores.[2]

After that was my old copy of Kenneth Roberts's historical novel about the American retreat from Canada in 1776 and the Saratoga campaign of 1777, *Rabble in Arms.* In it, Roberts (who probably deserved a Pulitzer for fiction but never won one) turned my twelve-year-old historical consciousness upside down by making Benedict Arnold out to be a hero. He showed (accurately) that Arnold's military skill accounted for the deferral of one British invasion of the northern United States and the defeat of another. Roberts described in terms more vivid than all but the best historians what it was like to fight a lake battle in upstate New York in late autumn, or be inoculated against smallpox, or deal with the stupidities of legislative politics. Roberts was but one of a whole series of historical novelists that included Walter Edmonds (*Drums along the Mohawk*) and (for younger readers) Esther Forbes (*Johnny Tremain*) who made the colonial and revolutionary past live.

Then there were the old copies of *American Heritage*, going back to the early 1960s. This magazine, which had been a small house organ of the American Association for State and Local History, was relaunched in 1954 in a handsome, 120-page hardcover format. The October 1961 edition was fairly typical. The senior editor was Bruce Catton, the prolific popular historian of the Civil War; the managing editor was Eric Larrabee, who later wrote one of the best studies of Franklin Roosevelt as commander in chief. Assistant and associate editors included Richard Ketchum and Stephen Sears, excellent historians of the Revolution and the Civil War, respectively. Authors in that issue included Hugh MacLennan, a prize-winning professor of English at McGill, writing about Canadian voyageurs; Mark Schorer, a Berkeley professor and biographer of Sinclair Lewis on the writing of *Main Street*; and John Lukacs, one of the most original historians of twentieth-century Europe, writing about George Bancroft, one of the fathers of American history. It wasn't fluff.

There was a progression here for a young person fascinated by the past, and with the ability to engage in it at a number of levels. And it unquestionably played a role in shaping my attitudes to politics. These were works of patriotic history, celebrating the American past and American heroes. They did not, nor did they need to, gloss over the stains and horrors. The heroes could be southern senators standing up to the Klan in the 1920s, or Chief Joseph leading his small tribe in a hopeless fight against the US Army. And the tales could include accounts of political corruption, ambiguous loyalties, and mayhem—

patriotic history does not have to conceal any of that, nor need it ignore the ambiguities of the past. But the key was that this was *my* history, to own and to celebrate, even though my grandparents were immigrants.

Particularly for Americans, patriotic history is a kind of glue for an extraordinarily diverse republic. Lincoln used a patriotic version of the revolutionary past and the founding generation to hold the Union together and provide meaning and redemptive hope to the slaughter of hundreds of thousands in the Civil War. And Lincoln in turn became a figure to inspire succeeding generations.

Patriotic history is more suspect these days than fifty years ago. In 2014 Kenneth Pomeranz, completing his term as leader of the American Historical Association, chose as the topic of his presidential address, "Histories for a Less National Age." While grudgingly conceding that nations or states remain important because they have armies, and acknowledging that historians might do some limited good by teaching about the United States, he generally welcomed the shift to spatially and temporally broader history, sweeping across continents and centuries. It is striking that just as he gave that address, the forces of nationalism—in Russia, China, western Europe, and most definitely in the United States—gave a chorus of roars that indicated that they were very far from dead. It was an instructive error for a historian to make.

Orwell famously observed in 1945 that nationalism is "the habit of assuming that human beings can be classified like insects," where patriotism is "devotion to a particular place and a particular way of life, which one believes to be the best in the world."[3] In practice, however, modern academic historians, who are wary of nationalism for reasons good and bad, often conflate it with patriotism. And this point is where some of the great divide between contemporary academic history and patriotic history has opened. When the academy questions the very utility of national history, by necessity it undermines the possibility of patriotic history as well.

Civic education requires knowledge of history, not only to know whence conventions, principles, and laws have come, but also to develop an attachment to them. And civic education is inextricably interwoven with patriotism, without which commitment to the values that make free government possible will not exist. Civic education depends not only on an understanding of fundamental processes and institutions (why there is a Supreme Court, why only Congress gets to raise taxes or declare war) but also on a commitment to those processes and institutions, and on some kind of admiration for the country that created them and the men and women who have shaped and lived within them. In a crisis, it is not enough to know how the walls were constructed and the plumbing laid out in the house that Madison, Washington, and Lincoln built. One has to think that the architects did remarkable work, that as their legatees we need to preserve the building even as we modernize it, and that it is a precious edifice like none other.

The triangular relationship among civic education, historical knowledge, and patriotism seems in our day to be broken. Survey after survey delivers dismal verdicts about what Americans know about the government under which they live. In one survey by the Annenberg Public Policy Center, barely a quarter of respondents could identify the three branches of government, for example—and one-third could not identify even a single branch.[4] More than half thought that illegal immigrants have no rights under the Constitution. Another survey indicated that only a third of Americans would pass the US citizenship test.[5]

The issue appears not to be a lack of civics courses per se, which are required during high school in the majority of states. Rather, the issue seems to be the unmooring of civics from history, and in particular, history in the curriculum at colleges and universities where the high school teachers of tomorrow are trained.

In a blistering article in the national security–oriented online publication *War on the Rocks,* my colleagues (able historians both), Francis

Gavin and Hal Brands, declare that the historical profession is "committing slow-motion suicide."[6] They point to studies showing a decline of 30 percent in history majors in the last ten years alone—the steepest slide in the humanities. The brunt of their critique is that the discipline of history has walked away from some of the subfields that matter most to the shaping of engaged citizens—politics, statecraft, and war.[7] Their fellow historians Frederik Logevall and Kenneth Osgood recently looked at H-Net, the leading website for academic jobs in history, and found a grand total of fifteen advertisements for tenure-track junior historians specializing in American political history.

Members of the historical profession might, with reason, push back on this bleak picture, noting the robust health of organizations like the Society for Military History. But the truth remains that traditional forms of history—political, diplomatic, and military—have been pushed to the margins of the field; that history departments have shrunk rapidly because students vote with their feet; and that churning out fewer history concentrators (who in turn are likely to be the future history teachers in junior high and high school) bodes poorly for the future of civic education. If, moreover, those smaller numbers of concentrators are themselves only scantily learned in the kinds of history that appeal to young people and that can help form them as citizens, the cycle becomes a vicious one. And if the nuts and bolts of American political and military history are not taught in universities, the chance that they will be passed to a younger generation diminishes further.

———

It is not that Americans have fallen out of love with their own past. Large numbers visit battlefields and museums—a million a year to Gettysburg, more than that to Mount Vernon, almost three quarters of a million to the National World War II Museum, and six-digit numbers even to more remote sites. Popular historians do well—David McCullough and Ron Chernow have repeatedly written best-selling historical biographies, while recent television series may not quite have drawn the 14-million-person viewership of Ken Burns's 1990 *Civil*

War series but have done respectably enough. *John Adams,* for example, drew around 2.5 million viewers.

The problem lies not in lack of interest, but in a tension between the academic historical community and both the reading public and popular writers. It is not enough to have best-selling books or television series about the American past, though those are welcome; there is a need for a general awareness of that past to be spread through college and university education and thence to high schools and junior highs. And while the history provided by the academy must be somewhat different than the history coming from Netflix or the airport bookstand, they cannot be too far apart.

That gap has not always existed. It was possible, for example, for Allan Nevins, an enormously prolific writer about the Civil War and a biographer of Charles Fremont, John D. Rockefeller, and Henry Ford, to be a tenured professor at Columbia and president of the American Historical Association—all this without a PhD, which would be unthinkable today. A contemporary who did have a doctorate, Harvard's Samuel Eliot Morison, was similarly popular, similarly prolific, and similarly influential.

The Morisons and Nevinses of the previous century believed that they had a duty to illuminate the American past for their fellow citizens. They could be nuanced and critical while respecting the patriotic uses of history. More recently, however, the weight in the academic historical profession has been hostile to anything that smacks of such an approach. In a critical review of McCullough's biography of Adams, Princeton historian Sean Wilentz lashed not only the author but also what he described as the *American Heritage* style, "brilliant in its detail, evocative in its storytelling, but crushingly sentimental and vacuous," which (he said) infected Ken Burns's *Civil War* as well.[8] Wilentz celebrated the now obscure (but worth reading) Bernard DeVoto, a once well-known popular historian, as an alternative to the likes of McCullough and Nevins.

These wars have continued. When in 2011 Harvard historian Jill Lepore published a book on the original Tea Party and its resonance today, she was taken to task by the dean of early American historians, Gordon S. Wood: "Americans," he wrote, "seem to have a special need for these authentic historical figures in the here and now. It is very easy for academic historians to mock this special need, and Harvard historian Jill Lepore, as a staff writer for the *New Yorker*, is an expert at mocking."[9]

After criticizing Lepore for her contemptuous tone toward a political movement (the 2010s Tea Party) that she despised, Wood argued that societies need memory, a useful and a purposeful past. Modern critical historical writing, he said, seeks simply to establish what happened. It is "all head and no heart," Wood wrote, and, citing his own teacher, Bernard Bailyn, argued that it was important to understand that such history could not meet a society's needs, and something else is required.

This is the nub of the matter. Even if the academy generated more historians (like Wood, Wilentz, and Lepore, for example) who can write compellingly and lucidly for lay audiences, and even if they turned their attention to politics of the kind that citizens need and average readers find interesting, there is bound to be a tension between the outlook of the modern analytic historian and that of the patriotic historian.

Patriotic history involves, for example, heroes. Most academic historians who write biography (not the most popular genre in universities) specialize in the study of clay feet. Hence David Herbert Donald's biography of Lincoln depicts a president stumbling from decision to decision and yet somehow presiding over a triumphant Union. Doris Kearns Goodwin—a popular historian—gives a much more sympathetic account in *Team of Rivals.* Perhaps because she had had closer connections to the world of actual politics, her book is the more popular and, one may even think, is in some ways the more essentially accurate portrait.

Americans need history that educates and informs, but also history that inspires. If, for example, one gives equal weight to John F. Kennedy's sordid sexual behavior and the soaring rhetoric of his inaugural speech; if one concentrates as much on the personal peccadilloes, inconsistencies, and mixed motives of the Founders as on the marvel that is the Constitution they created; if the shameful relocation of American citizens of Japanese ancestry to concentration camps gets more play than D-Day or Midway, history cannot serve that inspirational function. And then, in a crisis, you are stuck, because you have no great figures to remember, no memory of great challenges overcome, no examples of persistence and struggle to embrace.

A notable recent work of scholarship, Richard White's account of Reconstruction and the Gilded Age, *The Republic for Which It Stands,* is something of a warning. It is one in the excellent series produced by the Oxford History of the United States, which includes James McPherson's *Battle Cry of Freedom* (on the Civil War) and Wood's *Empire of Liberty* (on the early republic). Like the other volumes, it is lucid and masterly in its scholarship. But its relentless depiction of an irredeemably sordid past, blotted by the oppression of the African American population of the South, massacre of Indians, despoiling of the environment, horrors of tenement life, and political cupidity leaves the reader thinking that perhaps the only good thing to be said about the United States during this period is that, by contrast, it makes today's America look good.

One could write a history that acknowledges all those things yet also celebrates the great works of literature and engineering from Mark Twain to the Brooklyn Bridge, or the extraordinary political achievement of the reunification of a country that had experienced four years of unremitting bloodshed, or the heroism (quiet in one case, noisy in the other) of Booker T. Washington and the young Theodore Roosevelt.

Wood recognized in his review of Lepore's book about the Tea Party that the two forms of history—critical and patriotic—can coexist but rarely if ever coincide. Some particularly gifted historians can pull it off; David Hackett Fischer, for example, does that in his magnificent books, *Paul Revere's Ride* and *Washington's Crossing.* But for the most part, the two forms of history have different purposes and tap different skills and sensibilities. The challenge is the management of their coexistence, and in particular the recognition by scholars that both are necessary.

The popular and patriotic historians may grumble at reviews of their work by their academic colleagues but, in truth, pay them little heed. For the academic historians, however, the sentiments can be more acid. Jonathan Zimmerman, a professor at the University of Pennsylvania, put it sharply in a guarded defense of Ken Burns. "It's called sour grapes. Put simply, Burns has managed to engage a huge public audience. And that makes him suspect among members of our guild, who write almost entirely for each other. We pretend we don't envy his fame and fortune, but of course we do. We're like high-school kids who don't get asked to the prom, then say they never wanted to go in the first place."[10]

Unsurprisingly, Zimmerman began his career as a high school social studies teacher, closer to the real needs of the American public for historical education. He noted that writing for lay audiences often counts against a young historian, and he deplored the guild mentality of a history profession that too often looks down on public engagement. In so doing, he made a point that cannot be put too forcefully: unless history departments, and university administrators behind them, begin to weigh public engagement as a useful academic function, they are likely to pull their discipline further into bitter irrelevance.

A reversal of this trend is not inconceivable, particularly for faculty members who have tenure, but also in an era when higher education itself is being turned upside down and it's becoming harder to sustain departments that do not pay their way with student seats in classrooms. History departments' disdain of the last few decades for popular history and historians who engage the American public may not survive provosts unwilling to open new lines for expensive professors teaching less to fewer students.

Moreover, the educational establishment itself has, on occasion, changed its approach to history. After a series of criticisms, the College Board revised its course framework for Advanced Placement US History. The revised (2017) version is both sophisticated and sober, while offering ample opportunities to explore such learning objectives as "Explain how ideas about democracy, freedom, and individualism found expression in the development of cultural values, political institutions, and American identity."[11]

And then there is politics itself. In 2016 the political tide turned. Instead of a desperately unhappy conservative opposition to a liberal president turning to history for inspiration and consolation and meeting the scorn of liberal history professors, it was the liberals who found themselves looking for a usable past. They saw a president they believed to be a potential tyrant, and a Republican Party they saw mastering the legislative and judicial branches of government. They now needed the heroes and inspiring moments from the past to convince themselves that the country could get through difficult times.

Interestingly enough, it was Jill Lepore who found herself doing in a different way what she had disparaged the Tea Party movement for doing. In 2018 she published an ambitious and engrossing one-volume history of the United States, *These Truths*. It is filled with patriotic sentiment—"The United States rests on a dedication to equality, which is chiefly a moral idea, rooted in Christianity, but it rests too, on a dedication to inquiry, fearless and unflinching." She concluded with the old metaphors of the ship of state in a storm, with Americans called upon to fell majestic pines and "hew timbers of cedar and oak into planks" to rebuild the ship. Depending on one's literary tastes, the language was either florid or evocative, but it was clear that in the profound crisis Lepore saw in the Trump presidency, history had to come to the rescue. Possibly without recognizing it, she too had become a patriotic historian.

What, then, is to be done?

We can begin by recognizing that although America's renewed focus on STEM education for K–12 has had some beneficial effects, it is vital to pay heed to supposedly softer subjects, history foremost among them. Evidence suggests that the recent focus on testing (and therefore preparing for tests) and on STEM has come at the expense of civics, social studies, and history.[12] Education reformers should realize that the time may have come to rein in the obsession with formal testing and restore some balance to curricula.

While little can be done in the short run about what has happened to history as a discipline, or how history teachers are trained in universities, much can be done in summer workshops or through creative forms of part-time education, particularly online. If conventional universities do not offer adequate instruction in history-for-teachers, entrepreneurially minded competitors can do so, and with national reach via online education. All of these are opportunities for creative grant giving and philanthropy.

The federal government's role, however, is to be approached with care. Part of the strength of the traditional American education system was that it had been decentralized and competitive, and one can argue that attempts to create standardized tests and standards do as much damage as good. Particularly in the field of history, the temptations for ideological fiddling are too great to make conservatives, in particular, feel comfortable. But there are two areas in which there is good to be done.

The first is through the National Endowment for the Humanities, which has sponsored historical work to include workshops for teachers as well as original productions of videos and the like. The second, and even more important, is the role of the federal government in properly funding and sustaining national historic sites to include battlefields, monuments, and historical homes, as well as the Library of Congress and National Archives with their magnificent collections of historical documents. These offer many opportunities for the millions of Americans who are interested in engaging their past to do so.

There is also a role for entrepreneurship and philanthropy in bringing back some of the older material discussed at the beginning of this essay, and creating more that resembles it. Patriotic history may be imbibed in the classroom but it can also be found while camping on the Lewis and Clark trail, watching *The Civil War,* even by finding ways to get into the hands of a curious twelve-year-old a historical novel that she or he will never forget. Any good teacher, at any level, knows that the key to success lies in multiple ways to a young person's consciousness. "Material things, things that move, living things, human actions and account of human action, will win the attention better than anything that is more abstract," William James wrote in *Talks to Teachers.*[13] There is no more natural subject of fascination than history, particularly the history of one's own country, and particularly if that country is the United States.

Patriotic history is a sensitive topic. It can move in false and even dangerous ways. The Lost Cause narrative of the Civil War, for example, masked the reality of slavery as the central cause of the bloodiest conflict in American history. But if done well, as many historians; museum designers; custodians of national parks; and public and private institutions have done, history can both educate and inspire. And it is, in any case, inescapable. Without civics, our political institutions are reduced to valueless mechanisms; without history, there is no civic education; without civic education, there are no citizens; without citizens, there is no free republic. The stakes, in other words, could not be higher.

NOTES

1. David Spear, "Generation Past: The Story of Landmark Books," *Perspectives on History*, October 17, 2016, https://www.historians.org/publications-and-directories/perspectives-on-history/october-2016/generation-past-the-story-of-the-landmark-books.

2. Stacey Carpenter, "Landmark Books in Chronological Order," *picsandpapers .com*, March 20, 2014, accessed November 1, 2018, http://www.picsandpapers .com/landmark-books-in-chronological-order/.

3. George Orwell, "Notes on Nationalism," originally published in *Polemic*, no. 1 (October 1945), reprinted in *Essays*, ed. John Carey (New York: Alfred A. Knopf, 2002), 865–866.

4. "Americans Are Poorly Informed about Basic Constitutional Provisions," Annenberg Public Policy Center of the University of Pennsylva-

nia, September 12, 2017, https://www.annenbergpublicpolicycenter.org /americans-are-poorly-informed-about-basic-constitutional-provisions/.

5. "National Survey Finds Just 1 in 3 Americans Would Pass Citizenship Test," The Woodrow Wilson National Fellowship Foundation, October 3, 2018, https://woodrow.org/news/national-survey-finds-just-1-in-3 -americans-would-pass-citizenship-test/.

6. Hal Brands and Francis J. Gavin, "The Historical Profession Is Committing Slow-Motion Suicide," *War on the Rocks*, December 10, 2018, https://warontherocks.com/2018/12/the-historical-profession-is -committing-slow-motion-suicide/.

7. Fredrik Logevall and Kenneth Osgood, "Why Did We Stop Teaching Political History?" *New York Times*, August 29, 2016, https://www.nytimes .com/2016/08/29/opinion/why-did-we-stop-teaching-political-history.html.

8. Sean Wilentz, "America Made Easy," *New Republic*, July 2, 2001, https://new republic.com/article/90636/david-mccullough-john-adams-book-review. Richard Snow, editor of *American Heritage*, wrote a furious response: Richard Snow, "Has *American Heritage* Gone Soft?" *History News Network*, July 5, 2001, http://hnn.historynewsnetwork.org/articles/264.html.

9. Gordon S. Wood, "No Thanks for the Memories," *New York Review of Books*, January 13, 2011, https://www.nybooks.com/articles/2011/01/13 /no-thanks-memories/.

10. Jonathan Zimmerman, "What's So Bad about Ken Burns?" *The Chronicle of Higher Education*, October 3, 2017, https://www.chronicle.com/article /What-s-So-Bad-About-Ken/241364.

11. College Board, "AP United States History: Course Framework," 2017 edition, 26, https://secure-media.collegeboard.org/digitalServices/pdf/ap/ap -us-history-course-and-exam-description.pdf.

12. See, for example, Michael Hansen et al., *The 2018 Brown Center Report on American Education* (Washington, DC: Brookings, 2018), 9, https://www .brookings.edu.

13. William James, "What the Native Reactions Are," in William James, *Writings 1878–1899* (New York: Library of America, 1992), 741.

CHAPTER 3

What Causes—and What Might Cure—Illiberalism and Groupthink in Education?

By Robert P. George

COLLEGES AND UNIVERSITIES that are dedicated to liberal arts ideals have three fundamental purposes: the pursuit, preservation, and transmission of knowledge. Of course, there are other desirable ends that these institutions—and the schools that feed students into them—legitimately seek to achieve, but those are their fundamental and defining purposes. Other things that such institutions do (in the arts, for example, or in professional training, athletics, and the like) are, in a sense, founded upon them, and anything institutions do that undermines these purposes they should not be doing.

A grave threat to their pursuit today is posed by the politicization of the academy (and sometimes its feeder schools). The problem is most vividly manifest in the phenomenon of campus illiberalism. By that I mean the unwillingness of so many members of college and university communities to entertain, or even listen to, arguments that challenge the opinions they hold, whether those opinions have to do with climate science, racial or ethnic preferences, abortion, welfare policy, sexual morality, immigration, US foreign policy, the international economic order, or the origins of human consciousness.

At many institutions, speaking invitations are not even issued to dissenters from campus orthodoxies. If they are issued, dissenting speakers are sometimes "disinvited" under pressure from opponents of their views. Or, if not disinvited, they are pressured to withdraw under the threat of disruptive protest. If they do not withdraw, they may be interrupted, shouted down, even subjected to violent assault.

But it's not just outside speakers who are at risk. Faculty and student dissenters within campus communities are subjected to abuse and intimidation (as we have seen at Evergreen State and other places).

I do not wish to paint with too broad a brush. The situation is better or worse at different institutions. As it happens, it is not at all bad at my own institution. I have taught for more than three decades at Princeton, where I have never been subjected to intimidation or abuse (though I've had threats from off campus, one of which landed the perpetrator in a federal prison, and threats have been made against Princeton for having me on its faculty). But everyone knows the cases I have in mind at colleges around the country.

I describe this form of illiberalism as the "most vividly manifest" version of the problem I am discussing, for what gets public attention are denials and withdrawals of speaking opportunities, the disruption of meetings, and the shouting down of dissenting speakers. But these are merely some *manifestations*. The core of the problem is this: many institutions, postsecondary and K–12, are subverting the transmission of knowledge by failing to ensure that their students at every level are confronted with, and have the opportunity to consider, the best that is to be said on competing sides of all questions that are in dispute among reasonable people of goodwill. Instead, they permit prevailing opinions on campus to harden into dogmas that go largely unchallenged, leaving students with the false belief that there are in fact no disputes on these matters among reasonable people of goodwill. At the problem's core is the toxic thing that provides an environment in which illiberalism flourishes—namely, the phenomenon of groupthink.

Liberal arts education goes beyond learning facts and acquiring skills. It requires the engagement of the knowledge seeker with competing perspectives and points of view. It also requires certain virtues, including open-mindedness, respect for what John Stuart Mill called "liberty of thought and discussion," intellectual humility—humility of the sort one can possess only insofar as one accepts one's own fallibility—and love of truth. It is the task of colleges and schools, as institutions of learning, to expose students to competing points of view and to foster in them those virtues. That is necessary not because there are no truths to be known, but rather because the pursuit of truth and the deeper appropriation of truths and their meaning and significance require it.

Whatever is to be said about the predominance of certain views and their proponents on campuses, and the exclusion of others, the problem I am calling attention to here is less about unfairness to conservatives or others than about the need to avoid and, where it has set in, overcome groupthink. We owe that to our students—whether they like it or not.

It is a scandal when students graduate from a liberal arts program— or any educational program at any level—with no understanding (or, worse yet, grotesque misunderstandings) of the arguments advanced by serious scholars and thinkers who dissent from campus orthodoxies on issues such as those mentioned above. Even if the opinions that students may acquire in an environment of groupthink happen to be true, their ignorance of the arguments of dissenters will prevent them from understanding the truth as deeply as they should and *appropriating* it—that is to say, understanding *why* it is so and why competing views have nevertheless attracted the attention and even the allegiance of serious thinkers.

The great twentieth-century jurist Learned Hand famously said that "the spirit of Liberty is the spirit of being not too sure one is right." In making that point, he was not endorsing radical skepticism or relativism or anything of the sort. Rather, he was pointing to the need for intellectual humility in light of the inescapable reality of human fallibility. But what he says about the spirit of liberty is also true of the spirit of truth seeking—a sense of one's own fallibility, that one could be wrong, even in one's most fundamental beliefs; an openness of mind; a willingness to entertain criticism and to engage critics. All these things are essential to the truth-seeking project. And that means they must be cultivated in institutions whose mission includes the pursuit and transmission of knowledge.

In this environment, we can still advocate for our views and engage politically. I myself am highly engaged politically and have been so throughout my career in the academy. But politically engaged scholars and teachers, like all scholars and teachers, need to be highly cognizant of their own fallibility—even on matters about which they care deeply and causes in which they are profoundly emotionally invested. One must never imagine that one cannot possibly be wrong about this or that cherished conviction, or that one's political adversaries and intellectual critics cannot possibly be right. That is fatal to the truth-seeking enterprise.

I think the proper attitude for us to hold is the attitude Plato teaches us to adopt, especially in the *Gorgias*. We must always be on the lookout for, and open to, the person who will confer upon us the inestimable benefit of showing us that we are in error, where in fact we are in error. Such a person, in correcting our mistakes, does us the very best service. We need to see that, and we need to help our students see it. One who sees his intellectual adversary as an enemy to be defeated, rather than as a friend joined with him dialectically in the pursuit of a common aim—namely, knowledge of the truth—is already off the rails. He is in grave danger of falling into the ditch of sophistry.

A spirit of openness to argument and challenge, where it flourishes in an academic culture, is what immunizes academic institutions against groupthink and chases the groupthink away when it comes knocking at the door.

Part of the problem, of course, is that once groupthink has taken hold, those who are caught up in it don't recognize the problem. When is the last time you met somebody who said, "Yeah, you know what? My problem is that I'm caught up in groupthink. I tend to just think like everybody else around me thinks." The trouble with groupthink is that—like a fish swimming in water—when you're in it, you generally don't know you're in it. You may realize that not everyone shares your views, but you will suppose that those who dissent from them are irrational or ill-motivated. You will imagine that anyone who disagrees with you is a bigot or tool of nefarious interests—a fool or a fraud. Someone who is in groupthink could pass a lie detector test claiming that he is not in groupthink, but that doesn't mean he's not in groupthink. And wherever ideological orthodoxies settle into place, we have to worry about groupthink setting in. That's true whether or not campus illiberalism visibly manifests itself in dissenting speakers being excluded from campus or shouted down.

Viewpoint diversity has value as a kind of vaccine against groupthink, and as an antidote to groupthink when it begins to set in. Diversity of views, approaches, arguments, and the like is the cure for campus illiberalism. People who have the spirit of being "not too sure they are right"—people who want to be challenged because they know that challenging and being challenged are integral and indispensable to the process of knowledge-seeking—such people (whatever their own personal views) will want intellectual diversity on campus in order for the institution to accomplish its mission.

We all know that it's hard to get this intellectual diversity. I think there are several reasons for that, reasons that go well beyond deliberate discrimination in hiring and promotion against people who dissent from the regnant orthodoxies. I don't think such blatant discrimination (though, regrettably, it does occur) is the heart of the problem. The more fundamental—and difficult—challenge is that we human beings, frail creatures that we are, have trouble appreciating meritorious work and even good arguments when they run contrary to our own opinions, especially when we're strongly emotionally attached to those opinions.

As I see it, this isn't just a progressive or left-wing problem; it's a human nature problem. Any time an intellectual or political orthodoxy has hardened into place—it doesn't matter whether a left-wing or right-wing orthodoxy—it becomes very difficult for many people to draw the distinction between "work I disagree with despite its being really very good and challenging and interesting and important," and "work that goes contrary to what I just know to be true on issues that are important and critical to me and bound up with my sense of who I am as a [fill in the blank: progressive, conservative, feminist, libertarian, Christian, atheist . . .]." People can perceive challenges to the dominant opinions as outrageous attacks on truth, indecent assaults on essential values, threats to what is good and true and right and just, and intolerable violations of the norms of "our" community.

———

What to do? First, I address my friends in academia who are on the progressive side of the political divide, and who perceive the problem as I do, and who think something needs to be done about it: We need to expose, and protest, any *overt* discrimination based on viewpoint. Honorable progressives themselves need to be in the forefront of calling it out the moment it appears. Period. By both precept and example, we also need to strongly encourage our colleagues and students to be rigorously self-critical in ways that would enable them honestly to say, as I might say about the work of, for example, my colleague at Princeton, Peter Singer, "Well, you know, I'm really scandalized by his defense of the moral permissibility of infanticide, but there's an argument he makes that's got to be met. And the burden is on me to make the argument that our dignity as human beings comes by our humanity—our status as beings possessing, at least in root form, even in the earliest stages of development, the capacities for the types of characteristically human activities that give human beings a special kind of standing and inviolability." The burden is on me, in other words, to meet his challenge.

I want my progressive colleagues to take the same position about work by more conservative scholars, especially in these hot-button areas. But I acknowledge that it's hard to do, especially when dogmas and orthodoxies have hardened into place and one is not even hearing arguments against one's own positions. For when one is not hearing them, and everybody one knows tends to think the same thing about that body of issues, no matter how much diversity there is on other matters, we're again headed for groupthink.

Working up the motivation to think more critically gets much easier when, in the normal course of events, one is regularly challenged by thoughtful people who have different perspectives. So it's best for us not to get ourselves into this fix in the first place.

A growing number of prominent university leaders around the country—Robert Zimmer, president of the University of Chicago; Michael Roth, president of Wesleyan University; Christopher Eisgruber, president of Princeton; Carol Christ, chancellor of the University of California, Berkeley; Ronald Daniels, president of Johns Hopkins University; among others (most of whom are, by the way, self-proclaimed political progressives)—are publicly acknowledging the groupthink or "echo chamber" problem in American higher education and asking for help in doing something about it. Here, alumni and friends who want to help make a difference have a golden opportunity. They can join efforts to found or support campus initiatives aimed at bringing a wider diversity of views into the discussion and turning campus monologues into true dialogues. Centers and institutes have already been created at many top universities in the United States and Britain to do just that. And they are already having an impact.

Allow me a couple of examples of the value of intellectual diversity, drawn from my own experience. One is the James Madison Program at Princeton, which I have the honor to direct. Founded nineteen years ago, its impact on the intellectual culture of Princeton, precisely by bringing viewpoint diversity into our community in a serious way, has been remarkable. It gives me enormous satisfaction that this opinion is shared by many of my liberal colleagues who share none of my other opinions. They have praised the Madison Program for expanding the range of ideas and arguments heard on campus—and benefitting everybody in the process. The presence on campus of such an initiative ensures that there are people around who represent a wide spectrum of views.

The practical effect is that at discussions across the university in general, not just at the Madison Program's own events, people cannot simply suppose that everybody in the room shares the same assumptions or holds the same opinions. People know they must defend their premises—because they will be challenged. That makes for a different, and much better, and more serious, kind of engagement, which profoundly enriches the intellectual life of the entire community.

A second example, again from my experience, has been teaching together with my friend and colleague Cornel West. Understand that Professor West and I have deep disagreements (he's a democratic socialist, I'm a traditional conservative)—but what happens in our joint seminars is magical and the impact on our students is amazing. We collaborate across the lines of ideological and political difference in the common project of truth-seeking; knowledge-seeking; wisdom-seeking; engaging with each other and our students in a serious, respectful manner; striving to understand and learn from each other; treating each other not as enemies, but as partners in the dialectical process of seeking truth, knowledge, and wisdom.

And here is the thing that really matters: the students learn, and they learn how to learn. They learn to approach intellectual and political matters dialectically—critically engaging the most compelling points to be adduced in favor of competing ideas and claims. They learn the value and importance of mutual respect and civility. They learn from two guys with some pretty strong opinions, neither of whom is shy about stating them publicly, that the spirit of truth-seeking, like the spirit of liberty, is open to the possibility that one is in error.

What Cornel and I do is, I believe, part of the cure for campus illiberalism. Now, I've always prided myself as a teacher on being able to represent, accurately and sympathetically, moral and political views that I myself do not share. Let's say that I'm teaching about abortion, or something having to do with affirmative action, or marriage, or religious freedom, or campaign finance and the First Amendment, or the Second Amendment right to bear arms, or whatever it is, in my constitutional interpretation or civil liberties classes. I like to think that if someone came in who happened not to know which side I was on, they wouldn't be able to figure it out from my presentation of the competing positions and the arguments for and against them. That's not because I think professors should hide their views—and outside the classroom I do nothing of the sort! But I don't think classrooms should be used to proselytize or push a moral or political agenda or recruit adherents for one's causes. That is why, no matter how much I care about an issue, I strive in class to present the very best arguments, not only for my own positions, but for positions I strongly reject.

What I have learned in teaching with Cornel, however, is that as good as I think I am at this, I am not good enough. The evidence is simply that time after time in the course of our seminars I have found Cornel saying something, or making a compelling point in response to a point that I or one of the more conservative students has made, that simply would not have occurred to me—a point that needs to be seriously considered and engaged. Had Cornel not been there, even doing my best to represent his side, the point would not have been made, and the benefit to be conferred on all of us in grappling with it would not have been gained.

Cornel tells me that he has had precisely the same experience, time and again. He has found me making points or developing lines of argument that he says he had never considered and that simply would not have occurred to him, even though he shares my aspiration to represent as fully and sympathetically as possible positions and arguments from across the spectrum.

A healthy intellectual milieu is one in which students and scholars regularly encounter competing views and arguments; where intelligent dissent from dominant views is common and the value of dissent is understood and appreciated; where beliefs that can be supported by arguments and advanced in a spirit of goodwill are common enough that they do not strike people as reflections of ignorance, bigotry, or bad will—and people who do not share them do not experience them as personal assaults or outrages against community values.

It's great to have competing views among instructors in the classroom, yet many institutions cannot afford to provide that luxury on a regular basis. But diversity among faculty on campus, even if not in the same classroom, helps to cure campus illiberalism. It voids the tendency of people—students and faculty alike—who hold positions that happen to be dominant to suppose that the college or university is only for people like them, not for people who disagree with them. It sends a message that all who seek knowledge of truth and wish to pursue it in a spirit of civility and mutual respect are welcome here as insiders sharing the truly constitutive values and goals of the community, not outsiders who are, at best, merely to be tolerated.

Am I advocating "affirmative action" for conservatives? Not at all. I am pleading for attitudes and practices that will cure campus illiberalism without the need to give conservative scholars preferences in hiring and promotion. If conscious and unconscious prejudice against people who dissent from prevailing orthodoxies were defeated, if intellectual diversity were truly valued for its vital contribution to the cause of learning, the hiring and promoting problems would take care of themselves. We would not have departments of sociology or political science or history with forty-three liberals and one conservative (or, more likely, one libertarian). Nor would we have the embarrassments, and (as at Middlebury) the tragedy, of campus illiberalism.

———

Let me close with a plea to teachers, administrators, school board members, parents, and anyone else who is in a position to influence what goes on in K–12 and, especially, high school education. You are sending those of us who teach at the college level increasingly diverse students, and that's great. It's especially wonderful to see so many young men and women who are of the first generation in their families to go to college, and to see many, many children of immigrants from nations and cultures spanning the entire globe. Bravo! That's what we want.

But I'm also seeing something else, and it's not what we want or should want—students who are diverse in myriad ways and yet alike in their viewpoints and perspectives, students who have absorbed what I sometimes call the *New York Times* editorial board view of the world.

They think what, evidently, they think they are supposed to think, if they are to be regarded as urbane, sophisticated, "woke." They seem to have absorbed, uncritically, progressive ideology, and they embrace it zealously, obediently, and, alas, dogmatically as a faith, a kind of religion. Challenging its presuppositions and tenets is regarded not merely as wrong or even as heretical, but as, in many cases, quite literally unthinkable. In other words, they come to us already in groupthink. (I suppose that makes the job of any left-wing professors who actually do want to indoctrinate their students easy: they come preindoctrinated.)

This is bad. Sure, it makes it fun for people like me to shock and scandalize the youngsters, in the way I suppose it was fun for secular liberal professors of an earlier era to shock and scandalize students from devout evangelical backgrounds by teaching Darwinian evolution or introducing them to the historical-critical approach to understanding the Bible. But that's scarcely comforting. If teachers or schools are doing the indoctrination, they really must stop. And even if they aren't, schools need to teach students to question dominant or prevailing opinions among their peers and in their communities and equip them with the tools of critical thinking and logical reasoning that will make such questioning intellectually fruitful for them.

For starters, kids need to be taught that whatever they and their peers believe and take as what all "right-thinking" people believe is actually contested by fellow citizens of theirs who are no less reasonable people of goodwill than they themselves are. My experience with students in recent years tends to support the thesis that many are ignorant of this fact. Sure, they know that there are people who don't share the views of the editorial board of the *New York Times* (or the people on stage at the Academy Awards), but they are inclined to think that such people must be bigots or ignoramuses. And by saying that students need to "be taught" that there are reasonable people who do not share their outlook, I mean they must be taught *by example* as well as by precept. Teachers and schools need to model the tolerance, open-mindedness, willingness to challenge and be challenged, and other values that we need to see more of in our students at all levels and in our citizens. Young men and women in, say, New York public or private schools, or in San Francisco, or Chicago, should not have to wait for college to encounter libertarian, neo-conservative, and socially conservative arguments, authors, guest speakers, or for that matter, teachers. I have a sense that there are many schools in which conservative teachers are as rare and (if they exist at all) exotic as they are in universities. Whatever the reason for this state of affairs, it is not good.

A final word for schools and teachers: Especially in the domains of civic and moral education, students need to be equipped with a fund of basic knowledge, including, notably, a knowledge of American and world history, and with the skills to think deeply, critically, and for themselves. If schools are doing their jobs properly, they will be sending us students who can spot bias in, say, history textbooks, even if the bias is in a direction they themselves favor. Our job then will be to help them deepen their knowledge and further refine their critical thinking skills. Kids will come to us from high school already on their way to being independent thinkers, lifelong learners, and their own best critics. And that means they will also be on their way to being responsible citizens, fit to enjoy—and equipped to play their role in sustaining and passing along to future generations—the rich blessings of living in a democratic republic.

CHAPTER 4

Philanthropy and the Civic Education Challenge

by Adam Meyerson and Adam Kissel

O UR COUNTRY is in a civic literacy crisis. Survey after survey shows how little Americans know about ourselves.

Thirty-three percent of Americans cannot name a single one of the three branches of government, according to the Annenberg Public Policy Center.[1] Only 26 percent could name all three branches in 2017.[2] Only one-fourth can name more than one of the five freedoms vouchsafed in the First Amendment. (The same study showed that more than half could name at least two of the five cartoon *Simpsons*.)[3]

This ignorance has been accompanied by an erosion of civic norms. According to a Knight-Gallup survey of free expression on campus, 37 percent of college students think it is sometimes appropriate to shout down a speaker with whom they disagree.[4] Many in the media have abandoned the presumption of innocence, so central to the due process rights of the Fifth and Fourteenth Amendments.

In recent months, we learned that a majority of adults in every state—except one—would fail the civics portion of the US citizenship test, which is part of the oral interview required for naturalization. Applicants for citizenship are asked ten randomly chosen questions from a list of one hundred and must come up with their own answers. (It's not multiple choice.) Questions range from "What is the supreme law of the land?" to "What movement tried to end racial discrimination?" A passing score is six out of ten.[5] The Woodrow Wilson Foundation, using a multiple-choice version of this test with forty-one thousand adults, found that only Vermont squeaked by with a bare majority passing.

Most adults in all other states—about 60 percent overall—failed the exam.[6]

Though this crisis of ignorance is not new, it has worsened in the last two generations. Civics was a staple of public education for most of the twentieth century. The Campaign for the Civic Mission of Schools notes that "until the 1960s, three courses in civics and government were common in American high schools: *Civics* explored the role of citizens especially at the local and state levels, *Problems of Democracy* encouraged students to discuss current issues and events, and *US Government* focused on structures and function of government at the national level." Today, however, says the organization, "the civic picture in our schools remains bleak."[7]

This is a far cry from Americans' robust civic knowledge in the nineteenth century. In 1852 Frederick Douglass could say, in his famous address "What to the Slave Is the Fourth of July?":

> To say now that America was right, and England wrong, is exceedingly easy. Everybody can say it; the dastard, not less than the noble brave, can flippantly discant on the tyranny of England towards the American Colonies. . . . The causes which led to the separation of the colonies from the British crown have never lacked for a tongue. They have all been taught in your common schools, narrated at your firesides, unfolded from your pulpits, and thundered from your legislative halls, and are as familiar to you as household words. They form the staple of your national poetry and eloquence.[8]

Today, little of that is true. Many graduates of elite colleges often struggle to name England as our old adversary. Firesides, legislative halls, dinner tables, and the media are generally silent about US history, not to mention the core principles of American government.

Civic education has declined for many mutually reinforcing reasons.

First, during World War II and the Cold War, there was broad recognition that America's conflicts with Nazism, imperialism, and Communism were not just military conflicts but ideological clashes between systems of government. Complacency about the future of democratic self-government set in after the collapse of the Soviet empire, and there was less focus in our education system and our public discourse on the special value of the US Constitution. But with the rise of China, totalitarian forms of Islam, and a resurgent authoritarian and expansionist Russia, it is increasingly clear that our freedoms and democratic way of life cannot be taken for granted.

Second, schools and colleges have prioritized other knowledge and skills over civics. *Why Johnny Can't Read* focused the nation's attention on reading skills in 1955.[9] With the "Sputnik crisis," the technological and engineering revolutions of the twentieth century, and the rise of computer science, many people have seen America's future through the lens of science and technology. In 1983, the now-famous report *A Nation at Risk* argued that "a high level of shared education is essential to a free, democratic society" but focused almost all of its disciplinary attention on math, science, English, and foreign languages.[10]

Third is the extent to which, in recent decades, civic education has focused on civic engagement at the expense of foundational knowledge of constitutional principles. The National Action Civics Collaborative, for example, explicitly denigrates "traditional civic education" as "boring and ineffective, focusing on the basics of our political system" rather than on civic skills.[11] The Power Internship Curriculum at Temple University teaches kids about "Oppression, Power & Privilege AND Identity Politics" and substitutes "awareness" of civic "issues" for actual civic knowledge.[12]

This line of thinking can lead to impractical, imprudent, and ignorant civic action. Robert Pondiscio of the Thomas B. Fordham Institute wrote in March 2019, after young students confronted a prominent US senator about the urgency of pledging her support for the Green New Deal, that "encouraging children to be directly involved in activism" is "morphing from a valuable instructional strategy into a manipulative and cynical use of children as political props in the service of causes they understand superficially, if at all."[13]

Today, the high school course in US history is often the only place in the curriculum to learn civics. A 2018 survey by *Education Week* found that only eight states have a yearlong civics or government requirement separate from history in their schools, while twenty-eight require half a year and fourteen have no separate requirement at all. Alarmingly, eight states require neither a government course nor a history course.[14]

And unfortunately, all too many history teachers and textbooks oppose the goal of developing appreciation for the Constitution and its core principles. Parallel streams of anti-American sentiments during the Cold War, social upheaval beginning in the 1960s, the Gramscian "long march through the institutions,"[15] opposition to American intervention in Vietnam, disgust over civil rights violations in the segregated South, arguments that the American Dream is an inaccessible myth, complaints over economic inequality despite huge improvements in almost everyone's standard of living, and new narratives of America as an oppressor rather than a liberator—all have led to many teachers and professors being much less interested in promoting American ideals. We see this pessimistic perspective on American history summarized in Howard Zinn's widely used textbook, *A People's History of the United States*.

A further case in point—fortunately since rectified—were 2014's changes by the College Board to the framework of the Advanced Placement US History (APUSH) course and exam. National Association of Scholars president Peter Wood wrote that in the new framework, "The American Revolution [became] little more than a replacement of one ruling class by another. . . . Major figures ranging from Benjamin Franklin and James Madison to Martin Luther King Jr. [went] unmentioned."[16]

These changes produced an outcry from many historians, and the

College Board listened. Today, the APUSH framework is much better balanced, and the framework for Advanced Placement US Government and Politics is strong.

Another case in point is the stress on social justice, civic activism, and critical thinking skills rather than content knowledge in the National Council for the Social Studies (NCSS) national curriculum standards, first published in 1994, and in the NCSS College, Career, and Civic Life (C3) social studies framework, which remain quite influential in elementary and middle schools.

The decline of general education requirements at the college level, combined with extreme specialization in the history profession, has led to a fall-off in US history survey courses. The National Association of Scholars found that sixteen of the top fifty colleges "had mandatory or preferred survey courses in American history in 1964," but that number was zero in 1993.[17] The American Council of Trustees and Alumni (ACTA) found that only 18 percent of four-year colleges require a "foundational course" in US history or government, and that US history was not even required of history majors at 70 percent of top colleges.[18]

Today's hyperpolarization shows the sad result of civics failure. But the efforts of many philanthropists and nonprofit organizations demonstrate that Americans retain deep interest in preserving our core political institutions.

President John F. Kennedy put it succinctly in 1962: "There is little that is more important for an American citizen to know than the history and traditions of his country. Without such knowledge, he stands uncertain and defenseless before the world, knowing neither where he has come from nor where he is going."[19]

Indeed, we should know why we chose to be independent of a king and an unaccountable parliament. We should know why we chose representative government instead of direct democracy. For 230 years, the structure of our government and its amendment process have given more people more freedom and greater opportunity than any other political system in the history of the world. The Civil War–era amendments corrected the terrible injustice of slavery and provided for equal protection under the rule of law. The Nineteenth Amendment guarantees women the right to vote. And when there has been continuing injustice, as with racial segregation and discrimination, our core documents offer a vision and framework for peaceful reform. We should know why Dr. Martin Luther King Jr. did not refer to our Constitution as an instrument of oppression and injustice; on the contrary, in his "I Have a Dream" speech, he invoked "the magnificent words of the Constitution and the Declaration of Independence" as a "promissory note" that all men, black as well as white, "would be guaranteed the unalienable rights of life, liberty, and the pursuit of happiness."[20]

There is growing recognition today, across the political spectrum, of the fundamental importance of separation of powers, checks and balances, federalism, equal protection under the rule of law, and protection of minority rights. But Americans need to know these things, to understand them, to appreciate them. Success in learning the fundamentals will make our civic attachments deeper, civic skills stronger, and civic action wiser.

———

One of the greatest opportunities for private philanthropy over the next ten years is to take on this challenge and help strengthen understanding of core constitutional principles. Philanthropy directed toward private-sector organizations is crucial because government programs and requirements have not succeeded.

Already today, many of the brightest opportunities for Americans to engage in their own civic education come from philanthropic individuals, nonprofit groups, and private foundations.

For example, the four leading historical sites in Virginia are all run by private organizations. In 1853, Louisa Bird Cunningham took a boat down the Potomac River and viewed with horror and dismay the dilapidated home of America's first president. She wrote her daughter, "If the men of the country won't save Mount Vernon, the women should."[21]

More than 160 years later, the Mount Vernon Ladies' Association still owns and operates the site, funding it entirely through ticket sales and philanthropy, without a dime of government money. Thanks to the Ladies' stewardship and philanthropists including Karen Buchwald Wright and the Donald W. Reynolds Foundation, over 85 million people have visited this national treasure and have come to better appreciate the leadership of George Washington.

Meanwhile, in the 1920s, Colonial Williamsburg was restored and re-created due to the philanthropy of John D. Rockefeller Jr. and community organizations such as the Colonial Dames. The Colonial Williamsburg Foundation owns the property and receives no state or federal funding. Similarly, the Thomas Jefferson Foundation has run Monticello, and the private National Trust for Historic Preservation owns James Madison's Montpelier.

Civics-related philanthropy continues actively today. David Rubinstein, for example, has provided for public display of original copies of the Declaration of Independence, the Emancipation Proclamation, and the Magna Carta, as well as major restoration projects at the Washington Monument and Lincoln Memorial. He says, "People who are more informed about our country and our citizenry are going to be better citizens, and if we have better citizens, more informed citizens, we might have a better democracy."[22]

The Philanthropy Roundtable, where we work, is building a network of organizations and individual donors focused on dramatically increasing support for knowledge of the Constitution and civic principles. Donors can—and many already do—invest in great practitioners who work with teachers, young students, college students, and adults.

In the government sphere, the Joe Foss Institute has contributed to persuading dozens of states to require some form of the US citizenship exam for high school graduation. This bare minimum is just a start toward proper civics education.

In the nonprofit sphere, excellent resources and training for teachers and students are provided by the National Constitution Center, Bill of Rights Institute, Ashbrook Center, Jack Miller Center, and Gilder

Lehrman Institute, which has created an inventive curriculum using performances of the musical *Hamilton* and interactions with its cast to encourage student interest in the Founding Era.

Classically oriented charter school networks such as the Great Hearts Academies make understanding America's core documents a priority.

At the National Constitution Center, the Interactive Constitution website hosts in-depth analysis of constitutional debates, concept by concept and clause by clause, with leading progressive and conservative experts explaining where they agree and where they disagree. The center has also teamed up with the College Board to develop excellent lesson plans for Advanced Placement students, including a two-week module on free speech.

The Bill of Rights Institute has joined with OpenStax, a top provider of open educational resources, to publish a free textbook, able to reach about half a million APUSH students and many others every year. The institute's teacher network includes a quarter of the nation's social studies teachers.

At iCivics, online games put you in the ratification debates; or at a law firm deciding whether your client's constitutional rights have been violated; or in all three branches of government as a law gets passed, signed, and challenged in court; or on a jury; or in your naturalization interview.

The Boy Scouts and Girl Scouts reach large numbers of children through citizenship badges. For more advanced students, there are leadership programs like Boys State and Girls State, debate competitions, and deep consideration of Supreme Court cases through the Harlan Institute.

For donors who want to work with their own alma maters, almost every university has at least one strong political science professor to build with, and the sixty-thousand-member Federalist Society has more than two hundred chapters at law schools. Dozens of individual professors lead centers that teach constitutional principles. The entire School of Civic and Economic Thought and Leadership at Arizona State University focuses on statesmanship through deep consideration of ancient and modern perspectives.

A great remaining challenge, as the surveys show, is retention of civic knowledge into adulthood. College students forget what they learned in high school, and adults forget what they learned in college. Civic associations focus so much on volunteer efforts that they often leave the fundamentals behind.

One model focused on adults is the Leadership Program of the Rockies, which grounds opinion leaders in constitutional principles, whether they are in business, politics, education, or the media. More than fifteen hundred graduates have become influential ambassadors of political and economic freedom throughout Colorado, and the program is expanding into other states.

In addition to connecting with best-in-class practitioners, donors can encourage these organizations to coordinate their efforts. A multidimensional set of local efforts in a particular city can have a major impact. What would it take, for instance, to double the civic literacy rate among children and adults in that city?

What could happen in civic education with the next hundred million philanthropic dollars? Imagine these possibilities:

First, many of the best-in-class practitioners could multiply their impact per dollar if they develop their resources with a bolder, yet more efficient vision. They can promote a small number of core constitutional concepts that children and adults are likely to remember. They can broaden the reach of their best existing resources. And they can work to reform teachers' preservice training and later professional development so that civic education is endemic to the culture of teacher education rather than something undertaken after the fact.

Second, city-level interventions can be replicated in hundreds of communities, reaching not only children but also the adults who actually engage in civil society today.

Third, membership organizations and those with short-term

education programs can focus on ambassadorship kits for peer education about the Constitution. And we can do much more to celebrate the naturalization of new citizens through public events.

Fourth, engaging people in civil debate around contested questions of American government—such as the contours of First Amendment rights—can develop civic skills and address polarization while providing education in core ideas. By debating the Constitution, we understand it better and become better citizens.

Fifth, we need to know more about what's working in this realm, including better metrics of success. Careful long-term studies will provide information we need for widespread, generational change.

Ronald Reagan famously said in 1961:

> Freedom is never more than one generation away from extinction. We didn't pass it on to our children in the bloodstream. The only way they can inherit the freedom we have known is if we fight for it, protect it, defend it and then hand it to them with the well-thought lessons of how they in their lifetime must do the same. And if you and I don't do this, then you and I may well spend our sunset years telling our children and our children's children what it once was like in the United States when men were free.[23]

This language was rousing nearly sixty years ago. But today the grandchildren of that generation often cannot recognize the former Soviet Union on a map nor even know what it was.

Our work is cut out for us.

NOTES

1. "Civics Knowledge Predicts Willingness to Protect Supreme Court," Annenberg Public Policy Center of the University of Pennsylvania, September 13, 2018, https://www.annenbergpublicpolicycenter.org/civics -knowledge-survey-willingness-protect-supreme-court/.
2. "Americans Are Poorly Informed about Basic Constitutional Provisions,"

Annenberg Public Policy Center of the University of Pennsylvania, September 12, 2017, https://www.annenbergpublicpolicycenter.org/americans-are-poorly-informed-about-basic-constitutional-provisions/.

3. National Constitution Center, "What We Can Learn about the Constitution from the Simpsons," January 14, 2018, https://constitutioncenter.org/blog/what-we-can-learn-about-the-constitution-from-the-simpsons/.

4. Knight Foundation, "College Students Show Strong Support for First Amendment, but Some Say Diversity and Inclusion Is More Important to a Democracy Than Free Speech, Gallup-Knight Survey Shows," March 12, 2018, https://knightfoundation.org/press/releases/college-students-show-strong-support-for-first-amendment-but-some-say-diversity-and-inclusion-is-more-important-to-a-democracy-than-free-speech-gallup-knight-survey-shows.

5. "Study for the Test," US Citizenship and Immigration Services, accessed August 15, 2019, https://www.uscis.gov/citizenship/learners/study-test.

6. "When It Comes to American History Knowledge, Woodrow Wilson Foundation Finds Only One State Can Pass US Citizenship Exam," Woodrow Wilson National Fellowship Foundation, February 15, 2019, https://woodrow.org/news/one-state-pass-us-citizenship-exam/.

7. Jonathan Gould et al., eds., *Guardian of Democracy: The Civic Mission of School* (Philadelphia: Leonore Annenberg Institute for Civics and Campaign for the Civic Mission of Schools, 2011), 12, https://civicyouth.org/wp-content/uploads/2011/09/GuardianofDemocracy.pdf.

8. Frederick Douglass, "What to the Slave Is the Fourth of July?" Teaching American History, accessed August 15, 2019, http://teachingamericanhistory.org/library/document/what-to-the-slave-is-the-fourth-of-july/.

9. Rudolf Flesch, *Why Johnny Can't Read: And What You Can Do about It* (New York: Harper, 1955).

10. *A Nation at Risk: The Imperative for Educational Reform*, a report to the nation and the Secretary of Education by the National Commission on Excellence in Education, April 1983, https://www.edreform.com/wp-content/uploads/2013/02/A_Nation_At_Risk_1983.pdf.

11. "The Challenge: Our Democracy Is Broken," National Action Civics Collaborative, accessed August 15, 2019, https://actioncivicscollaborative.org/why-action-civics/the-challenge/.

12. "Power Internship Curriculum (Fall Cycle)," University Community Collaborative, Temple University, July 2007, http://actioncivicscollaborative.org/wp-content/uploads/2013/07/UCC_POWER_Curriculum.Overview.pdf.

13. Robert Pondiscio, "Kids as Political Props," *Flypaper*, Thomas B. Fordham Institute (blog), March 6, 2019, https://fordhaminstitute.org/national/commentary/kids-political-props.

14. "Data: Most States Require History, But Not Civics" *Education Week*, October

23, 2018, https://www.edweek.org/ew/section/multimedia/data-most-states-require-history-but-not.html.

15. Originating with Rudi Dutschke, the term reflects Antonio Gramsci's idea that dominant groups lead culture and the subsequent cultural Marxist strategy of turning a culture toward Marxism by dominating, over time, the culture's institutions.

16. Peter Wood, "APUSH: The New, New, New History," *Academic Questions* 28, no. 2 (2015), https://www.nas.org/blogs/dicta/apush_the_new_new_new_history.

17. *The Dissolution of General Education: 1914–1993* (New York: National Association of Scholars, 1996), 28, https://www.nas.org/storage/app/media/images/documents/report_the_dissolution_of_general_education_1914_1993.pdf.

18. *No US History? How College History Departments Leave the United States out of the Major* (Washington, DC: American Council of Trustees and Alumni, July 2016), 2, https://www.goacta.org/images/download/no_u_s_history.pdf.

19. John F. Kennedy, "JFK on Our Nation's Memory," *American Heritage* 59, no. 4 (2010), originally published in 1962, https://www.americanheritage.com/jfk-our-nations-memory.

20. Martin Luther King Jr., "I Have a Dream," address delivered at the March on Washington for Jobs and Freedom, August 28, 1963, https://kinginstitute.stanford.edu/king-papers/documents/i-have-dream-address-delivered-march-washington-jobs-and-freedom.

21. Louisa Bird Cunningham (1853); American Association of University Women, October 12 Luncheon Meeting, accessed August 15, 2019, https://newlondon-ct.aauw.net/2016/08/23/october-12-luncheon-meeting/; A Southern Matron, "To the Ladies of the South," *Charleston Mercury*, December 2, 1853. (This article was actually written by Ann Pamela Cunningham.) https://www.mountvernon.org/education/primary-sources-2/article/charleston-mercury-on-december-2-1853/.

22. *Patriotic Philanthropy: A Conversation with David Rubenstein*, video of interview given by Jeffrey Rosen at the Philanthropy Roundtable 2018 Annual Meeting at Palm Beach, Florida, October 26, 2018, https://www.youtube.com/watch?v=wWmn6F-ho3c.

23. Ronald Reagan, "Encroaching Control," speech given to the Phoenix (AZ) Chamber of Commerce, March 30, 1961, https://archive.org/details/RonaldReagan-EncroachingControl.

PART 2

Character, Purpose, and Striving

CHAPTER 5

The Education of Character

by Peter Wehner

WHEN I began working as a speechwriter in early 1987 for then–secretary of education William J. Bennett, his agenda consisted of the "Three Cs": content, school choice, and character. In some respects, it was the last of these, character, that was the most contentious.

Bennett argued—more than any of his predecessors or successors—that it was the role of schools to shape not only the intellect but also the character of the young, to "help them develop reliable standards of right and wrong to help guide them through life."[1]

That view, he pointed out, was uncontroversial for most of American history. From the beginning, character education was a fundamental part of the mission of American education; to disregard the former was to deracinate the latter. Or so it was widely thought, until right around a half-century ago.

———

The *New England Primer*—known as "the little Bible of New England"—was the first primer used throughout colonial America. Fewer than one hundred pages long, it advanced a Puritan ethic, relying on rhymes ("In Adam's Fall / We Sinned all"), pictured alphabets, catechisms, and religious maxims. (Over the decades, and influenced by the Great Awakening, the emphasis shifted from God's wrath to God's love.) Eventually millions of copies were printed, and they shaped the moral landscape of America.[2]

John Phillips, the founder of Phillips Exeter Academy, expressed a commonly held view when, in 1781, he defined the new school's mission. "Above all," he stated, "it is expected that the attention of instructors to the disposition of the minds and morals of the youth under their charge will exceed every other care; well considering that though goodness without knowledge is weak and feeble, yet knowledge without goodness is dangerous, and that both united form the noblest character, and lay the surest foundation of usefulness to mankind."[3]

In the eighteenth century, according to Michael Josephson, a leading champion of character education, parents "valued character, and they expected public schools to help their children become both smart and good." Educators embraced this responsibility gladly, reports Josephson: "There was no effort to separate the teaching of knowledge from the teaching of virtue."[4]

In his landmark 1818 Report of the Commissioners for the University of Virginia, Thomas Jefferson described the purposes of education, which included improving one's "morals and faculties"; to "instruct the mass of our citizens in these their rights, interests and duties, as men and citizens" and "develop the reasoning faculties of our youth, enlarge their minds, cultivate their morals, and instill into them the precepts of virtue and order"; and "generally to form them to habits of reflection, and correct action, rendering them examples of virtue to others and of happiness within themselves."[5]

As the nineteenth century unfolded, the common school, the forerunner of the public school designed by education reformer Horace Mann, saw the moral instruction of students as one of its central purposes. There were differences over how exactly that should be done—for example, whether to include the Bible as part of the curriculum, whether specific denominational teaching should occur, and whether there was too much focus on Protestant-centered morality—but it was nevertheless assumed that an emphasis on inculcating moral habits was a strong component of education.[6] Indeed, the common schools came into being in part as a response to threats of social fragmentation and moral and social decay.[7]

Through much of the twentieth century, the importance of character education was still more or less a given, despite a variety of philosophical movements like logical positivism that challenged the view that public institutions, including schools, should instill ethical standards and moral principles.[8]

But the latter half of the century was something of an inflection point, for it was then that the so-called values clarification and cognitive moral development[9] movements began to take hold in primary-secondary education.

At the heart of values clarification was the belief that morality was subjective rather than objective, that neutrality on moral questions was the teacher's proper stance, and that the goal of education was not to instill traditional virtues but to help students clarify their own values and create their own value systems. The focus was on moral autonomy at the expense of moral authority. On questions of ethics, teachers became facilitators more than instructors.[10]

That view isn't as fashionable now. In fact, Lawrence Kohlberg, widely viewed as the father of values clarification and an influential Harvard psychologist who criticized traditional moral education on the grounds that it was "indoctrination"—"undemocratic and unconstitutional," in his words—revised his own views, admitting in 1978:

> The educator must be a socializer teaching value content and behavior, not merely a Socratic facilitator of development. In becoming a socializer and advocate, the teacher moves into "indoctrination," a step that I originally believed to be invalid both philosophically and psychologically. . . . I no longer hold these negative views of indoctrinative moral education, and I now believe that the concepts guiding moral education must be partly "indoctrinative." This is true by necessity in a world in which children engage in stealing, cheating and aggression. . . .[11]

By then, however, the damage was done, and the widespread consensus that schools should engage in moral education was fractured.

Since then, there has been something of a renewed interest in character education, although the results of purposeful character education programs are somewhat mixed, with some studies reporting success[12] while others[13] have found that for the most part they don't produce any improvements in student behavior or academic performance.

As one might expect, much of the success of moral formation in schools depends on the quality of the curriculum and training, how effective the implementation is, whether there is assessment and accountability, whether role models and mentors play a prominent role, and how much buy-in there is, not only from students, teachers, and school leaders but also from parents and the wider community.

A recent book by the University of Virginia's Institute for the Advanced Studies in Culture, *The Content of Their Character: Inquiries into the Varieties of Moral Formation*, explores how American high schools directly and indirectly inculcate moral values in students. In order to do this, researchers visited schools in each of ten sectors: urban public, rural public, charter, evangelical Protestant, Catholic, Jewish, Islamic, prestigious independent, alternative-pedagogy, and home schools. The results "point to a new model for understanding the moral and civic formation of children and to new ways to prepare young people for responsibility and citizenship in a complex world."[14] That model, however, has not been widely embraced and replicated. To the contrary.

The issue of character education is not simple, not in our increasingly diverse, multiethnic, pluralistic nation. To be sure, some people, including some within the education establishment, don't think schools should pay much attention at all to cultivating the moral life of their students. But that's hardly a majority view.[15]

The more common concern is whose values do we teach—when might respect for authority undermine individualism and justice?—and how do we teach them. For example, what role, if any, should religious teachings play in moral education? There is also the pressure that teachers feel to focus on academic standards, leaving little time and energy to focus on character education, as well as the understandable fear educators have of being drawn into contentious social and political debates. Teachers also tell me that increasingly parents take the side of their children when schools attempt to hold them accountable for misconduct. Enforcing discipline in the classroom has never been harder.

In addition, people are shaped by a host of factors, from genetics and the biomedical roots of human behavior to the environments—family, neighborhood, and so on—in which they grow up. How character is shaped is a complex matter, then, and often too much responsibility is placed on schools when it comes to the formation of character. Character education programs, if done well, can do some good for some number of students, but even that good can be washed away—by neglect, by abuse, by peer groups, and by heredity. In general, parents are greater moral influences on their children than are schools, yet we know that the children of responsible and attentive parents can go astray.

But neither is character education a hopeless undertaking, something beyond our reach and our wit. For the remainder of this essay, then, let us focus not on how we should go about teaching character education but on the prior question, which is *why* moral education matters—because I'm not sure that we're as clear on that as we should be. (A friend of mine recently told me, "Even the language of character sounds like a dead language—like one is speaking Latin.")

———

One compelling argument for instilling character in the young is that it's essential for academic achievement. It is impossible to teach or learn in a setting where students are rude, undisciplined, and in charge. If self-control doesn't exist in a classroom, chaos will prevail—and chaos is the enemy of intellectual excellence. Self-control—the mastery over one's passions, impulses, and desires—is a basic virtue, but not a natural one. It needs to be taught.

We know that self-discipline is among the most important traits when it comes to student success—this is particularly true for the iPhone generation, when the temptations to distraction are greater than ever—and schools that are disorderly and characterized by disruption will fail. According to neuroscience researchers Sandra Aamodt and Sam Wang, authors of *Welcome to Your Child's Brain*, "Childhood self-control is twice as important as intelligence in predicting academic achievement."[16]

But there's much more to character development than its academic utility. Character is essential to a fulfilled life and ordered liberty, something the ancient Greeks and the American founders both understood. For Aristotle, true happiness was to be found in living well, in attaining excellence in character, in exhibiting virtue. Those are the highest goods, he believed, and the only way to achieve inner harmony. This was consistent with the views of Socrates, who believed that those who are not virtuous cannot be happy.

When we give it even a moment's thought, most everyone agrees that good character—qualities like courage, compassion, empathy, kindness, honesty, respect for others, trustworthiness, loyalty, fidelity, friendship, fairmindedness, honor, perseverance, and self-control— are integral to a good life. Those who embody these virtues never regret having done so. "The ultimate joys are moral joys," David Brooks wrote in his marvelous book *The Road to Character*.[17]

This understanding of things can't be proven like a mathematical equation, and I suppose people who are fundamentally corrupt and malicious can claim that they possess inner harmony and are at peace with themselves and the world. I just don't believe them, and I rather doubt they believe themselves.

The reason, I would say, is teleological: We are made to live a certain way. We are born with a moral sense, an innate understanding of right and wrong, and (to borrow from C. S. Lewis) our souls are made to conform to moral reality. There are ramifications when we do, and when we don't.

Here is David Brooks again:

> Occasionally, even today, you come across certain people who
> seem to possess an impressive inner cohesion. They are not
> leading fragmented, scattershot lives. They have achieved
> inner integration. They are calm, settled, and rooted. They
> are not blown off course by storms. They don't crumble in
> adversity. Their minds are consistent and their hearts are
> dependable. . . . These are the people who have built a strong
> inner character, who have achieved a certain depth. In these
> people, at the end of this struggle, the climb to success has
> surrendered to the struggle to deepen the soul.[18]

The reason we should strive for the cultivation of good character
isn't for reasons of prudishness or priggishness, not because we are
censorious and killjoys. It is rather because good character leads to
human flourishing. Because there is not only honor to be found in
living a moral life, but joy too.

Yet even that is not the whole story. In a free society like the United
States, where external constraints on how we live our lives are limited,
internal constraints are all the more necessary.

James Madison, the most important figure in the creation of the
Constitution, put it this way in Federalist Paper #55: "As there is a
degree of depravity in mankind which requires a certain degree of
circumspection and distrust, so there are other qualities in human
nature which justify a certain portion of esteem and confidence.
Republican government presupposes the existence of these qualities
in a higher degree than any other form." He added, "Were the pictures
which have been drawn by the political jealousy of some among us
faithful likenesses of the human character, the inference would be,
that there is not sufficient virtue among men for self-government; and
that nothing less than the chains of despotism can restrain them from
destroying and devouring one another."[19] Later, at the Virginia ratifying convention of 1788, Madison said:

I go on this great republican principle, that the people will have virtue and intelligence to select men of virtue and wisdom. Is there no virtue among us? If there be not, we are in a wretched situation. No theoretical checks—no form of government can render us secure. To suppose that any form of government will secure liberty or happiness without any virtue in the people, is a chimerical idea. If there be sufficient virtue and intelligence in the community, it will be exercised in the selection of these men. So that we do not depend on their virtue, or put confidence in our rulers, but in the people who are to choose them.[20]

Thus Madison believed, as did the entire founding generation, that republican government could not thrive without a virtuous citizenry. The American founders believed this was a vital task, but knew that it wasn't an easy one.

Irving Kristol, one of the consequential intellectuals of the latter half of the twentieth century, wrote that we moderns are much more negligent than the founders were about the complicated ways in which the transformation of a community of individual sinners into a good community takes place and "uncomprehending as to the constant, rigorous attentiveness necessary for it to take place at all."[21]

Which returns us to character education. Our schools are but one institution of many that are tasked with shaping the moral lives of the young. The philosopher Martin Buber, while cautioning not to overestimate what the educator can do to develop character, wrote, "Education worthy of its name is essentially education of character. For the genuine educator does not merely consider individual functions of his pupil, as one intending to teach him only to know or to be capable of certain definite things; but his concern is always the person as a whole, both in the actuality in which he lives before you now and in his possibilities, in what he can become."[22]

Society can't create virtuous citizens without the help of schools; but schools can't create virtuous citizens without the help of society, individual communities, and parents. Students' character and ethics will only be made a priority for schools if they are a priority in the hearts and minds of adults—and too many adults have forgotten that virtue, the good life, and the good society are links in a golden chain.

We can't will the end—citizens of good character—without willing the means to the end: inculcating virtue in the young through moral precept, through example and habit, through rewards and punishment, through conversations and stories.

We've done it reasonably well before; we need—urgently—to do it again.

NOTES

1. William J. Bennett, *Our Children and Our Country: Improving America's Schools and Affirming the Common Culture* (New York: Simon and Schuster, 1988), 9.

2. *Encyclopaedia Britannica*, "The New-England Primer," accessed August 15, 2019, https://www.britannica.com/topic/The-New-England-Primer.

3. "Academy Mission," Phillips Exeter Academy, accessed August 15, 2019, https://www.exeter.edu/about-us/academy-mission.

4. Robert Tatman, Stacey Edmonson, and John R. Slate, "Character Education: An Historical Overview," *Character Counts* (blog), accessed August 15, 2019, https://charactercounts.org/character-education-an-historical-overview/.

5. *Founders Online*, "Report of the Board of Commissioners for the University of Virginia to the Virginia General Assembly, (4 August) 1818," accessed August 15, 2019, https://founders.archives.gov/documents/Madison/04-01-02-0289.

6. Graham Warder, "Horace Mann and the Creation of the Common School," VCU Libraries Social Welfare History Project, accessed August 15, 2019, https://socialwelfare.library.vcu.edu/programs/education/horace-mann-creation-common-school/.

7. Encylopedia.com, "Common School Movement," accessed August 15, 2019, https://www.encyclopedia.com/history/united-states-and-canada/us-history/common-school-movement.

8. *Encyclopaedia Britannica*, "Logical Positivism," accessed August 15, 2019, https://www.britannica.com/topic/logical-positivism.

9. Dr. Veritas, "Kohlberg's Theory of Moral Development," *American College of Pediatricians* (blog), September 4, 2017, https://www.acpeds.org/kohlbergs-theory-of-moral-development.

10. For a thoughtful discussion of the values clarification movement, see Edwin J. Delattre and William J. Bennett, "Moral Education and the

Schools," *The Public Interest*, Winter 1978, https://www.nationalaffairs
.com/public_interest/detail/moral-education-in-the-schools.

11. Richard M. Lerner and Jasna Jovanovic, eds., *Cognitive and Moral Development, Academic Achievement in Adolescence*, 2nd ed. (New York: Routledge, 2016), 84.

12. Marvin W. Berkowitz and Melinda C. Bier, *What Works in Character Education: A Research-Driven Guide for Educators* (Washington, DC: Character Education Partnership, 2006), https://characterandcitizenship.org/images /files/wwcepractitioners.pdf.

13. Sarah D. Sparks, "Character Education Found to Fall Short in Federal Study," *Education Week*, October 21, 2010, https://www.edweek.org/ew/articles /2010/10/21/09character.h30.html.

14. James Davison Hunter and Ryan S. Olson, eds., *The Content of Their Character: Inquiries into the Varieties of Moral Formation* (New York: Finstock and Tew, 2018).

15. One anecdote: A church class I attend on Sunday mornings is located at a public middle school in McLean, Virginia. The walls of the classroom have posters that include a code of conduct that emphasizes being courteous, on time, on task, prepared, respectful, and striving for excellence; that urges students to think before they speak by asking if what they're going to say is true, helpful, important, necessary, and kind; and that urges students to be ready, kind, respectful, thoughtful, and "your best." As you enter the classroom, there is a poster on the door that simply states, "Have Courage and Be Kind." Obviously, moral education is being encouraged.

16. Sandra Aamodt and Sam Wang, "Building Self-Control, the American Way," *New York Times*, February 17, 2012, https://www.nytimes.com/2012/02/19 /opinion/sunday/building-self-control-the-american-way.html.

17. David Brooks, *The Road to Character* (New York: Random House, 2015), 15.

18. Ibid., xvi.

19. Yale Law School Lillian Goldman Law Library, "The Federalist Papers: No. 55," accessed August 15, 2019, http://avalon.law.yale.edu/18th_century/fed55 .asp.

20. University of Chicago Press, "Representation: James Madison, Virginia Ratifying Convention," accessed August 15, 2019, http://press-pubs.uchicago .edu/founders/documents/v1ch13s36.html.

21. Irving Kristol, *Reflections of a Neoconservative: Looking Back, Looking Ahead* (New York: Basic Books, 1983), 82.

22. Martin Buber, "The Education of Character," *CrossCurrents* 1, no. 2 (1951): 16–25, https://www.jstor.org/stable/24455638?seq=1#page_scan_tab_contents.

CHAPTER 6

Restoring Purpose and Patriotism to American Education

by William Damon

A S ANY TEACHER will tell you, motivation is key to learning. Highly motivated students will find ways to acquire knowledge and skills even in suboptimal circumstances. Students who have little interest in learning will be hard to teach no matter how well furbished the school.

The gold standard of motivation is *purpose,* because purpose is enduring and resilient. A purpose is a long-term goal that a person sees as both personally valuable and important to the world beyond the self.[1] A purpose motivates one to accomplish short-term goals that serve that purpose. If a student is dedicated to a long-term purpose such as becoming a doctor, the student is likely to pursue short-term goals such as studying biology, passing tests, going to college, and gaining admission to medical school. Along the way, that student will learn a lot.

The human species is built in a way that requires purpose for optimal functioning. This was the groundbreaking insight of Austrian psychiatrist Victor Frankl in his mid-twentieth-century masterpiece *Man's Search for Meaning.* Frankl rejected the reductionist views of fellow Austrian Sigmund Freud, contending that people are not primarily shaped by base emotional desires, early experiences, past traumas, or nagging conflicts, but rather are driven by what they believe in—actually, *we drive ourselves* to accomplish purposes that inspire us and give our lives meaning.

In the half-century since Frankl's theory created a forward-looking line of thinking in psychology, research has confirmed the essence of his insights. Legions of studies have shown that, beginning in early adolescence, people committed to purposes show high levels of achievement, energy, resilience, health, emotional stability, and subjective well-being.[2]

Purpose is not a sole elixir for the good life; many other character strengths and skills are needed. Purpose alone does not ensure either good sense or ethics. But purpose ranks high on the list of character strengths that young people should acquire for productive and fulfilling lives.

Yet American schools today (with notable exceptions) are failing to encourage the all-important development of purpose among their students. My message in this essay is that the reforms most needed in American education are the kind that would improve the capacity of schools to help students find purpose in their studies and beyond.

In advocating for the cultivation of student purpose, I am emphasizing the importance of motivation, interest, agency, and individual choice. I believe schools are responsible for offering a broadly conceived education that imparts the moral, civic, and character strengths that enable young people to become productive citizens who dedicate themselves to the achievements they aspire to and the causes in which they believe. In K–12 education, this approach lies squarely in the camp that's been known as "educating the whole child." The assumptions behind it include a conviction that the cognitive skills and knowledge that are central to the educational mission can only be developed when students are motivated to learn, and that students will only be motivated to learn if they find personal meaning in the subjects they are offered. The whole-child approach also assumes that educators are responsible for more than cognitive learning in their students. Moral issues such as honesty and fairness arise in every classroom daily, and educating students to deal with such issues in an honorable manner is an essential part of a school's responsibility. So too are issues related to personal well-being and good citizenship.

I write as a developmental psychologist, not a political scientist or policymaker. My research focuses on purpose across the life span. When I argue that schools should promote, and not deter, students' acquisition of purpose, I consider this to be a position warranted by findings of developmental science rather than by an ideological stance or policy-wonk preferences.

But I cannot ignore one policy-linked irony of consequence: federal policy in the United States over the past quarter century has pushed K–12 schooling further and further away from whole-child education and toward a narrow curriculum and obsessive focus on test scores.

This counterproductive push took shape with legislation enacted in 1994—the Goals 2000 law and the Improving America's Schools Act, which enshrined standards and tests in just two subjects (reading and math) as the basis for judging school quality and effectiveness. The push strengthened with 2002's No Child Left Behind Act, was reinforced in several ways in 2009's Race to the Top program and was only slightly eased in 2015's Every Child Succeeds Act.

If one were intentionally to try to design a policy aimed at impeding student purpose, it would be hard to find a more injurious approach. The policy strongly shaped choices that educators made, or felt compelled to make, in school districts throughout most of the country. It's distressing to think of the vast number of students who, during their formative years for acquiring purpose, were subjected to the miseducative instructional choices promoted by this centralized, top-down, coercive, narrowly conceived, federal policy approach.

———

From our studies and those of other researchers, we know a lot about the conditions that foster purpose.[3] Here are the essential ones:

- Opportunities to participate in activities that one finds worthwhile, gratifying, and interesting
- Opportunities to discover and further develop one's talents
- Discovery of aspects of the world that need to be remedied or improved

- Opportunities to do so by making efforts to contribute something of value to the world
- Observations of mentors who are making such efforts in a purposeful way
- Instruction that fosters moral and character strengths such as
  honesty, diligence, and future-mindedness

What did twenty-five years of federal policy signal—and seek to
coerce—as the top priority for US schools?[4] None of the above. The
policy's most striking limitation was a narrowing of the curriculum
that resulted from the emphasis that those who designed the initiative
placed on the particular academic skills that they considered necessary for future employment. These skills centered on basic literacy and
numeracy. These skills are obviously important, and schools should
teach them in a rigorous way. I am in favor of teaching and testing for
these skills in order to keep improving them. But the federal incentive
system relied so strongly on testing for these, and only these, limited
skills that many school-based educators felt forced to focus on those
skills exclusively. "Peripheral" subjects such as art, music, theater, civics, geography, history, and creative writing were deemphasized and
even eliminated in many places. I have heard of schools that dropped
their music teachers, or stopped funding their theater programs, in
order to gain an advantage in the narrow types of student test scores
that counted in the federal incentive regime. I was told of schools that
no longer devoted resources to activities that foster students' interests in entrepreneurship, such as projects designed to acquaint them
with business skills and practices, and of schools that were not able
to continue funding instructive extracurricular activities such as the
school newspaper.

It is in such "peripheral" subjects that many students find personal
meaning and interest. The narrowing of the curriculum drastically
reduced the chances that such students would find purpose in their
academic work.

Perhaps it might be argued that it doesn't matter whether students find subjects such as art and music meaningful, since these subjects—unlike, say, algebra—won't land the student a job. It may be that this was the mind-set of the policymakers in the Clinton, Bush 43, and Obama administrations who shaped and continued to reshape this policy. But think about it for a moment. In terms of national GDP, one of the largest industries in the United States is the entertainment media, which draw on skills such as those fostered by various arts. Who is to say that students who avidly throw themselves into learning the arts have fewer employment opportunities than those who feel constrained in school to study subjects—the STEM constellation, for example—that government policymakers speculate will make them employable? Equally misdirected, removing entrepreneurship education from the classroom eliminates an entire direction for employment possibilities—a direction that, as the Network for Teaching Youth Entrepreneurship has shown, can appeal to many young people who otherwise find little of interest in traditional academic work.

Students who feel forced to learn become poor learners, and poor learners don't make for successful workers. Nor do such students end up feeling purposeful or fulfilled. A high school student we interviewed in one of our studies put it this way when speaking of her experience in a school that did not offer her anything matching her interests and personal aspirations: "I feel like a bird in a cage."

So we come to whole-child issues of well-being, motivation, emotional stability, and mental health. Federal policy during this prolonged period took no interest in such issues, and none was measured during the policy's reign. But we have evidence of how the cohort of students subject to such cramped schooling have fared in these essential personal qualities. A 2017 assessment by the American College Health Association reported that the current crop of college students expressed frighteningly adverse conditions related to their subjective well-being, mental health, and overall adaptation to college life.[5] Over 80 percent felt "overwhelmed by all [they] had to do" in college and "exhausted" by their academic workloads. Three in five felt "overwhelming anxiety" in college, and two in five "felt so depressed that it was difficult to function." Over half reported feeling "hopeless." It is hard to argue, in this time of lavish college facilities and grade inflation, that this contrast can be accounted for by harsher higher education environments. There may have been other causes that contributed to the personal difficulties of college students in 2017, but one thing is certain: the cumulative effect of federal K–12 education policy since the end of the twentieth century has done nothing to arm students with character strengths that could allay such difficulties.

Even regarding the limited set of abilities that Uncle Sam emphasized, learning conditions promoted by the policy were counterproductive. The policy operated by creating incentives for schools to improve scores on tests that held little interest or meaning for most students. Teachers, naturally, were induced to teach to the test, especially in schools and districts most vulnerable to the incentive/disincentive structure of the program. This led to deadly instructional practices such as drill and rote regurgitation, and objectives such as short-term learning rather than understanding and commitment. In keeping with the overall cynicism that the incentive scheme fostered, it also led to corruption in the behavior of some teachers and administrators. There were widely covered cases of fudging student scores, misreporting data, and other instances of actual cheating on the part of school staffers trying to give their own schools an advantage. So much for moral education by example.

Despite the highfalutin titles on these various federal laws—"No Child Left Behind," "Race to the Top," "Every Student Succeeds," and so on—the policy regimen was fundamentally dishonest. Toward what "top" was this program racing? The policy's provisions paid no attention to excellence, giftedness, outstanding performance, or originality. Nothing in the policy was directed to learning that leads to innovation and creative achievement—capacities that are important for both individual success and the national interest. For anyone paying attention to this policy's deceptive title, the cynicism surrounding the venture could only have increased. As if symbolically underscoring the moral void in federal education policy, the Obama administration closed down the Department of Education's character education desk as soon as it took office.

Which brings up the essential but fraught matter of moral and character education. Although most parents would like to see schools impart virtues such as honesty and responsibility to their children, character education in public education has been hindered by progressive resistance to instruction that makes claims about right and wrong in the face of cultural variation (even when such claims focus on values such as truth and obligation that virtually all cultures respect). There are recent signs of a reawakening, but we have a long way to go before American schools return to their once unquestioned mission of fostering character and virtue.

———————

Perhaps the most glaring failure of public schools has been their inability to accomplish another classic mission of American schooling—namely, citizenship education. This mission is as crucial now as ever; yet most schools today are failing at it, if they are even trying. Civics is one of the "peripheral" subjects deemphasized by the single-minded focus on basic skills during the recent heyday of the narrow curriculum.

During this period, the National Assessment of Educational Progress found that only one in four high school seniors scored at least "proficient" in knowledge of civics. For fourth and eighth graders across all academic subjects tested, civics and the closely linked subject of history came in last: "A smaller proportion demonstrated proficiency in civics than in any other subject the federal government has tested."[6] After some high-profile public figures such as Sandra Day O'Connor called this situation a "crisis," the neglect of civics among public schools has abated somewhat: in recent years, Florida, Texas, California, and other states have added beneficial civics materials to their public school curricula. Still, many key concepts have not been addressed, and doing so will require taking on a number of misplaced biases that are widespread in education circles today.[7]

In civics, as in all subject areas, students learn well only when they find the ideas personally meaningful. Genuine citizenship education requires building a sense of civic purpose among students.[8] The signs of civic purpose are knowledge of how one's government works, an understanding of the principles underlying the present social order, a historical perspective on the social order, and commitment to the preservation and improvement of one's civic society. In the United States, such a commitment means participation as a citizen in a democratic republic and a dedication to traditional American ideals such as liberty and equality.

Accordingly, there are motivational as well as cognitive dimensions essential for civic purpose. The key motivational component is a positive attachment to one's society—that is, a sense that one cares about the society enough to contribute to it and, if necessary, to sacrifice for it. Since the time of the ancient Greeks, this aspect of civic purpose has been called *patriotism*.

Unfortunately patriotism is not a popular word in education circles. In fact, patriotism is one of the most politically incorrect words in education today. If you think it's hard to talk about morality and values in schools, try talking about patriotism. Educators often confuse the patriotic love of country with aberrant nationalism or with the militaristic chauvinism that twentieth-century dictators used to start wars and manipulate the masses. There is little awareness among educators and intellectuals that it was the patriotic resistance to dictatorships by citizens of democracies that saved the world from tyranny in the past century and is the best hope of doing so in the future. Some examples of antipatriotic sentiments among educators today include the following statements that I have quoted in previous writings:[9] "This is not a form of allegiance that people need"; patriotism "motivates more death than justice" and "propagates the myth that America stands for the rule of law and stands for democracy"; it "can hardly be innocent: it is reproducing institutions which possess vast armaments"; "an education that takes national boundaries as morally salient reinforces . . . irrationality, by lending to what is an accident of history a false air of moral weight and glory"; "This nationalistic view is abhorrent."

Educators at every level of schooling see patriotism as antithetical to a global perspective on humanity and thus an enemy of the humane goals of peace and justice. Many educators urge schools to teach children to become "citizens of the world" rather than of a single nation, and to adopt a "cosmopolitan" perspective rather than identifying themselves as Americans. Indeed, there is a turning away from American identity as a desirable mark of citizenship education. Consider this statement by a university professor: "Long-standing notions of democratic citizenship are becoming obsolete, even as we cling to them. . . . American identity is unsustainable in the face of globalization. Loyalties are moving to transnational communities defined many different ways: by race, ethnicity, gender, religion, age, and sexual orientation."[10]

As global citizens, it is argued, students' identification should be with the humanity of the world. While the lofty ideals of cosmopolitanism and world citizenship are understandable, they do not in themselves provide a realistic route to civic education. For one thing, the serious tasks of citizenship that students need to learn are all played out on a local or national level rather than a global one. We do not pay taxes to the world, we do not vote for a world president or senator, we do not serve in a world army or peace corps, and we are not called to jury duty in any world courtroom. When we write e-mails to our congressional representatives or vote and campaign for candidates running for elective office, these activities are part of our national civic life, not part of any global event. As the philosopher Michael Walzer wrote, "I am not a citizen of the world. . . . I am not even aware that there is a world such that one could be a citizen of."[11] Eleanor Roosevelt, hardly considered a provincial chauvinist in her time, emphasized the standing of the nation-state as every citizen's primary identification when she proposed the Universal Declaration of Human Rights to the United Nations in 1948.[12] Again, what was once seen as progressive advancement of liberty is now castigated as reactionary. One result of this ideological turnaround has been the resistance of American education to promoting in our students a civic purpose and a felt attachment to our broader society.

In much of education today, American history and social studies are taught from a critical perspective. Yes, it is important that young people learn about mistakes their society has made and how the society can do better in the future. But it is always important to attend to context and development sequence—that is, placing the criticism in context of the country's achievements and principles, and presenting the criticism after the student has fully understood what is being criticized. Many students today learn about what is wrong with our country without gaining knowledge of its successes. Why would a student exert any effort to master the rules of a society that the student has gained no respect for and thus no interest in being part of?

To acquire civic purpose, students need to care about their country. As a foundation for citizenship education, schools should begin with the positive and emphasize reasons for caring enough about our society to participate in it and try to improve it. In this way, American students and those who teach them can share civic purposes energized by a motivating spirit of patriotism.

NOTES

1. For more details on this definition, now widely used in developmental science, see William Damon and Matthew J. Bundick, "Purpose," in *The Sage Encyclopedia of Lifespan Human Development*, ed. Marc Bornstein (Thousand Oaks, CA: Sage Publications, 2018).

2. Stanford University Center on Adolescence, "Journal Articles," accessed August 15, 2019, https://coa.stanford.edu/publications/journal-articles.

3. See Stanford University Center on Adolescence, "Publications," accessed August 15, 2019, for comprehensive findings: https://coa.stanford.edu /publications/publications.

4. As a vast and sprawling program that relied on incentives and disincentives rather than specific instructional mandates, there was considerable variation in the ways these federal policies were implemented, from state to state and district to district. But there was a common set of aims that guided the incentives and disincentives, and these produced a set of practices that

generally conformed to the initiative's narrow vision. The numerous critics of the initiative identified the same limitations that, in effect, operated as antidotes to students' acquisition of purpose.

5. American College Health Association, *American College Health Association-National College Health Assessment II: Reference Group Executive Summary Fall 2017* (Hanover, MD: American College Health Association, 2018), https://www.acha.org/documents/ncha/NCHA-II_FALL_2017_REFERENCE _GROUP_EXECUTIVE_SUMMARY.pdf.

6. Institute for Education Sciences, National Center for Education Statistics, "NAEP: National Assessment of Educational Progress," accessed June 11, 2014, https://nces.ed.gov/nationsreportcard/.

7. For recommendations regarding needed civic education improvements, see the consensus report from eight experts on youth citizenship development. Heather Malin et al., *Youth Civic Development and Education: A Conference Consensus Report* (Stanford, CA, and Seattle, WA: Stanford Center on Adolescence and Center for Multicultural Education, University of Washington, 2014), https://coa.stanford.edu/sites/g/files/sbiybj1076/f/civic_education _report.pdf.

8. Heather Malin, Parissa J. Ballard, and William Damon, "Civic Purpose: An Integrated Construct for Understanding Civic Development in Adolescence," *Human Development* 58, no. 2 (2015): 103–30.

9. William Damon, *Failing Liberty 101: How We Are Leaving Young Americans Unprepared for Citizenship in a Free Society* (Stanford, CA: Hoover Institution Press, 2011).

10. Ibid.

11. Michael Walzer "Spheres of Affection," in Martha C. Nussbaum, *For Love of Country?* (Boston, MA: Beacon Press, 2002), 125.

12. Mary Ann Glendon, *A World Made New: Eleanor Roosevelt and the Universal Declaration of Human Rights* (New York: Random House, 2001).

CHAPTER 7

Race, Discipline, and Education
by Heather Mac Donald

IN 2018, juvenile crime in Chicago was spiking. Carjackings had nearly tripled since 2015, and the share of juveniles committing them had grown from 35 percent in 2016 to 60 percent in the first five months of 2018. This surge was the result of a 2016 change in the criminal law that eliminated the automatic transfer of young carjackers to adult court. Now, sixteen- and seventeen-year-olds who used guns to steal occupied cars were merely getting probation. If a teen carjacker's criminal history was particularly egregious, he might face a few months in juvenile detention hall. "The kids have become enlightened to the [lack of] consequences," said Cook County's chief juvenile court judge.

Meanwhile, in downtown Chicago, youth mobs were running riot. Large groups of teens regularly swarmed across major intersections, jumping on the tops of cars caught in the stampede. Over the 2018 Memorial Day weekend, teens ran down Michigan Avenue punching people and vandalizing stores; a group of eight to ten boys knocked a fifteen-year-old boy to the ground, then stomped on his head and kicked his ribs, back, and face, before emptying his pockets and taking his shoes. The police made almost no arrests during the melee, preferring to avoid confrontation. Earlier that year, gunfire erupted during a fight between two groups of youths in the Water Tower Place mall.

"The city is lost," a federal prosecutor told me. "We have never had crimes like this downtown—people getting shoved and robbed at 3 p.m. It's just brazen." This prosecutor has started avoiding the Magnificent Mile on Saturday afternoons. "I'm scared to be downtown," she said. A Chicago police detective with twenty-four years on the job observed, "The kids who are mobbing downtown are the same ones doing the carjackings. This generation of kids has grown up with no one daring to touch them."

The New Orleans district attorney reported a similar breakdown of social control in his city. "Kids are terrorizing New Orleans," DA Leon Cannizzaro told me. "There is a lot of pressure now not to incarcerate. We put a lot of youth and adults in diversion programs. But there has got to be accountability. Without that, they become brazened, hardened individuals."

The lowered sanctions on juvenile criminals in Chicago, New Orleans, and elsewhere belonged to a wider push to reduce criminal penalties across the board. For the last five years, activists and academics have pressured legislatures into lessening the sanctions on criminal behavior or decriminalizing it altogether. From California to New York, serious theft, shoplifting, turnstile jumping, drug dealing, public urination, and littering, among other offenses, have been downgraded from felonies to misdemeanors or taken off the books entirely. A host of other criminal justice procedures—whether bail, police pedestrian stops (also known as stop, question, and frisk), or fines for skipping out on court—have come under attack as well.

A parallel process of desanctioning has been underway in the schools, and to the same effect: a rise in violent and antisocial behavior. The driving force in all these changes, whether in the education or the criminal justice system, has been the concept of "disparate impact." Any law enforcement or school disciplinary practice that disproportionately affects blacks and Hispanics is deemed racist. The vast majority of teen carjackers and robbers in Chicago, New Orleans, and other big cities are black, as are the majority of violent adult street criminals. (Blacks, for example, commit homicide at eight times the rate of whites and Hispanics combined.) Laws penalizing those behaviors, therefore, will disproportionately affect blacks (and, to a somewhat lesser extent, Hispanics). According to the proponents of disparate-impact analysis, however, the problem lies not with the behaviors that trigger that disparate impact, but with the laws and penalties themselves. By virtue of having disparate impact, they reflect bias and should be changed or eliminated.

The effect of disparate-impact analysis on education is arguably even more consequential than in the area of criminal justice, since schools are the last opportunity to correct an individual's antisocial behavior before he enters society as an adult.

Academics like UCLA's Daniel Losen have argued for years that school disciplinary practices were racist because black and Hispanic students were disproportionately suspended and expelled. Nationally, black students are suspended at nearly three times the rate of white students. Losen and his fellow antidiscipline researchers take such disparities as prima facie evidence of teacher and principal bias against so-called students of color. (Asians rarely get counted as students of color because they are academically successful.) Higher suspension rates for minority students are said to create a "school-to-prison pipeline." Suspended or expelled minority students have little choice but to become involved in street crime, it is argued, thus increasing their chance of ending up in prison.

Yet the school-to-prison pipeline conceit reverses cause and effect. It is the same lack of self-control that leads violent and disruptive students to be removed from class that also results in higher rates of crime and imprisonment. But suggesting that disparate disciplinary rates reflect different rates of school misbehavior has been taboo. It is simply assumed that black, Hispanic, white, and Asian students all behave identically in class but are treated differently by teachers and principals because of their race and ethnicity. Observational studies of student behavior are practically nonexistent because of the ban on acknowledging behavioral differences among demographic groups. But all available evidence points to the existence of large disparities in conduct. According to federal data, for example, black male teenagers between the ages of fourteen and seventeen commit homicide at nearly ten times the rate of white male teenagers of the same age. (The category "white" in these homicide data includes most Hispanics; if

Hispanics were removed from the white category, the homicide disparity between black and white teens would be much higher.) That higher black homicide rate indicates a failure of socialization; teen murderers of any race lack impulse control and anger-management skills. It is fanciful to think that the lack of socialization that produces such elevated rates of criminal violence would not also affect classroom behavior.

In the 2018 "Indicators of School Crime and Safety" report produced by the US Justice and Education Departments, black students self-reported being in a physical fight at school at over twice the rate of white students. Schools that were 50 percent minority or more reported weekly gang activity at nearly ten times the rate of schools where minorities constituted 5 to 20 percent of the population. (Reports of gang violence in schools with less than 5 percent minority populations were too few to be usable statistically.) Widespread weekly disorder in classrooms was reported in schools with at least 50 percent minority populations at more than five times the rate as in schools with 5 to 20 percent minorities. More than four times as many high-minority schools reported weekly verbal abuse of teachers compared with schools with a less-than-20 percent minority student body. (Again, widespread disorder and teacher abuse in schools with less than 5 percent minority populations were too low to be statistically reliable.)

These data all support the conclusion that "students of color" act out more than white and Asian students. (White students are also disciplined far more than Asian students, and boys far more than girls. The race activists have never accused schools of antiwhite and antimale bias, however, apparently accepting that Asian students and girls possess more impulse control and show more respect for authority than white students and boys.)

—————

In 2011, the US Commission on Civil Rights held hearings on school discipline. These, too, confirmed behavioral disparities. Teachers from urban districts described a range of violent and highly disruptive student conduct. A high school English teacher in Alexandria, Virginia, no longer tries to intervene in fights between black girls, he told the commission. "We've had staff members injured separating them. There's an anger in those girls, where there's no fathers in the home . . . that is almost unbelievable."[1] An eighth-grade social studies teacher from Allentown, Pennsylvania, said that it was "not terribly unusual . . . for one student to throw a chair at another during the middle of class because the second student made a nasty verbal comment."[2]

Academic-bias researchers complain that black students are punished more often for "subjective" offenses. These allegedly bias-inviting subjective infractions include defiance, disobedience, and classroom disruption, as opposed to, say, the "objective" offense of smoking. This objective-versus-subjective distinction is ad hoc and largely factitious. And given black family breakdown, with the attendant loss of child socialization, it is predictable that black students would be more prone to insubordination and classroom disruption. Another witness at the 2011 Civil Rights Commission hearing described some of the "subjective" offenses that urban teachers routinely encounter: "Calling out, engaging in conversation across the room, dancing at one's seat, loud singing, choral singing, exchanging insults . . . talking back to the teacher, use of obscenity, insulting the teacher . . . standing up and telling stories to the class, wandering around the classroom . . . touching other students, [and] leaning into the hall and addressing passers-by."[3] It is absurd to suggest that such behavior, which prevents other students from learning, is less serious than smoking.

In any case, "objective" metrics of problem behavior show similar racial disparities. The rate of chronic truancy (defined as eighteen or more unexcused absences a year) is five times higher for black elementary school students in California than for white students. Such truancy grows out of the same chaotic home environments that produce classroom disobedience.

Nevertheless, school districts across the country have been radically reducing punishments for serious student misbehavior, and doing so in the name of social justice. "Restorative circles" and yoga have replaced out-of-school suspensions and expulsions. School districts have hired costly school-climate transformation directors and equity overseers. The results have been the same as in the criminal justice arena: not greater justice, but greater violence and chaos. Students know that the rules have changed and that there are no longer consequences for their behavior. An eighth-grade girl taunted a middle school remedial teacher who had tried to reprimand her for continuously talking over him: "I'm going to torture you. I'm doing this because I can't be removed," she said, as the teacher recounted to the US Civil Rights Commission.[4] In Des Moines, teachers started leaving for new jobs after the school district demanded that disruptive students be kept in the classroom. Students hit teachers and other students with little consequence, reported the *Des Moines Register* in late 2016.[5] A nine-year-old boy was repeatedly struck by a fellow student, but the teacher felt powerless to do anything lest she be accused of discriminating against a minority student.

In 2018, a cell-phone video captured a classroom assault emblematic of the postdisciplinary era. A physics teacher in Texas had dared to confiscate a student's smart phone. "Give me my fucking phone. This is the last time asking your stupid ass," the teen yelled, towering over the teacher, who was sitting frozen behind his desk, the very image of cowering submission. The student aggressively swept the papers on the teacher's desk to the floor, then violently shoved him in the face. Still impassive, the teacher silently pushed the phone across the desk back to the student, who grabbed it with a self-righteous shrug and strode away. The school principal explained that it "was just a bad day the student was having," and commended the teacher's response.

A substitute teacher who worked in Los Angeles's inner-city schools documents similar insubordination in his recent book, *Sit Down and Shut Up: How Discipline Can Set Students Free*.[6] One student, recounts author Cinque Henderson, shoved a pregnant teacher in order to grab her laptop and watch a video. The dean then interrogated the *teacher* about why the student was not "jibing with her." An instructor from

Miami–Dade County told Henderson, "It is virtually impossible to discipline a student. I know we are losing a generation of kids of color as a result of allowing them to run wild."

Teachers are fleeing urban schools because of students' "chaotic unchecked behavior," Henderson writes. Students know that the rules have changed and that there are no longer consequences for their behavior. Henderson told two thirteen-year-old girls to go to the principal's office for insubordinate behavior. They refused. After ten minutes of defiance and the ineffective intercession of a campus aide, one finally said, "C'mon, let's go. Nothing's going to happen to us anyway." Henderson calls the tolerance for cursing at teachers the broken windows of public education: evidence of a collapsed school environment ruled by emotional chaos, where test scores are invariably rock bottom.

In New York City schools, violence and disrespect increased after school suspensions were reduced by fiat. A student was stabbed and killed in history class in a New York school where teachers had already reported a drop in discipline. The district attorney in St. Paul called the rise in attacks on teachers a "public health crisis." The district attorney in Syracuse forced schools to return to traditional disciplinary policies after a teacher was stabbed. In Charlotte, students brought guns and drugs more frequently to school, and teachers were attacked. Student assaults in Durham increased more than 50 percent in 2017. And education suffered as well. Wisconsin schools that adopted nonpunitive disciplinary measures had lower reading and math achievement than schools that stuck with traditional discipline.

This desanctioning movement was already well underway before 2014, when guidance from the Obama Education and Justice Departments threatened schools with litigation and the loss of federal funding if they did not bring down black and Hispanic disciplinary rates to the same level as whites and Asians. But that guidance strengthened the clout of pricey equity consultants and antiracism advocates, who redoubled the pressure on school district leaders and principals to not remove black and Hispanic students from class for serious misbehavior. In late 2018, Trump's education secretary Betsy DeVos rescinded the Obama guidance on school discipline, but K–12 education has become so permeated by identity politics and racial victimology that many districts will continue with their desanctioning policies anyway.

Pace the race advocates, this new state of affairs constitutes an actual school-to-prison pipeline. Schools are usually the last chance to civilize children if their family has failed to do so. Schools accomplish that civilizing mission through the application of a color-blind behavioral code, neutrally enforced, that communicates to students that their behavioral choices have consequences. Students learn that society will hold them responsible for their actions. If, instead, a school tolerates disruptive impulses and, worse, conveys that race is an excuse for bad behavior, that school not only does not arrest an antisocial, criminogenic tendency, it contributes to it. The teen carjackers in Chicago and rampaging youth in New Orleans likely faced little punishment in school before encountering that same lack of punishment from the criminal justice system.

In 1965, Daniel Patrick Moynihan warned about the effects of family breakdown. Almost three decades later, in a much-quoted article titled "Defining Deviancy Down," he wrote:

> [A] community that allows a large number of young men to grow up in broken families, dominated by women, never acquiring any stable relationship to male authority, never acquiring any set of rational expectations about the future—that community asks for and gets chaos. Crime, violence, unrest, unrestrained lashing out at the whole social structure—that is not only to be expected; it is very near to inevitable.[7]

The very reason why black students act out at disproportionate rates—the disintegration of the marriage norm—is precisely why strict school discipline and high expectations for behavior are so crucial. Self-control is essential for functioning in modern society. If it hasn't been learned at home, schools must be all the more insistent in demanding it in the classroom.

Excusing insubordination and aggression in the name of racial equity is not a civil rights accomplishment. The third-party victims of such behavior are themselves disproportionately minority—whether fellow classmates who cannot learn, or law-abiding residents of high-crime neighborhoods who have to worry about taking their children safely to school without being carjacked or caught in a drive-by shooting. But the alleged beneficiary of a racial double standard in conduct—the student who is exempted from strict discipline—is also a victim, since he will be handicapped in life by his failure to learn self-restraint and respect for authority.

The majority of black leaders today have chosen to play the race card rather than to call for personal responsibility in their own community. Rather than urging students to crack the books in order to close the academic achievement gap, they demand that colleges implement racial preferences to admit black students with far lower academic skills than their white and Asian peers. Rather than demanding that criminals face severe punishment for their predation, they blame a racist criminal justice system for the disproportionate share of black prisoners. And rather than encouraging students to obey their teachers and pay attention in class, they promulgate the preposterous idea that teachers—arguably the most social justice–marinated profession in the country—discipline minority students out of racial bias rather than the need to maintain order in their classrooms.

This swerve away from self-help and personal responsibility betrays the august traditions of black leadership, embodied by Frederick Douglass, Booker T. Washington, W. E. B. Du Bois, and Martin Luther King Jr., all of whom celebrated bourgeois values of comportment and high standards of achievement. They would likely have regarded the disparate-impact conceit with disdain.

Tragically, no progress in stemming the social catastrophe of family breakdown has been made since 1965, when Moynihan predicted that the march toward full racial equality would stall unless the practice of marriage returned to the black community. But double standards in behavior and in achievement only perpetuate the racial divide, rather than help close it. The highest mission of education is to pass on knowledge of a culture's greatest accomplishments and to develop in students gratitude for the beauty that has been bequeathed to them by past generations. But that transmission of culture can only occur if students first learn to civilize themselves.

NOTES

1. US Commission on Civil Rights, "US Commission on Civil Rights Briefing," February 11, 2011, 36, https://www.usccr.gov/calendar/trnscrpt/BR_02-11-11 _School.pdf.
2. Ibid., 7, 23.
3. Ibid., 9.
4. Ibid., 11.
5. Mackenzie Ryan, "Des Moines School Discipline Reform Stirs Backlash," *Des Moines Register*, November 26, 2016, https://www.desmoinesregister.com /story/news/education/2016/11/26/des-moines-school-discipline-reform -stirs-backlash/91745014/.
6. Cinque Henderson, *Sit Down and Shut Up: How Discipline Can Set Students Free* (New York: St. Martin's Press, 2018).
7. Daniel Patrick Moynihan, "Defining Deviancy Down," *The American Scholar* 62, no. 1 (1993): 17–30, 26.

CHAPTER 8

Educating the Gifted

by Michael Barone

I WAS BORN in 1944, on the day that Franklin Roosevelt and Winston Churchill, meeting in Hyde Park, agreed that they would not tell Joseph Stalin about the Manhattan Project that was developing the atomic bomb. I entered kindergarten in 1949, in the Detroit Public Schools, in a dark-green, two-room, temporary building across the street from a farm, on 7½ Mile, just a half mile north of the now-famous city limit of Eight Mile. While I was a kindergartener, the city of Detroit achieved its maximum population in the 1950 Census of 1,849,568—nearly three times its population today. Enrollment in the Detroit Public Schools (DPS) peaked at three hundred thousand; today, it is about fifty thousand, with fifty thousand more students in charter schools.[1]

This was also arguably the peak era of what I have called Big Unit America, in which Big Government, Big Business, and Big Labor were widely trusted, and large bureaucratic organizations governed the country's workplaces and schools alike. These were the Big Units that had won World War II and were building the unexpected prosperity of postwar America, institutions whose competence and expertise Americans respected, even as they occasionally chafed and grumbled at their rigidity and rules—not to the point, however, of complaining about the remoteness of their leaders.

The Detroit Public Schools were such an institution, with uniform textbooks and spiral notebooks, a standard curriculum and standard district-wide rules. When I was in the second or third grade, boys liked to wear Civil War–style blue or gray hats. DPS banned them, and I couldn't wear mine to school. In retrospect, there was good reason for the ban: for the children of the white and black southerners who thronged to work in the city's booming factories, those caps could be fighting words. That wasn't the case in my school, in the far reaches of the city, a neighborhood with a heavy Jewish population. But the citywide rule had to be enforced anyhow.

Other rules did too. I had apparently learned to read before kindergarten, and by second grade was reading at a sixth-grade level. My mother, who had taught first grade for a year herself, felt obliged to intervene repeatedly with my teachers and the principal's office so that I could take advanced books out of the school library, for the rules did not encourage special treatment of gifted or advanced students—quite the contrary. American public schools at the turn of the twentieth century had catered to gifted students, and a high school diploma then required mastery of what we would regard as college-level (or higher) material today. But in the 1920s and 1930s, the gospel of progressive education looked askance at such elitism and promoted in the name of egalitarianism a curriculum that was accessible to the great mass of students.

By the time I was in third grade, my mother had had enough. She enrolled me in an elite private school in suburban Bloomfield Hills, with smaller classes and more individual attention than I could receive from the rule-bound, mass-educating, public schools of Detroit. She ended up sending me and my two sisters each to different schools: a practitioner of school choice avant la lettre.

In my case, as it happened, this was just a few years before a sharp change in the education of gifted children. Progressive education advocates, it has been said, sought to educate the masses to be constructive and docile workers in enormous bureaucratic and industrial organizations, small cogs in very large machines. A massive military and heroic mass production had, after all, won the war for America but it was also apparent that advanced technology had been essential for victory and would be even more so if another major war should come (as they then seemed to, every twenty years or so). The atomic bomb, developed by creative physicists and brilliant engineers, many of them refugees from Europe, had persuaded Japan to surrender without the million casualties military leaders expected from an invasion: brains, not masses, made the difference. And the Cold War also seemed to be a battle of brains: the Soviets developed an atomic bomb just four years after ours, a hydrogen bomb virtually simultaneously with ours, and rockets that appeared to shoot up in the stratosphere earlier and more reliably than ours. In October 1957, when they fired off a rocket that put a satellite—Sputnik—into orbit around the earth before the United States could do so, there was something like panic in America—a panic that made it seem suddenly necessary to make maximum use of our gifted young people.

That imperative had already registered at Cranbrook School, where I was part of the class that took standard ninth-grade courses in the eighth grade, with a view toward taking calculus and advanced science courses in eleventh and twelfth grades rather than leaving them for college. This was part of a much wider trend, seen in other elite private schools and some public schools as well, particularly in the elite central-city high schools—Bronx Science and Stuyvesant in New York, Boston and Roxbury Latin, Central High in Philadelphia, Cass Tech in Detroit, Hyde Park in Chicago, Lowell in San Francisco—as well as the high schools of high-income suburbs such as Scarsdale and Great Neck in New York, New Trier on Chicago's North Shore, the Main Line outside Philadelphia, and Birmingham outside Detroit. The National Merit Scholarship Program started in 1955, and the now-huge Advanced Placement program was also born—and launched in many of the same schools—in the late 1950s.

As one writer put it, "The field of gifted education continued to evolve mainly in response to the changing needs of the country, especially after the Soviet Union's launch of Sputnik in the late 1950s."[2] Another chronicler wrote, "Interest in science during the 1950s and 1960s sparked funding for the most talented students in math and science, resulting in many education acts, including the National Defense Education Act (1958)"[3] and expansion of National Science Foundation funding. (I was offered an NSF stipend to get a PhD in history at Harvard but opted for law school at Yale instead; I'm not sure how this improved either American science or American defense.)

Did these policies work? I venture to say the answer is yes, and in support of that proposition cite a fact that may seem unrelated but actually I find entirely pertinent. The only year in American history that has seen the birth of three presidents was 1946: Bill Clinton was born in August of that year, George W. Bush in July, and Donald Trump in June—almost exactly nine months after V-J Day. All three were also members of the high school graduating class of 1964, the class that produced the highest SAT scores in history.

The year 1946 is generally taken as the beginning of the postwar baby boom (though Strauss and Howe's *Generations* places it in 1943, which would include 1944ers like me) and, given the sharp increase in births that year, almost certainly a disproportionate number of 1946ers were firstborns, who tend to score higher than younger siblings on intelligence tests. We can glimpse the dawning not only of an intellectual elite but also of a set of educational arrangements designed to sustain it.

But the emphasis on educating the gifted did not last. Although Advanced Placement and National Merit Scholarships continued, as did a modest collection of "exam schools," by the early 1960s American leaders were shifting their focus from foreign policy and the struggle with the Soviets to domestic policy and the need for economic and civil equality for blacks, especially, and the poor more generally. And the success of the civil rights movement in convincing the majority of Americans of the need for change—the oppressed teaching the oppressors—convinced many of the otherwise illogical proposition that people living in poverty were the people who could most helpfully teach society how to end poverty.

In the process, many programs aimed at educating the gifted fell to the wayside. The biggest federal program of aid to K–12 education, 1965's Elementary and Secondary Education Act (ancestor of today's Every Student Succeeds Act), targeted the disadvantaged, with the hope that extra funding would somehow produce the kind of upward mobility among discriminated-against blacks that the public school systems of New York and other big cities had produced a generation or two before among discriminated-against Jews and (if to a lesser extent) others descended from the Ellis Island immigrants of 1892–1924. Spending increased, spurred especially by the growing teacher unions, but the results were otherwise disappointing, as *A Nation at Risk* made clear in 1983.

Over the next three decades, the thrust of education reformers was primarily directed at improving the performance of disadvantaged and minority students, as well as children with disabilities, with little to no concern about improving the performance of the gifted. The No Child Left Behind Act (NCLB; 2002), which passed with impressive bipartisan support, embodied this approach in its very title. As a Fordham Institute research team wrote in 2016, NCLB "meant well, but it had a pernicious flaw: It created strong incentives for schools to focus all their energy on helping low-performing students get over a modest 'proficiency' bar." As Chester Finn and Amber Northern wrote two years earlier, "The pre–Common Core era has not done well by high achievers in the United States. Almost all the policy attention has been on low achievers. Meanwhile, it ignored the educational needs of high achievers." Neglect of the gifted, they concluded, was "one of the wrongs perpetrated on K–12 education during the NCLB era."[4]

The federal intervention was not fruitless. Reading and math achievement rose in the late 1990s and early 2000s, but then it stalled, with National Assessment of Educational Progress (NAEP) scores showing little change over the last decade. And, as Michael Petrilli has written, "More than half of our students graduate from high school without the academic preparation to succeed in what's next."[5]

Yet the situation of gifted students, at least for many of them, is not as dire today as in the early 1950s. Though seldom mentioned in polite, politically correct company, students with high test scores tend to be geographically and demographically concentrated—in upscale, that is, high-income / high-education portions of the nation's metropolitan areas plus some smaller university towns. Demographers have noted that Americans seem to be engaging in more assortative mating—high-test-score individuals marrying high-test-score individuals—than was the case in the first half of the twentieth century. At a time when college students were mostly male, highly educated men often married lesser-educated women. Today, however, as any reader of the *New York Times* wedding announcements is aware, highly educated, high-ability people tend to marry their intellectual and educational equals, and as readers of Charles Murray's *Coming Apart* are aware, modest-ability people and those with fewer education credentials often don't marry at all.

Paradoxically, perhaps, our increasingly fair society tends to have increasingly less social and educational mobility: Assortative mating means that gifted children tend to start off where in a fair society they should end up. The upward mobility of the children and grandchildren of Ellis Island immigrants has some parallel today in the mobility of the children and grandchildren of Asian immigrants—especially but not only coastal Chinese and high-caste Indians—against whom college admissions officers are practicing racial and ethnic discrimination of a kind eerily similar to what their counterparts once practiced against Jewish applicants. Similarly, the extraordinary success of Asian youngsters in gaining admission to New York's most selective public high schools has prompted Mayor Bill de Blasio to insist that their decades-old, exam-based admissions process be altered to ensure entry to many more lower-scoring blacks and Hispanics.

Yet as Petrilli notes, "We are not going back to a time when urban schools had the 'exclusive franchise' to operate schools within their geographic boundaries."[6] Public charter schools now serve over 3 million students and show no sign of going away, despite the efforts of teacher unions and Democratic politicians. Scholarship programs work hard to identify and aid students with high intellectual gifts and modest economic backgrounds. The Advance Placement (AP) program continues to grow—and diversify—without apparently compromising its rigorous standards. And the affluent parents of what is probably a large majority of gifted students are able in one way or another to exercise school choice on behalf of their children, whether by sending them to private schools, navigating them into public charter and "exam schools," or buying homes in high-achieving school districts.

These gifted children do not depend on an active federal government or the bureaucrats of a giant district to gain an education suitable to their abilities. Parents and philanthropists are doing a pretty good job of it, aided by the steady expansion of school choice.

The cultural variety and educational pluralism of our nation today leaves a growing number of gifted children from middle-class families better served than the uniformities of the midcentury left their counterparts more than sixty years ago. That, however, still leaves in the lurch a great many just-as-able children of the left-out parts of America today, including rural whites as well as disadvantaged minorities trapped in dire but unyielding urban neighborhoods. Many lack experienced "navigators" at home and quality school opportunities nearby. Some nonetheless prevail. Charles Murray, raised in Newton, Iowa, and admitted to Harvard in 1961 thanks to high College Board scores, was one such student; J. D. Vance, raised in Middletown, Ohio, and academically successful at Ohio State and Yale Law School (but only after four years' service in the Marine Corps), was another.

Murray wrote about the plight of such students in his 2008 book *Real Education: Four Simple Truths for Bringing America's Schools Back to Reality*,[7] noting that standardized tests were developed in the 1950s in order to identify able youngsters and steer them toward a rigorous college education. That was a praiseworthy effort toward a meritocratic education system that would advance young people on the basis of ability and achievement rather than birthright. Yet birth still matters hugely in the "coming apart" society that Murray characterized just four years later. And Vance's bestselling 2016 book, *Hillbilly Elegy: A Memoir of a Family and Culture in Crisis*,[8] shows how contingent his own success was on happy accident.

Some gifted youngsters create their own opportunities—or simply get lucky—but for most the education system has to provide them.

That it's doing better at this today than a few decades back doesn't mean the job is done, and it's a job that conservatives should—for at least three clear reasons—want to help complete.

First, because of the human capital challenge. A successful, growing, wealth-producing, and internationally competitive economy in the modern world cannot afford to waste the top talent that it could be cultivating.

Second, to further opportunity, encourage meritocracy, and advance social mobility instead of coming further apart, we need to realize that it's the *smart* poor kids with the greatest potential to be upwardly mobile, provided their potential is recognized and cultivated.

And, finally, because those of us who yearn to diminish identity politics, quotas, affirmative action, and other symptoms of social and cultural division and instead strengthen the American "unum" have an obligation to ensure that that potential is in fact recognized and cultivated in our K–12 arrangements throughout this vast land.

Notes

1. Citizens Research Council of Michigan, *Public School Enrollment Trends in Detroit*, Memorandum 1141, June 2016, http://crcmich.org/PUBLI-CAT/2010s/2016/enrollment_trends_in_detroit-2016.pdf.

2. "A Brief History of Gifted and Talented Education," National Association for Gifted Children, accessed August 15, 2019, http://www.nagc.org/resources-publications/resources/gifted-education-us/brief-history-gifted-and-talented-education.

3. "What Is Gifted Education?—History, Models, and Issues," Study.com, accessed August 15, 2019, https://study.com/academy/lesson/what-is-gifted-education-history-models-issues.html.

4. Chester E. Finn, Jr. and Amber M. Northern, "Can Gifted Education Survive the Common Core?" *Flypaper,* Thomas B. Fordham Institute (blog), February 20, 2015, https://fordhaminstitute.org/national/commentary/can-gifted-education-survive-common-core.

5. Michael J. Petrilli, "The End of Education Policy," *Flypaper,* Thomas B. Fordham Institute (blog), November 15, 2018, https://fordhaminstitute.org/national/commentary/end-education-policy.

6. Ibid.

7. Charles Murray, *Real Education: Four Simple Truths for Bringing America's Schools Back to Reality* (New York: Three Rivers Press, 2008).

8. J. D. Vance, *Hillbilly Elegy: A Memoir of a Family and Culture in Crisis* (New York: HarperCollins, 2016).

CHAPTER 9

Focusing on Student Effort

by Rod Paige

A MONG THE FOUNDATIONAL elements that underpin America's greatness, our system of public education is clearly among the most important. Recognition of the importance of a high-quality education system dates back to the nation's beginning.

Thomas Jefferson declared on multiple occasions that an educated citizenry is essential not only to personal attainment but also to the healthy functioning of a republic and the betterment of society. In a letter to James Madison, he expressed his hope that "above all things, the education of the common people will be attended to . . . [as I am] convinced that on their good sense we may rely with the most security for the preservation of a due degree of liberty."[1] Years later, he wrote to a colleague that "if a nation expects to be ignorant and free, in a state of civilization, it expects what never was and never will be."[2]

Such thinking on the part of the nation's founders—along with the heroic actions of civil rights leaders, presidents, and others over the years who have shared this belief in the importance of a quality public education for all—forged a system that helped to power the United States to world leadership.

Looking at the current status of that system, however, it is clear that we have lost our way. Former education secretary Arne Duncan has used the term "stagnation" to characterize the current state of affairs.[3] Those who find this characterization exaggerated and overly pessimistic need only look at the data. Although trend results from the National Assessment of Educational Progress (NAEP) show some gains in the early grades, progress in the upper grades has been minuscule—less than one point average score change per year from the early 1970s to 2012 (see table 9.1).[4]

TABLE 9.1

NAEP Long-term reading and math achievement trends, 1971–2012

Subject / Age Group	Average Scale Score		Change in Average Score over Entire Period	Average Score Point Change Per Year
Reading	1971	2012		
Age 17	285	287	+2 points	.0488
Age 13	255	263	+8 points	.1951
Age 9	208	221	+13 points	.3171
Math	1973	2012		
Age 17	304	306	+2 points	.0513
Age 13	266	285	+19 points	.4871
Age 9	219	244	+25 points	.6410

Source: National Center for Education Statistics

Furthermore, in the most recent round of NAEP assessments (2017), only 37 percent of twelfth graders were proficient readers, just 25 percent were proficient in math, and merely 22 percent were proficient in science.[5]

Results from international assessments are just as bleak. The United States is not among the highest-performing nations in any of the subjects tested by the Programme for International Student Assessment (PISA) or the Trends in International Mathematics and Science Study (TIMSS). In most subjects, our students perform in the middle or lower ranks among Organisation for Economic Co-operation and Development (OECD) member nations. That means the United States is no longer a world leader in education—and it is falling further behind as other countries continue to make gains while we stagnate. The only area in which we are an undisputed leader is education spending.

Given such evidence, Duncan's word choice is fully warranted.

Stagnation conveys a state of suspended activity in which there is no growth or development—a failure to progress.

The key questions we therefore need to ask ourselves today are: Why have our school reform efforts yielded so little? What should we do now? And why do so many leaders—including conservatives—continue to ignore the importance of student effort and responsibility in our nation's attempts to improve educational outcomes?

Complacency about the quality of America's education system was shattered in 1957 when the Soviet Union launched Sputnik into orbit. National fears that our foremost Cold War foe was beating the United States in the space race resulted in unprecedented federal investments in math and science education. Another outcome was a substantial increase in the federal government's role in public education—a source of tension ever since.

Almost three decades later, fears about the caliber of public education in the United States were stoked once again when a commission formed by President Ronald Reagan's education secretary, Terrel Bell, published its grim findings in the landmark report *A Nation at Risk: The Imperative for Educational Reform.* Released with great fanfare, the report issued an eloquent call to action:

> History is not kind to idlers. The time is long past when America's destiny was assured simply by an abundance of natural resources and inexhaustible human enthusiasm, and by our relative isolation from the malignant problems of older civilizations. The world is indeed one global village. We live among determined, well-educated, and strongly motivated competitors. We compete with them for international standing and markets, not only with products but also with the ideas of our laboratories and neighborhood workshops. America's position in the world may once have been reasonably secure with only a few exceptionally well-trained men

and women. It is no longer. . . . The educational foundations of our society are presently being eroded by a rising tide of mediocrity that threatens our very future as a Nation and a people. . . . If an unfriendly foreign power had attempted to impose on America the mediocre educational performance that exists today, we might have viewed it as an act of war.[6]

A Nation at Risk sparked a deluge of education reforms and investments, all of which promised to reclaim America's preeminence in public education. Even so, twenty years later, the Hart-Rudman Commission on National Security concluded that US education was still in serious crisis. Its report began with a forceful statement: "American power and influence have been decisive factors for democracy and security throughout the last half-century. However, after more than two years of serious effort, this Commission has concluded that without significant reforms, American power and influence cannot be sustained."[7]

"In the next quarter century," the authors declared, "we will likely see ourselves surpassed, and in relative decline, unless we make a conscious national commitment to maintain our edge."[8]

In the nearly two decades that have passed since the Hart-Rudman report, still other commissions and groups have issued similarly stark warnings about the weaknesses of the US education system and the resulting threats to our nation's security. In response, billions have been spent on education reforms at federal, state, and local levels. Scholars Eric Hanushek and Paul Peterson estimate that, since 1980, the federal government alone has spent almost $500 billion (in 2017 dollars) on compensatory education and another $250 billion on Head Start programs for low-income preschoolers.[9] At the same time, we have seen vast state, local, and philanthropic investments in improving public education. Big-city mayors have stepped up to involve themselves in public school governance, and courts have compelled states to devote more resources to the least affluent school districts.

Yet despite all of these increases in resources and activities, a large segment of the nation's youth—especially minorities and low-socioeconomic students—continues to experience high educational failure at an unreasonably high rate. Achievement gaps between socioeconomic groups have not significantly diminished.[10] And we continue to fall further behind many of our international peers.

Can the education system adapt? Evidence is mounting that Americans are growing frustrated by its failure to do so. The growth of competitors to traditional public schools such as charter schools, voucher initiatives, and homeschooling are signs of the public's waning confidence and strong desire for alternatives. (Others are simply giving up on the system and seeking out education refuges for their own children—private and posh suburban retreats that are the schooling equivalent of gated communities.)

Given both the undeniable evidence and the apparent consensus that our reform efforts to date have not lived up to hopes or expectations, it is high time to ask an important question. Playing off the title of Charles Payne's acclaimed book *So Much Reform, So Little Change: The Persistence of Failure in Urban Schools,* why has so much reform resulted in so little change . . . and what must we do differently?[11]

My experiences as the son of public school educators and as a teacher, college dean, school board member, district superintendent, and US secretary of education have lead me to believe that there are three distinct (though intersecting) categories of ways to improve teaching and learning:

- Increase the *quality* of instruction—that is, make it better.
- Increase the *quantity* of instruction—that is, do more of it.
- Increase the *quality* and *quantity* of the energy that the learner puts into the learning process—that is, increase student effort.

Over the years, US school reform efforts have focused almost exclusively on the first two categories while almost entirely disregarding the third. We have seen extraordinary efforts to improve the quality of instruction—more rigorous teacher certification, new curricula, new academic standards, "highly qualified teacher" rules, performance evaluations, merit pay, and so on. Efforts to increase the quantity of instruction have also been widespread: longer school days, more school days, and more time on task.

Without a doubt, high-quality instruction, high standards, and more time on task are essential components of improving learning and academic achievement. But I believe, and decades of cumulative evidence show, that they are insufficient. As we have seen, the results of reforms focused only on these elements have fallen short. I believe they are bound to continue falling short until and unless we also pay serious attention to the third category. As Henry Ford famously admonished, "If you keep on doing what you have always done, you will keep on getting what you have always got." Accordingly, if we want to get a different result, we need to change our thinking and doing. It is time to reform our approach to school reform.

———

Student underperformance has many sources, of course, but I am certain that a central reason our nation's heroic attempts to improve academic achievement have yielded so little can be boiled down to one word: effort. Too many students are investing far too little of themselves in their learning. I firmly believe that school reform cannot and will not succeed unless and until it takes student effort into serious consideration.

Today, American educational practices rest on the assumption that the teachers' role is to teach and the students' role is to sit there and let teachers bear primary responsibility for their learning. Generally speaking, we let students treat their classes like spectator sports.

This contrasts sharply with how things work in other helping professions. Psychotherapists, physicians, and social workers, for example, are responsible for the care and expertise they provide to their patients and clients, but they understand that they cannot achieve the desired outcomes alone. Those they serve share responsibility for the desired end result, whether it is becoming healthier, dealing with an emotional or mental health issue, or confronting an addiction.

Consider a client who is working with a weight-loss expert to lose fifty pounds. No matter how committed and talented the expert is, or how much expertise he or she possesses, the client's goal of losing fifty pounds is not going to happen without substantial effort on the client's part to control his or her diet, to exercise, and so forth. Progress is contingent on the person assuming ownership of the problem that needs to be solved.

Put simply, other helping professions treat achievement as a two-way street. This is not the case in our education system, however. There, we place responsibility for outcomes almost solely on schools and teachers, and their levels of expertise and talent are seen as *the* key determinants of student success.

The emphasis on high-quality instruction is understandable. Researchers have demonstrated the impact of teaching on student outcomes, and I believe that teacher talent as well as strong school leadership is crucial. But I submit that we will never achieve the learning outcomes we want without also focusing on the effort that students put forth.

I am not alone in thinking this. In the early 1990s, Harold Stevenson and colleagues published the findings of their intensive research into Asian schools, teachers, and students and how their beliefs and practices differed from those of their US counterparts. A journalist summarized Stevenson's key findings this way:

> At the core of many of the differences is the far greater emphasis that Americans place on innate ability in determining achievement. Asians stress effort. Every child is assumed to be able to master the full curriculum. Those who are slower are expected to work harder, not to achieve less. The belief in effort as the key to success engages parent, child, and teacher in a shared endeavor.[12]

Stevenson urged education leaders in this country to learn from Asian schools and warned of the devastating consequences that would result if they did not.

Tommy Tomlinson and Christopher Cross followed this line of inquiry by probing the reasons for American students' passivity in an insightful article titled "Student Effort: The Key to Higher Standards." "For fear of blaming the victims," they wrote, "[American] educators have been reluctant to endorse strategies requiring hard work from students as a condition for learning. US students are working far below their potential because they experience no reason to do otherwise."[13]

Taking this a step further, Tomlinson and Cross added, "Recent reformers have overlooked the simple truth that *to learn more, students have to work harder. With proper support and an understanding of what's at stake for them, they will*" (emphasis added).[14]

To be sure, a subset of American students—not a sizeable percentage, in my estimation—do put forth exceptional effort to learn and to achieve academic success. Some are internally driven; others are pressed to do so by their parents. The question is how to bring such effort to scale—that is, how to make it the rule rather than the exception.

Based on my strong belief in the power of student effort, I propose that school reform must expand its focus beyond the quality and quantity of instruction, and on the roles of teachers and school leaders. In particular, education reformers need to figure out how to:

- Help students accept personal responsibility for their learning, which becomes increasingly vital as they mature.
- Help students understand that achievement is determined at least as much by effort as by ability.
- Help students and teachers understand and appreciate the connection between effort and achievement.
- Help staff understand that student motivation drives their level of effort and that increasing student effort therefore requires increasing student motivation.

What can education leaders and policymakers do to bring these changes about?

In a 2018 *Education Next* article, Fordham's Adam Tyner and Michael Petrilli offered some compelling thoughts. While acknowledging that it's difficult for policymakers to "move the needle" on students' intrinsic motivation, they wrote:

> Another approach . . . is to hold students themselves accountable for their performance by ensuring that their work is tied to real consequences. This approach is based in research and used throughout much of the world. By giving students a greater and more immediate stake in their schoolwork and their learning, such student-accountability policies could bridge the gap between effort and reward.[15]

I am taken with the powerful idea that students will increase their effort if they understand what's at stake. Thus, I believe that reformers would be wise to ask what policies and practices will help students grasp what a high-quality education offers them and what conditions a poor education imposes and will continue to impose throughout their lives. They would also be wise to consider the counterproductive impact of rolling back accountability tied to consequences for the individual—for example, eliminating end-of-course exams that require students to demonstrate knowledge and skills in certain subjects before receiving a high school diploma.

Conservatives have long espoused the importance of personal responsibility and accountability, but many have been strangely silent on this issue. I believe it is our duty to champion efforts to increase the role of student responsibility and accountability in K–12 education—and to ensure that our education system ceases to be a passive endeavor that yields so many young people so little in terms of results.

I also believe we must reform school reform by rethinking school culture—beginning with asking ourselves what kind of culture our schools currently embody, what this says about what we value most, and what kinds of behaviors and habits it reinforces.

Amanda Ripley's eye-opening book, *The Smartest Kids in the World*, captures the very different school cultures experienced by students in different countries, one of whom is a bookish American teenager named Tom. A reviewer recaps Ripley's observations regarding the contrast between Tom's experience and that of his peers in Wroclaw, Poland:

> In Tom's hometown high school . . . sports were "the core culture." In Wroclaw, "sports simply did not figure into the school day; why would they? Plenty of kids played pickup soccer or basketball games on their own after school, but there was no confusion about what school was for—or what mattered to kids' life chances."[16]

Researchers have found strong evidence of the ways in which people's social environment shapes their behavior. As Linda Cox Story asserts in her dissertation on this topic, "The school is the principal social environment of adolescents; thus, the school environment necessarily influences the behaviors of students to some degree."[17] I would only replace her qualifier "to some degree" with "to a great degree."

What reform-minded leaders and policymakers therefore must decide is what they want the school environment to convey. If they want it to convey that learning is important and that education is the path to economic and social success, then the school environment must portray that—and only that—using a variety of visual and auditory communications to consistently reinforce the theme of economic empowerment through education.

The beliefs and attitudes of school staff, particularly leaders and teachers, are also powerful cultural forces within a school. They must believe that all children can learn at high levels and hold high expectations for all students, and their behaviors need consistently to convey these beliefs.

Many elements shape the character of a school, but few hold more power than the beliefs and attitudes of the adults in the building. I therefore propose that in reforming school reform, we not only need to reshape school culture and reorient the use of school time. We also need to ensure that administrators have the authority to build a school staff composed of individuals who believe, act, and display behaviors that vividly demonstrate to students that they believe all students can and will achieve, that a high-quality education is the path to a high-quality life, and that they are there to help students achieve.

Decade after decade, one commission after another has issued powerful warnings about America's education system. One study after another has revealed our weaknesses relative to other high-achieving countries and urged us to learn what we can from others who are succeeding where we are not.

In response, we have invested mightily and tried a host of reforms. Yet despite all of this, we've still fallen far short of the vision that so many leaders in our history have put forth as the key to democracy and the betterment of society: the vision of a high-quality education for all.

Clearly, the time has come for us to reform our approach to reform, not persist with more of the same. It is time for us to expand our thinking beyond the quantity and quality of teaching and learning, and to finally do what we have long ignored: acknowledge and address the pivotal role of student effort in the education process.

Put simply, we must put individual responsibility and accountability at the center of our reform efforts, which means embracing policies and practices that encourage and reward effort and persistence. To those who see this as blaming the victim, I vehemently disagree. Unless and until we embrace individual effort and responsibility and forthright accountability on the part of students, we will never achieve the outcomes we urgently desire.

Notes

1. "Letter to James Madison from Thomas Jefferson, 20 December 1787," Founders Online, National Archives, accessed August 15, 2019, https:// founders.archives.gov/documents/Madison/01-10-02-0210.

2. "Letter to Charles Yancey from Thomas Jefferson, 6 January 1816," Founders Online, National Archives, accessed August 15, 2019, https://founders. archives.gov/documents/Jefferson/03-09-02-0209.

3. See, for example, Arne Duncan, "The Threat of Educational Stagnation and Complacency," remarks at the release of the 2012 Program for International Student Assessment (PISA), December 3, 2013, https://www.ed.gov/news/ speeches/threat-educational-stagnation-and-complacency.

4. Data here include public and private schools. NAEP scores range from 0 to 500. Several administrative changes were initiated beginning with the 2004 assessment, including allowing accommodations for students with disabilities and for English language learners. To assess the impact of these revisions, two assessments were conducted in 2004, one based on the original assessment and one based on the revised assessment. In 2008 and 2012, only the revised assessment was used. National Center for Education Statistics, "The Nation's Report Card: Trends in Academic Progress 2012 (NCES 2013-456)," accessed August 15, 2019, https://nces.ed.gov/programs/coe/pdf /coe_cnj.pdf.

5. "The Nation's Report Card," accessed August 15, 2019, https://www.nations reportcard.gov/.

6. National Commission on Excellence in Education, *A Nation at Risk: The Imperative for Educational Reform*, a report to the nation and the secretary of education by the National Commission on Excellence in Education, April 1983, https://www.edreform.com/wp-content/uploads/2013/02/A_Nation _At_Risk_1983.pdf.

7. US Commission on National Security for the 21st Century, *Road Map for National Security: Imperative for Change* (March 15, 2001), accessed August 16, 2019, vii, https://tinyurl.com/yyqxdvvv.

8. Ibid., xiv.

9. Eric A. Hanushek and Paul E. Peterson, "The War on Poverty Remains a Stalemate," *Wall Street Journal*, March 17, 2019, https://www.wsj.com/arti cles/the-war-on-poverty-remains-a-stalemate-11552847932?mod=search results&page=7&pos=1.

10. Ibid.

11. Charles M. Payne, *So Much Reform, So Little Change: The Persistence of Failure in Urban Schools* (Cambridge, MA: Harvard Education Press, 2008).

12. Jessica Matthews, "Lessons from Asian Schools," *Washington Post*, November 30, 1992, https://www.washingtonpost.com/archive/opinions/1992/11/30 /lessons-from-asian-schools/dbe54869-7f39-45a4-aa2d-0aecebee498e/.

13. Tommy Tomlinson and Christopher Cross, "Student Effort: The Key to Higher Standards," *Educational Leadership* 49, no. 1 (1991): 70.

14. Ibid., 69.

15. Adam Tyner and Michael Petrilli, "The Case for Holding Students Accountable: How Extrinsic Motivation Gets Kids to Work Harder and Learn More," *Education Next* 18, no. 3 (2018): 28.

16. Annie Murphy Paul, "Likely to Succeed," *New York Times*, August 22, 2013, https://www.nytimes.com/2013/08/25/books/review/amanda-ripleys -smartest-kids-in-the-world.html.

17. Linda Cox Story, "A Study of the Perceived Effects of School Culture on Student Behaviors," *Electronic Theses and Dissertations, East Tennessee State University* (Paper 2249, 2010), accessed August 16, 2019, http://dc.etsu.edu /etd/2249.

CHAPTER 10

From Help to Need

A New Education Agenda

by Arthur C. Brooks and Nathan Thompson

A PERSISTENT UNEASE has lodged itself in the heart of modern American life.

While worsening polarization and increasingly rancorous policy disputes are clear enough for anyone to see, a sense of pessimism felt by many citizens runs still deeper than any kind of temporal political problem. The country's future is cited as a greater source of stress for more Americans than either financial or employment concerns.[1] Three-quarters of the populace either doesn't feel needed or useful in the work they do, or perceives that they are not valued by the nation's decisionmakers and institutions.[2] Just 37 percent of American adults believe that their children will have better lives than their own.[3]

In other words, Americans appear to be losing hope in the promise of America. A creeping suspicion that the United States has become a stalled engine—a mighty vessel in danger of running aground—pervades popular discourse. We see this in everything from public protests against global economic engagement and the American free enterprise system to the overwhelming frustration with our nation's leaders that saturates news coverage and social media feeds. Public rhetoric suggests that the American Dream is dying a slow death, suffocated by a fundamentally broken economic system, the outsourcing of jobs and capital to foreign lands, and newly calcifying socioeconomic divisions here at home.

And yet, while this American unease is ubiquitous, it finds itself seemingly at odds with the picture painted by the economic data.

As we write, the United States is in the midst of the second-longest economic expansion in its history,[4] with unemployment rates close to their lowest levels in nearly fifty years.[5] A clear majority of Americans sees their standard of living continue to rise, and inequalities in the provision of basic material necessities continue to shrink.[6] Robust economic growth has brought hundreds of thousands of individuals into the workforce, contributed to rising wages over the last two years, and lowered the unemployment rate for those without a high-school diploma to a mere 60 percent of its long-term average.[7] Economic growth is strong.

But these topline numbers are not the only reasons why one might reject the now-common claim that the American economy is rigged against those least likely to succeed. There is persuasive evidence that economic mobility has not stalled in the way most people think,[8] as well as evidence that the so-called 1 percent has not claimed a permanent seat atop the American economy.[9] Moreover, while income inequality is often viewed as a rising threat to economic mobility, it has actually decreased by 5 percent over the last decade.[10] Finally, while the reputation of free trade has suffered of late, a closer examination of the facts reveals that it is hardly the disruptive force it is often made out to be.[11] Although trade has caused concentrated disruption in certain communities, it is the culprit behind just a fraction of overall job churn in the American economy—not to mention functioning as the source of millions of new American jobs.

The startling disparity between our dismal outlook on the country's future, on the one hand, and its economic health, on the other, might lead one to believe that we are living in two different countries: one comprising people who only listen to the news or spend time scrolling through social media feeds, and one comprising economists. In the former land, journalists speak with ordinary people who convey an experience of deep-rooted anxiety about the health of the nation and their own ability to pass opportunity on to the next generation. In the latter country, economists relay the data they observe, which tell them that, by and large, the nation is in good health. How is it that perceptions and reality can be in such conflict? What are we getting wrong?

The truth of the matter is that while broad economic statistics inspire a sunny assessment of the state of the union, it does not follow that healthy figures for the whole of the country reflect evenly spread flourishing across its particular pockets. In reality, entire segments of American society have been left out of the system of earned success.

In the ten years following the Great Recession, almost all income growth accrued to the highest quintile of the income distribution, leaving millions with stagnant wages. Furthermore, as pathbreaking work from social scientists Robert Putnam, Charles Murray, and Raj Chetty has documented, Americans have been segregating geographically along socioeconomic lines. In important ways, growing geographic divisions have blinded our nation's leaders to the problems faced by Americans navigating the most difficult socioeconomic circumstances, fueling populist sympathies among those who feel most forgotten. Such a political development is not unprecedented; as research has shown, financial crises often lead to an increase in the representation of populist political parties.[12] However, the core challenge with such a development is not that a receding tide of opportunity has created an income gap. It's that too many Americans sense that they are not *needed* in their own families and communities. Substantial elements of America are suffering from a "dignity deficit."

How can we be sure of this? Here's what to look for: An attenuated sense of dignity is lethal to one's ability to envision a better tomorrow. If you are not needed by your family, your community, or your country, despair sets in. In such circumstances, misery and even death are often not far behind—and that is exactly what we are witnessing to an upsetting degree.

The United States is in the midst of the deadliest overdose epidemic in its history. Opioid-related deaths have skyrocketed to record rates: ten times the number of deaths per 100,000 members of the population as compared with the heroin epidemic of the early 70s.[13] At the same time, suicides have spiked to record numbers.[14] An economy that stalled for 80 percent of Americans for a decade combined with the hopelessness rippling out from concentrated areas of medical crisis are conditions wholly indicative of a dignity deficit.

If it is true that particular areas of the country face mounting barriers to opportunity and thus to dignity, one might reasonably ask why the tools traditionally used to overcome these barriers are not serving as they once did. As such, it should come as no surprise that concerns about our fellow citizens' abilities to achieve the American Dream are particularly acute with respect to the role of education and inequalities in educational attainment. Over the last decade, median hourly wages have grown nearly 8 percent for individuals with a college degree, while they have flatlined or risen by just over 2 percent for individuals with some college education or a high school diploma, respectively.[15] As the United States enters the heart of the twenty-first century, the acquisition of necessary training for productive participation in the labor force has not received the attention it deserves from policymakers. And for the majority of Americans who do not earn a college degree, such a landscape makes prospects for a better future feel understandably dim.[16]

What is the solution to this problem?

One popular answer is simply to give people more education and push them into a four-year college. Central to such a plan is government-funded college tuition for any student who wants to attend a public university—"college for all," in common parlance. In this telling, a university education is the linchpin of employment success and economic mobility in twenty-first-century America, making free college the single best way to address the challenge before us. If America wishes to remain economically competitive, the argument goes, it should imitate its counterparts in much of the developed world and provide a free college education for its young people. Though expensive, universal college is a both critical and common-sense investment that will pay for itself in the form of increased human capital, productivity, and growth, while closing the dignity deficit for those who struggle most to find opportunity in this society.

The second option, particularly in the event that a policy of "more education" fails, is to fall back on universal basic income (UBI) or a similar form of welfare program. If we can raise the income standard of those on the margins of society, goes the reasoning, we will eventually be able to push more people into college—the aim of option one. A UBI would redistribute larger amounts of income in order to rectify society's economic imbalances—oftentimes traceable to differences in education—directing income from highly skilled workers to those who have been shut out of the economy, with the hope that they might be able to put that money toward building a better life.

Unfortunately, even from a pure policy standpoint, both UBI and college-for-all are inadequate responses to the dual challenges of equipping individuals to earn their success and closing the dignity deficit.

Notwithstanding the devaluing of earned success that a form of greatly expanded welfare would precipitate, two outstanding issues remain. The first is the massive expense it would incur (some estimates place it around $3 trillion annually; others closer to $4 trillion), all without serving populations that need government assistance the most.[17] As a program primarily serving childless, nonelderly, and nondisabled households—not the aged, infirm, or parents of young children—UBI would divert resources away from the most vulnerable members of society to those who are not truly indigent. However, the greatest flaw in a plan to expand welfare payments is that it would do nothing to fix underlying structural problems with respect to people's abilities to earn their success and pass on opportunity to their children. If we are concerned with preparing individuals to become self-sufficient, an expanded welfare state does nothing to directly address a shortage of human capital.

A more-education approach generally and a college-for-all approach specifically take on an appropriate challenge: the lack of preparedness among America's citizens for participation in the modern economy. And yet, while these approaches identify a legitimate challenge, the solution on offer—paying full freight for individuals who wish to attend a public university—fundamentally misunderstands the realities of America's education landscape. Three important data points help us understand why. The first is that while the number has grown in recent decades, only 33 percent of Americans age twenty-five and older possess a bachelor's degree or higher, meaning that two-thirds of American adults over twenty-four have not, and likely won't ever, earn a college degree.[18] This is the case for reasons ranging from a simple lack of interest to a lack of preparedness (as well as cost, of course). But essential for the policymaker to understand is the structural nature of the matter: an attempt to push more students into college would be fundamentally at odds with the facts of American participation in higher education.

The second challenge is that many colleges do not, on average, accomplish what they set out to do: graduate students in four years with skills that employers want. In the case of the average American college student, acquiring a bachelor's degree from a private institution takes nearly six years (or just over five years at a public institution), oftentimes leaving students with few skills and tens of thousands of dollars in loan debt.[19] Moreover, a shocking 47 percent of individuals who begin a four-year college program do not graduate within even six years.[20] In other words, putting more people in college is hardly a guarantee that more students would earn a degree. Furthermore, many jobs today don't even require a college degree. According to estimates from the New York Federal Reserve, 44 percent of graduates who have taken "good jobs" (paying $45,000 or more a year) do not use or need the skills acquired during their years as college students.[21]

The final challenge—and what may be the single greatest indictment of a proposal to simply expand education access and funding—is that free college tuition is a regressive policy in practice.[22] For example, since England moved away from a free college model and introduced tuition fees two decades ago, the country has seen increased per-student funding, rising enrollments, and, most importantly, a narrowing of the participation gap between wealthy and poor students.[23] As counterintuitive as it may seem, charging tuition increases educational access for those who need it most. College-for-all, on the other hand, ends up being little more than aid for the already-college-bound.

In terms of cost and likely impact, the cases for UBI and college-for-all do not stand up to scrutiny as solutions to America's woes. But this is not fundamentally why these policy proposals are misguided.

While one could criticize UBI or college-for-all on any number of policy grounds, the deepest flaw of each springs from the same mistake: *they address the wrong problem.* To be clear, the shared—and most fundamental—flaw of such ideas is derived not from any particular misreading of policy or error of arithmetic. If a massive glut of spending on welfare or higher education in the present moment would solve underlying structural socioeconomic problems, both would be worth considering. But money per se isn't the issue. Rather, the problem is philosophic, for the real challenge the United States faces is not economic inequality; it is an inequality of earned success and dignity. And what both of these approaches are solutions to is the problem of *helping* more people rather than the more appropriate, and far more urgent, problem of building a society in which more people are *needed.*

The philosophic difference between helping someone versus needing that person cannot be overstated. The former suggests a conception of our fellow citizens as merely incidental to our lives, as if they are individuals we might pass on the street and wish well, but forget only a moment later. The latter, however, sees our fellow citizens, and especially those on the margins of society, as necessarily integral to our own lives and communities, understanding that genuine societal progress is achieved only when those individuals' communities, colleagues, and families need and value them.

To close the dignity deficit, then, we have to first solve a philosophic problem, not a policy problem. Those of us in the world of policy so often err by first trying to solve a policy problem when in fact it is an underlying philosophic problem that causes us to repeatedly travel down dead-end roads. In this way, we err because we attempt to solve society's problems in reverse order—starting with policy and then articulating philosophy, rather than the other way around.

With an understanding of the importance of first solving the philosophic problem, we can see that framing policy questions in terms of needing rather than helping should alter the way we think about and craft education policy in America.

When all we have to do is *help* others, indefinitely providing them with direct financial assistance or more education funding, it is far easier to tolerate slapdash solutions that do little more than throw money at problems. This allows us to remain distant enough from recipients of state spending to avoid taking any responsibility for their flourishing if their lives aren't ultimately changed for the better. But a commitment to building a society in which every last person is *needed* can and should open our eyes to a whole new set of possibilities for education in America. Such a commitment would free us from tired loyalties to existing models of education, or to a clinical and uncreative dependence on an impersonal state. This kind of philosophic framing places important demands on us of which we would otherwise be free. A philosophy of neededness requires us to become more engaged in our communities, more aware of our local education landscapes, and more willing to reexamine political commitments that may be well intended but that serve to maintain a counterproductive status quo.

Almost all people don't want to just be helped. We all grasp the necessity of material provision, of course, but one can be provided for while simultaneously being disposable. It is the indignity of feeling disposable that plagues so many Americans today. And a world in which so many people do not feel needed is one in which the rapid onset of hopelessness, opioid addiction, and the collapse of community feel not merely possible, but probable. In response to such a world, what America needs today is not a well-intended exercise in profligacy but a new education movement grounded in a philosophy of neededness.

What would such a movement look like?

To begin, policymakers must break out of what has become a narrow and self-limiting understanding of intelligence and ability. It is no secret that K–12 education in the United States is far too frequently geared toward test-taking and standardized assessments of knowledge. This is not all bad, for basic skills in math and reading are essential in most professions. However, by limiting our understanding of what it means to be educated to "possessing the capacity to succeed in STEM careers," we overlook other skill sets—basic critical-thinking aptitude and visuospatial ability among them—that are equally in demand in many fields. Whether in farming, advanced manufacturing, or other technical realms, there is not just a need for statisticians and physicists. As psychologists Jonathan Wai and David Uttal observe, by testing students so narrowly, we blind ourselves to the skills that many young people possess and that businesses require, leading society to "neglect many potential innovators and even 'future Einsteins and Edisons' from disadvantaged backgrounds."[24]

Similarly, a tight focus on a narrow set of aptitudes often leads to an emphasis on grade performance that comes at the expense of subject mastery, leaving students less prepared for career success regardless of whether they attend college. Rather than funneling K–12 pupils into a testing process that either fails to measure the range of human intelligence, or that privileges numerical scores and letter grades over genuine competence, we should be thinking more creatively about how to uncover and nurture their abilities. This is the guiding philosophy of organizations such as the Mastery Transcript Consortium (MTC), a network of public and private high schools that facilitates a more personalized, mastery-focused approach to education.[25] While the MTC aims to place many of its students in college, it is nevertheless an example of the kind of thinking that we should be more open to when crafting holistic ways to assess and develop the abilities of America's young people.

A second step in building an education movement based on need-edness is to provide students—especially in high school—with legitimate paths to pursue other than college, as well as ensuring that they have greater access to information about those alternative paths. At a practical level, this means much greater investment in career and technical education (CTE) programs, apprenticeships, and public-private partnerships between local businesses and high schools, all of which offer paths to viable careers and steady incomes without the necessity of a college degree.

Recognizing the value of these programs, many localities and businesses are taking steps to embrace nontraditional education paths. For example, P-TECH, a school initiative launched by IBM, offers students the chance to simultaneously earn a high school degree and an industry-recognized associate degree or other credential, complemented by relevant work experience.[26] Rather than attend a conventional college, these students graduate from high school prepared to make a tangible and rewarding impact in their local community and labor force. Another outstanding example of public-private partnerships comes from Huntington Ingalls Industries, which builds ships, submarines, and aircraft carriers for the US Navy. The firm has established partnerships at every level of education near its facilities in Virginia and Mississippi, including an apprentice school in Newport News that integrates classroom work with hands-on learning.[27] These are exactly the kinds of programs that the United States should be investing in, insofar as they take advantage of the broad array of human aptitudes without necessitating college completion.

If these programs are to succeed, however, students must also be made aware that they exist. To that end, schools should be proactive in providing students with relevant information about skills and technical education available to them aside from the college-only path. One way to do so may be to increase the number of counselors available to students—but not *college* counselors. A call for greater investment in nontraditional pathways should be accompanied by a similar investment in tailored guidance toward those paths. Given the enormous amount of money spent per pupil in the United States, alongside the fact that the average student-to-school-counselor ratio is 482-to-1, a greater focus on counseling that does not push ill-prepared students into college may be one way to improve awareness about these other programs and pathways.[28]

Finally, to build a neededness movement in education policy, a cultural challenge must be addressed: the glorification of higher education. Fighting against this trend will not be easy, but it is critical. College degrees are worthy aims for many and, on average, offer the surest path to self-sufficiency. But policymakers must be more attentive to the fact that equality of human dignity is not conditional upon college completion, and they must be careful not to build a system that fails to serve the majority of our citizens—who have not, and likely will not, attend college—because they have elevated a single ideal of a worthy life above all the rest. Moreover, we should resist the urge to put college on a pedestal, given that a degree is simply not necessary for many jobs in the modern economy. That's why it is so important that companies from Google to Whole Foods to Bank of America no longer require such degrees for every job.[29] Other employers would do well to follow their lead. If our leaders become advocates not merely for a more credentialed public, but for a functionally more educated public, we might be able to loosen the stranglehold that a college-for-all mentality has on the rhetoric of many of the country's policymakers. The result, one would hope, would be a country that acknowledges the dignity of all work and strives to facilitate opportunities for all Americans to earn their success, with or without a degree.

In the end, what American policymakers must realize is that the first step to doing away with our culture's help-first, college-or-bust mentality is solving the different philosophic problem of neededness. Once we have addressed this problem, we will find ourselves more able to both tackle our cultural obsession with higher education and take specific steps to improve noncollegiate opportunities in America.

Of course, such an approach is deeply pragmatic. It will strengthen the country's economy, build out additional paths to prosperity, and provide those on the periphery of society with more opportunities to make a living and give their children and grandchildren better lives than their own. These benefits are desirable. But more than larger paychecks and enhanced skills, what makes an education movement based on neededness worth investing in is that it will help our country restore the one thing that so many find themselves without today: dignity.

NOTES

1. American Psychological Association, "APA Stress in America Survey: US at 'Lowest Point We Can Remember'; Future of Nation Most Commonly Reported Source of Stress," press release, November 1, 2017, https://www.apa.org/news/press/releases/2017/11/lowest-point.

2. "Study: Voters Frustrated That Their Voices Are Not Heard," Congressional Institute, February 3, 2017, https://www.conginst.org/2017/02/03/study-voters-frustrated-that-their-voices-are-not-heard/.

3. Ben Popken, "Only 37 Percent of Americans Think Their Kids Will Be Better Off," *NBC News*, June 6, 2017, https://www.nbcnews.com/business/consumer/only-37-percent-americans-think-their-kids-will-be-better-n768706.

4. Sho Chandra and Vince Golle, "The US Economy Has Hit a Milestone," *Bloomberg*, May 1, 2018, https://www.bloomberg.com/news/articles/2018-05-01/as-u-s-expansion-hits-endurance-milestone-here-s-what-s-next.

5. Avie Schneider, "US Unemployment Rate Drops to 3.7 Percent, Lowest in Nearly 50 Years," *NPR*, October 5, 2018, https://www.npr.org/2018/10/05/654417887/u-s-unemployment-rate-drops-to-3-7-percent-lowest-in-nearly-50-years.

6. Jim Norman, "Americans' Ratings of Standard of Living Best in Decade," *Gallup*, September 12, 2017, https://news.gallup.com/poll/218981/americans-ratings-standard-living-best-decade.aspx.

7. Michael R. Strain, "Protect the Gains Made by Low-Skilled Workers," *Bloomberg*, November 1, 2018, https://www.bloomberg.com/opinion/articles/2018-11-01/low-skilled-workers-make-gains-that-need-protecting.

8. Mark J. Perry, "Some Amazing Findings on Income Mobility in the US Including This: The Image of a Static 1 and 99 Percent Is False," *Carpe Diem*, November 16, 2017, http://www.aei.org/publication/some-amazing-findings-on-income-mobility-in-the-us-including-this-the-image-of-a-static-1-and-99-percent-is-false/.

9. Russ Roberts, "Do the Rich Get All the Gains from Economic Growth?" *Medium*, October 23, 2018, https://medium.com/@russroberts/do-the-rich-capture-all-the-gains-from-economic-growth-c96d93101f9c.

10. Michael R. Strain, "Don't Believe the Naysayers: Capitalism Is Healthier Than It Appears," *The Guardian*, June 12, 2019, https://www.theguardian.com /commentisfree/2019/jun/12/dont-believe-the-naysayers-capitalism-is -healthier-than-it-appears.

11. Michael R. Strain, "You Can't Be Pro-Jobs without Being Pro-Trade," *Bloomberg*, December 10, 2018, https://www.bloomberg.com/opinion /articles/2018-12-10/elizabeth-warren-is-wrong-about-jobs-and-trade.

12. Manuel Funke, Moritz Schularick, and Christoph Trebesch, "Going to Extremes: Politics After Financial Crises, 1870–2014," *European Economic Review* 88 (2016): 227–60.

13. "Overdose Death Rates," National Institute on Drug Abuse, accessed August 16, 2019, https://www.drugabuse.gov/related-topics/trends-statistics /overdose-death-rates.

14. "Suicide Statistics," American Foundation for Suicide Prevention, accessed August 16, 2019, https://afsp.org/about-suicide/suicide-statistics/.

15. Elise Gould and Heidi Shierholz, "Average Wage Growth Continues to Flatline in 2018, While Low-Wage Workers and Those with Relatively Lower Levels of Educational Attainment See Stronger Gains," *Economic Policy Institute*, July 18, 2018, https://www.epi.org/blog/average -wage-growth-continues-to-flatline-in-2018-while-low-wage-workers -and-those-with-relatively-lower-levels-of-educational-attainment-see -stronger-gains/.

16. Liz Hamel, Elise Sugarman, and Mollyann Brodie, "Kaiser Family Foundation / CNN Working-Class Whites Poll," *Kaiser Family Foundation*, September 23, 2016, https://www.kff.org/other/report/kaiser-family-foundationcnn -working-class-whites-poll/.

17. Hilary W. Hoynes and Jess Rothstein, "Universal Basic Income in the US and Advanced Countries," *National Bureau of Economic Research,* Working Paper No. 25538 (February 2019); Nathan Heller, "Who Really Stands to Win from Universal Basic Income?" *The New Yorker*, July 2, 2018, https ://www.newyorker.com/magazine/2018/07/09/who-really-stands-to-win -from-universal-basic-income.

18. "Highest Educational Levels Reached by Adults in the US since 1940," United States Census Bureau, press release, March 30, 2017, https://www.census.gov /newsroom/press-releases/2017/cb17-51.html.

19. "Time to Degree–2016," *National Student Clearinghouse Research Center*, September 18, 2016, https://nscresearchcenter.org/signaturereport11/.

20. Elizabeth Chuck, "Just Over Half of All College Students Actually Graduate, Report Finds," *NBC News*, November 18, 2015, https://www.nbc news.com/feature/freshman-year/just-over-half-all-college-students -actually-graduate-report-finds-n465606.

21. "The Labor Market for Recent College Graduates," *Federal Reserve Bank of*

New York, July 17, 2019, https://www.newyorkfed.org/research/college-labor
-market/college-labor-market_underemployment_jobtypes.html.

22. Noah Smith, "Free College Would Help the Rich More Than the Poor," *Bloomberg*, October 30, 2017, https://www.bloomberg.com/opinion
/articles/2017-10-30/free-college-would-help-the-rich-more-than-the-poor.

23. Richard Murphy, Judith Scott-Clayton, and Gillian Wyness, "The End of Free College in England: Implications for Quality, Enrolments, and Equity," *National Bureau of Economic Research*, Working Paper no. 23888 (September 2017).

24. Jonathan Wai and David H. Uttal, "Why Spatial Reasoning Matters for Education Policy," *American Enterprise Institute*, October 4, 2018, http://www.aei
.org/publication/why-spatial-reasoning-matters-for-education-policy/.

25. "About Us," Mastery Transcript Consortium, accessed August 16, 2019, https://mastery.org/about/about-us/.

26. "About," P-TECH, accessed August 16, 2019, http://www.ptech.org/about/.

27. Tamar Jacoby, "Business Steps Up," *American Enterprise Institute*, March 28, 2018, http://www.aei.org/spotlight/business-steps-up/.

28. Alanna Fuschillo, "The Troubling Student-to-Counselor Ratio That Doesn't Add Up," *Committee for Economic Development*, May 4, 2018, https://www
.ced.org/blog/entry/the-troubling-student-to-counselor-ratio-that-doesnt
-add-up.

29. Courtney Connley, "Google, Apple and 12 Other Companies That No Longer Require Employees to Have a College Degree," *CNBC*, October 8, 2018, https://www.cnbc.com/2018/08/16/15-companies-that-no-longer-require
-employees-to-have-a-college-degree.html.

PART 3

Schools, Families, and Society

CHAPTER 11

School Choice and the Toughest-Case Kids
by Naomi Schaefer Riley

"**F**ROM THE START, I really try to instill in our team that families need to be our partners," Jessica Nauiokas, the head of Mott Haven Academy, tells me. But she knows there's a good chance that won't happen. A third of the kids at this ten-year-old charter school in the Bronx reside in foster homes and another third are from families receiving preventive services, meaning they are being watched by the Administration for Children's Services and could be removed into state custody at any time. Nauiokas adds, "In the event a child comes from the type of family where that parent's support isn't going to set them up for school success, we have to find workarounds for that."

The biggest successes of the education reform movement over the past few decades have been rooted in the important idea that we need to give more power to parents to choose their children's educational paths—to escape the monopoly of underperforming neighborhood public schools and move their sons and daughters either to public charter schools or private schools with the use of vouchers or scholarship funds. But for the hundreds of thousands of children whose parents can't be or won't be partners, it is time for conservatives to start thinking about workarounds.

This is not to detract at all from everything that education reform has accomplished. In return for providing astonishing academic results, not to mention some of the strongest community support, inner-city Catholic schools and high-performing charter-school networks asked only that parents and caregivers act as allies. These adults—often single mothers, aunts, grandmothers, and so on—did not need to be wealthy or educated, only aware and committed. They didn't have to help their kids with homework, only ensure that their children would put in a good-faith effort. They didn't need to promise that their children would always behave well—just that if their children didn't act appropriately, they would support the school's decisions about the consequences.

The results of this bargain have in many cases exceeded reformers' expectations. Especially in high-performing charter networks like Success Academy, the KIPP schools, and Democracy Prep, students have surpassed their peers in wealthy suburbs; they have gone on to elite colleges; and their completion rates are also surprising many critics.

What has become clear is that kids from poor families with single parents living in chaotic and crime-ridden neighborhoods can do good, even superlative academic work. As David Whitman writes in *Sweating the Small Stuff: Inner City Schools and the New Paternalism*, "Most of these paternalistic schools . . . are founded on the premise that minority parents want to do the right thing but often don't have the time or the resources to keep their children from being dragged down by an unhealthy street culture."[1]

And so the teachers and administrators at these schools manage their expectations. Whitman explains, "Parents' chief role at no-excuses schools is helping steer their children through the door—paternalistic schools are typically schools of choice—and then ensuring that their children get to school on time and do their homework."[2]

But when schools do not have partners in the home—at least one adult willing to be responsible for getting kids to school on time, for ensuring that they get a good night's sleep and do a little homework—it is hard for the no-excuses model to work. Not only would youngsters from these homes be unlikely to succeed without a stable adult at home, they would be unlikely even to apply for a scholarship, a voucher, or a lottery spot.

It is not uncommon to hear those who oppose the reforms of the past quarter century criticize the no-excuses model citing exactly this reason. But the fact that a school model can serve most of a population is not a reason to throw it out. Let me be clear: *choice is worth pursuing because it helps a great many students, but we need another set of policies and practices for the worst off.*

In fact, these no-excuses schools have provided us with a unique opportunity in the history of American education. Not only can we now give many kids in poor circumstances the chance to succeed in elementary and high school, and even higher education; we can also focus more of our attention on those children who are truly at sea, who have no adults in their lives ready to take responsibility for their future, and we can seek ways that schools can work to make up for some of their deficits.

There are 437,000 kids in foster care in America today, a number that's been rising for the past few years, thanks in part to the opioid epidemic. (While there are hundreds of thousands of other children also at risk, it is worth focusing on this unique population because it is large and we actually know a lot about it.) For these kids, the future looks bleak. According to Child Trends, a nonprofit research group:

> Children in foster care are more likely than other children to exhibit high levels of behavioral and emotional problems. They are also more likely to be suspended or expelled from school, and to exhibit low levels of school engagement and involvement with extracurricular activities. Children in foster care are also more likely to have received mental health services in the past year, to have a limiting physical, learning, or mental health condition, or to be in poor or fair health.[3]

We should be quick to note that not all of these problems are the result of being in foster care. They are more likely the result of circumstances that put kids in foster care to begin with. But if they are neither reunited with their biological family nor adopted—that is, if they age out of foster care—the results get worse. Of this population:

38 percent had emotional problems, 50 percent had used illegal drugs, and 25 percent were involved with the legal system. Preparation for further education and career was also a problem for these young people. Only 48 percent of foster youth who had "aged out" of the system had graduated from high school at the time of discharge, and only 54 percent had graduated from high school two to four years after discharge. As adults, children who spent long periods of time in multiple foster care homes were more likely than other children to encounter problems such as unemployment, homelessness, and incarceration, as well as to experience early pregnancy.[4]

Children in foster care are not the only kids in thoroughly dysfunctional home situations. There are tens if not hundreds of thousands of others who have been in state custody in the past or are receiving "preventive services" because they are at risk of being removed from their homes.

I do not suggest that kids in these circumstances are ineligible to attend charter schools or Catholic schools. Many do and are better off for the interaction with qualified, caring teachers for longer hours each day. Leaders at Democracy Prep, Success Academy, Public Prep, and other such schools are regularly in contact with the Administration for Children's Services in New York, for instance, reporting trauma and doing all they can to keep kids who are removed from their homes anchored in the same school community. But many schools of choice are simply not equipped to handle the kind of trauma or mitigate the kind of instability that these kids are experiencing at home.

———

Haven Academy, for its part, offers kids some of the same lessons they would get at other charter schools, such as the importance of maintaining eye contact with other people while they are speaking. But

Haven also spends considerable time, for instance, helping kids to learn empathy. Haven is run by the New York Foundling, the city's oldest foster-care agency, which offers it a unique perspective on these situations. And the Foundling also acts as a referral agency, suggesting to families with children at risk that they send their children there.

At the beginning of each year, teachers make visits to students' homes in order to better understand the environment they are coming from and enable the students to meet teachers in a place where they feel more comfortable. Teachers also try to build relationships there with parents or guardians to the extent that's possible.

Like many New York schools, Haven also has a pre-K program. Conservatives have rightly noted that the evidence for most pre-K programs is shaky at best. But there are important reasons to get this particular population into a school environment sooner rather than later. For example, teachers can keep a better eye on their development and report any instances of abuse or neglect.

When students enter the building at Haven, certain physical differences from other schools are immediately obvious. Classrooms are relatively small, but they also have "cozy corners" where students can go to calm down or be alone for a few minutes. At any time during the day, there are additional small rooms where children who are having bigger problems controlling themselves can go with an adult. The rooms are equipped with special "scoop rocker" chairs for children who need to rock in order to self-soothe. The school also has very specific safety plans for when a student is out of control, including getting other children out of the way.

But this is all a last resort. Kindergartners receive teddy bears at the beginning of the year that they can care for and dress. Teachers use the toys to teach children about empathy and caring for others. They also use the RULER program, an acronym standing for five skills of emotional intelligence: recognizing, understanding, labeling, expressing, and regulating emotions. When they enter a classroom, students are asked to rate their own emotional state, both their level of "energy" and their level of "pleasantness" on a graph. And then they are taught how to be conscious of and shift themselves to a state that is more appropriate for learning.

The school's efforts to maintain a calm atmosphere extend well beyond encouraging self-regulation. Instead of a buzzer or bell between classes, two minutes of Bach are played through the school's speakers. The school has its own counseling staff and is regularly in touch with both biological and foster parents as well as the child's ACS caseworker. The bureaucracy of child welfare agencies often makes it difficult for schools to find out what is really going on in the home lives of these children. Schools may even make reports of maltreatment but then not learn what happened. Still, schools have to find workarounds for kids to help them function even if they are not sure what is going on at home.

This is also true in the area of discipline. After the Obama administration issued guidelines for schools that aimed to reduce racial disparities in suspensions and suggested that schools do more to mediate disputes between students, many school leaders suggested that the results will not be fair for the kids who are actually in school to learn. As Success Academy founder Eva Moskowitz wrote in the *Wall Street Journal*:

> Suspensions convey the critical message to students and parents that certain behavior is inconsistent with being a member of the school community. Pretend suspensions, in which a student is allowed to remain in the school community, do not convey that message. Many students actually feed off the attention they get for misbehaving. Keeping these students in school encourages that misbehavior.

Indeed, she continues, "minority students are also the most likely to suffer the adverse consequences of lax discipline—that is, their education is disrupted by a chaotic school environment or by violence."[5]

But what happens when sending a child home is likely to result in no supervision for those days—or worse? More important, perhaps, many of the kids at Haven have no idea what it means to have logical consequences for their actions and there is little expectation that adults can be trusted at all. As Nauiokas explains, "It's not about, well, we're going to call your parent and then you'll be disciplined at home. If it happened at school it should be consequenced at school." If you misbehave at recess, you lose recess. If you misbehave on a field trip, you won't be able to go on future field trips. If you destroy property, you'll have to work to repair it. Particularly for children at younger ages, she says, we want to "help kids start becoming more informed agents. When they break a rule, they know what's going to happen to them." This is often very different from what is going on at home.

Defenders of the status quo in education will often say that schools cannot make up for all of the deficits that lower-income children experience in their homes, that schools cannot become their de facto families. Yet many schools, most often parochial schools, push back against this.

Some years ago, I interviewed a young man about his transition from a dangerous neighborhood public school to a local Catholic school thanks to a scholarship he received. The biggest difference, he told me, is that the latter "felt like a family"—like school was a continuation of home. It was clear from the beginning that his parents and teachers were working together. He explained that his parents didn't say, "Oh, your teachers will do their job and we'll do ours. . . . It was the same vision."

Sometimes school is the only thing that can make a particular family's situation work out. I met a family of Sudanese refugees in Omaha. The mother had passed away. The father had to go to Alaska to find work, and the oldest sister was attending the University of Nebraska while taking care of six younger siblings. Had the local Catholic school not surrounded her and all of the children with help and support, it's hard to see how any of this would have been feasible.

For kids in foster care—whether they are living in group homes, with relatives or nonrelatives (often for just a few weeks before moving on to the next place)—some schools are trying to create what a stable family life would look like. At Haven, lunch is served family style with a teacher at each table participating in conversations and encouraging children to ask each other to pass the potatoes. But Haven is by no means the only school to take on these challenges. Monument Academy opened in 2015 in Washington, DC, as a charter school with a five-day boarding program, where several kids live with house parents at the school, eat their meals together, help with chores, and learn to get along in a family setting. Unfortunately, Monument's board decided to close the school at the end of the 2018–19 school year due to safety violations on the campus. Given the difficulty of the population they are working with—many of the kids had been expelled from other schools—perhaps this is not surprising. Fortunately, the school was thrown a last-minute lifeline by the DC Public Charter School Board and was allowed to continue operating into the following school year. One hopes its new leadership will learn from past mishaps and sustain this important work for children in the nation's capital who need this kind of school.

The SEED Academies are also boarding programs. In Florida, child welfare officials can refer kids to SEED Miami to ensure that kids who are in foster care or whose families are receiving preventive services get first priority for admission.

It's relatively easy for a typical school to tell a parent that a child seems distracted in school because of a toothache or that the child's breathing seems labored when running around the playground. But if there's no one at home who will follow up, some schools may simply have to take on these responsibilities themselves. Monument, for example, has partnered with Georgetown University to provide some medical and dental care to children at school.

Leaders of no-excuses schools have found themselves having to defend the concept of "paternalism," a word David Whitman says they do not like to use. At KIPP academies, for instance, the administration talks about giving students "choice-filled lives," which is a kind of euphemism for a "bourgeois, middle-class future." Sure, you can choose to be homeless and unemployed, but we would also like to offer you the "choice" of having a meaningful career that allows you to support a family. The problem is that when parents are not in the picture as partners, when school leaders cannot simply say they are simply doing for these kids what their parents want but cannot accomplish, they must defend a more expansive form of paternalism, one in which school leaders and child welfare officials are making choices for children about their futures.

Whitman contrasts no-excuses schools with, say, the Indian boarding schools of the nineteenth and twentieth centuries, which were involuntary (though there's evidence that many Native American parents did want to send their children to these institutions). But for the hundreds of thousands of kids with no stable adult presence in their lives, we are going to need involuntary solutions or we are going to have to exercise even more paternalism in pushing kids into these environments and then ensuring that teachers and administrators take on the role of family as much as possible.

As conservatives, our first impulse is often to remove responsibility for such matters from schools. As James Q. Wilson wrote, "Paternalism seems to have democracy as its enemy and bureaucracy as its friend."[6] Indeed, too often school administrators have abused these powers to contradict parents' teachings about family matters in realms such as sex education, or to belittle families' religious beliefs. We are rightly suspicious of the kind of paternalism that public bureaucracies have tried to exercise over the lives of families. (Indeed, some libertarian-minded folks would like to reduce the presence not only of schools but also of child welfare services in the lives of these children.)

For children without a consistent adult presence in their lives or who have experienced severe trauma at home, school may be as close as they get to a family and conservatives need to find a way to live with that. When it comes to functioning adults (or even partially functioning ones), democracy can work, but when it comes to children, we are stuck with bureaucracy. The question, though, is how to ensure that these involuntary forms of heightened paternalism do not turn into Dickensian institutions and that they are run in such a way as to give these children the advantages they need instead of warehousing them to keep their disadvantages out of public view.

We should encourage some no-excuse model charters and parochial schools to expand their capabilities, whether that means providing more counseling for students, showing them how to live in a family, helping them access medical care, or providing them with a place to live. Parochial schools, because of their religious missions, may be best equipped to handle this kind of education, but charter schools whose mission is to aid such children can also accomplish a lot. What's clear is that putting these students into a standard-issue "special education" setting and expecting classroom teachers to figure something out has not worked.

Lest conservatives worry that all this talk about trauma-informed care and social emotional learning is code for lower academic standards, the leadership at Haven and Monument know that the schools have an important academic mission as well. Over the years, however, their ability to keep these two in balance has been a challenge. Many kids come to Haven already behind in their classes. They have missed significant amounts of school because of being transferred among different schools. And even children who are capable of doing the work have often been placed into special-ed classes because of their behavioral issues.

There's no clear-cut public policy answer to helping at-risk kids succeed in school. Conservatives are on the right path with their focus on encouraging new models of charter schools and providing public and private scholarship funds to be used in private schools that may be better equipped to handle these challenges.

The temptation may be simply to continue replicating charter schools that are part of already successful networks. But it is vital that

we also figure out how to serve students whose parents are not partners. Like other charters hoping to scale up, Monument is putting
information about its strategies and successes in the public domain
for other schools to use. Because Washington, DC has a generous
funding model for charters, Monument has not had to raise many
extra dollars. But other states that are attempting to serve this population should ensure, with their own funding mechanisms, that a school
like Monument could open inside their borders as well. Arizona, Florida, and North Carolina all have voucher programs for kids in foster
care to attend private schools. In 2018, Oklahoma expanded a program
for special-needs kids to include foster children too.

If these youngsters are to have any chance at success in life, they
must catch up academically. And we need to find ways for them not
only to finish high school but also to get some postsecondary training.
The First Star program of South Jersey, supported by the Pascale Sykes
Foundation, is now in its third year, with about 30 tenth and eleventh
graders spending several weeks each summer at Rowan University.
There, students take at least one college-level class for course credit in
addition to learning their way around a campus. Students also participate in a year-round program that meets every couple of weeks, where
they receive tutoring for the SAT, advice about college applications,
and the opportunity to work on group projects, like creating a robot or
a radio program. Students also make group visits to colleges.

The federal government also helps children who were in foster
care via the Fostering Adoption to Further Student Achievement Act,
which allows students adopted on or after their thirteenth birthday to
exclude their parents' income from their federal financial aid forms.
And the Chafee Grant finances state-administered vouchers of up to
five thousand dollars per year for former foster care children.[7]

A middle-class mother in Brooklyn recently asked me about my
research and wondered aloud if she could afford to take in a foster kid
or even adopt out of foster care. Her only son was about to graduate

college, and she had a little extra room in her apartment. But then she asked how she would afford college for another child. Ensuring that states put money into an education account that follows the child rather than depending on foster families to foot these costs is a vital part of caring for these young people. Doing so will also make fostering and adopting out of foster care more feasible for many middle-class parents who wouldn't want to give these kids any less than they would give their biological children.

Not all these kids will go on to college. In 2017, America Works signed a contract with New York City's Human Resources Administration to aid hundreds of former foster youths in Brooklyn and the Bronx. The four-decade-old organization holds that the first step to getting people to be independent, productive citizens is getting them a job. America Works has placed a half-million people in jobs with an average starting wage of ten dollars per hour plus benefits. In New York City, more than half of these workers were still employed after six months. Its clients, according to founder Peter Cove, include "single parents, drug and alcohol abusers, the mentally handicapped, the homeless [and] military veterans with posttraumatic stress disorder."[8]

The program simulates a workday. Participants are required to be there from nine to five. If they show up twenty minutes late or forget to clock out, their caseworkers will explain why this is a problem. And America Works provides counseling and help with working out transportation, childcare, and other factors that may get in the way of employment. With former foster youth, America Works is helping them with high-school equivalency exams and even college courses. It's teaching them how to make a household budget.

It's tempting for conservatives to avoid talking about the educational options for the most at-risk kids. Because the no-excuses model has worked so well and because conservatives tend to believe that parents are the best arbiters of decisions about their children's education, we have not fully engaged the question of what to do with kids who don't have a stable adult presence in their lives. The concern about getting public schools too involved in the personal and family lives of students has also made us wary of institutions that serve these kids in a more complete way. And our worries that a focus on the social and emotional aspects of kids' lives will detract from giving them the academic tools they need to succeed has kept many of us from grappling with the questions of how schools can heal the wounds that these vulnerable kids have suffered. But it's time to grapple.

NOTES

1. David Whitman, *Sweating the Small Stuff: Inner-City Schools and the New Paternalism* (Washington, DC: Thomas B. Fordham Institute, 2008), 28.
2. Ibid., 20.
3. "Foster Care," Child Trends, accessed August 15, 2019, https://www.childtrends.org/wp-content/uploads/2015/01/indicator_1421553426.6.html.
4. Ibid.
5. Eva S. Moskowitz, "Turning Schools into Fight Clubs," *Wall Street Journal*, April 1, 2015, https://www.wsj.com/articles/eva-moskowitz-turning-schools-into-fight-clubs-1427930575.
6. James Q. Wilson, "Paternalism, Democracy, and Bureaucracy," in *The New Paternalism: Supervisory Approaches to Poverty*, Lawrence M. Mead, ed. (Washington, DC: Brookings Institution Press, 1997): 330–343, 337.
7. "College Financial Aid Resources for Former Foster Youth," Voice for Adoption, March 29, 2013, http://fosteringsuccessmichigan.com/uploads/misc/VFA_College_Financial_Aid_Resource_Sheet.pdf.
8. Peter Cove, "What I Learned in the Poverty War: Work, Not Welfare, Uplifts the Poor," *City Journal*, Autumn 2012, https://www.city-journal.org/html/what-i-learned-poverty-war-13513.html.

CHAPTER 12

Can Education Ease America's "Men without Work" Crisis?

by Nicholas Eberstadt

AMERICA IS IN the grip of a historic crisis that, despite its manifest importance, somehow managed to remain more or less invisible for decades: the collapse of work for adult men, and the retreat from the world of work by growing numbers of men of conventional working age. According to the Bureau of Labor Statistics, "work rates" were actually somewhat lower for American men at the end of 2018 than they had been in 1939 (see table 12.1).[1] In other words, Depression-style work rates are still characteristic today for the American male. Unlike the Great Depression, however, today's work crisis is not an unemployment crisis. Only a small fraction of today's workless men are actually looking for employment. Instead, we have witnessed a mass exodus of men from the workforce altogether. At time of writing, some 7 million civilian noninstitutional men between the ages of twenty-five and

TABLE 12.1

US MALE "WORK RATES" TODAY VERSUS SELECTED DEPRESSION YEARS

YEAR	EMPLOYMENT-TO-POPULATION RATIO, MEN 20–64 (PERCENTAGE OF CIVILIAN NONINSTITUTIONAL POPULATION)	EMPLOYMENT-TO-POPULATION RATIO, MEN 25–54 (PERCENTAGE OF CIVILIAN NONINSTITUTIONAL POPULATION)
2018 (December)	80.0	85.9
1940	81.3	86.4
1930	88.2	91.2

Source: Nicholas Eberstadt, using data from the US Census Bureau and the Bureau of Labor Statistics

fifty-four ("prime working age") were neither working nor looking for work—four times as many as were formally unemployed.[2] And while employment trends are certainly problematic nowadays for women, too, both the duration and the magnitude of the work crisis have been far more acute for men.[3]

Among economists and policy analysts who have examined these unsettling trends, the general consensus is that declining male workforce participation in modern America is mainly explained by structural economic change, which has caused an especially dramatic drop in jobs for less-educated workers. Exemplifying this received wisdom is the Council of Economic Advisers' 2016 report on declining male labor force participation rates (or LFPRs).[4] As that study put it:

> The fall in participation for prime-age men has largely been concentrated among those with a high school degree or less. . . . Reductions in labor supply—in other words, prime-age men choosing not to work for a given set of labor market conditions—explain relatively little of the long-run trend. . . . In contrast, reductions in the demand for labor, especially for lower-skilled men, appear to be an important component of the decline in prime-age male labor force participation.[5]

If this assessment is more or less correct, it would be hard to overstate the importance of education and training as instruments for addressing our men-without-work crisis. If our rapidly modernizing economy is displacing those with limited education and skills, redoubled efforts to improve the quality of our educational system, to increase our population's educational attainment, and to improve the training of those already in the workforce would seem imperative to forestall further deterioration in the US male employment profile, much less to turn these trends around.

But what if that assessment is not correct? In this essay, I take issue with the conventional diagnosis of the men-without-work problem and consequently with the usual prescription—that is, more and better education and training—or, rather, with the expected efficacy of that prescription. There can be no arguing against more and better education for America—more and better education win on their own merits; they offer our society and her citizens all sorts of incontestable benefits. But as an instrument for redressing the long-term "flight from work" by men in modern America, more and better education may prove to be of more limited utility than many suppose.

———————

All observers agree about the general facts concerning the collapse of work for men in modern America, and there is no contesting the exceptionally poor trends for less-educated men in the workforce over the past half-century and more. Between 1965 and 2015, the percentage of prime-age US men not in the labor force (NILF) shot up from 3.3 to 11.7 percent, and the overall situation has only fractionally improved since then: NILFs still accounted for 10.7 percent of the prime male population in November 2019. But the decline in work was much worse for men with lower levels of educational attainment than with higher levels. Over this same half-century, work rates fell for prime age men in all educational groups, but by around 2 percentage points for men with graduate school training, as against nearly 18 points for those without such a diploma. By 2015, over one in seven prime-age men with just a high school diploma were neither working nor looking for work—and for those without a high school diploma, the ratio was worse than one in five. In 1965, LFPRs were actually higher for those with high school degrees than those with graduate training; half a century later, LFPRs were about 10 points lower for high school graduates than prime-age men with graduate training—and a chasm of nearly 20 points separated work rates for college grads and high school dropouts.

These trends are widely taken as prima facie proof that America's crisis of work for men is mainly a demand-driven, skills-sensitive problem—a matter of evaporating local jobs (and in particular, jobs requiring limited skills) in an increasingly dynamic and globalized marketplace. But a careful look at America's male worklessness problem suggests that there is much more to the story.

Four key facts about declining male labor force participation in the United States demonstrate that the prevailing "demand side" narrative needs to be revised and qualified—perhaps quite considerably.

1. *There is the uncanny regularity of the prime-age US male's long march out of the labor force since the 1960s* (see figure 12.1).[6] This monthly exodus from the workforce has been so steady since 1965 that it almost traces a straight line. The tempo of workforce withdrawal appears to be almost completely unaffected by the tempo of national economic growth, which varied considerably over this period. Recessions—including even the Great Recession—seem to have scarcely any impact on the trend. The striking steadiness of this exodus, year in and year out, is fundamentally inconsistent with a demand-side explanation for declining LFPRs.

2. *There is the pronounced and increasing geographic disparity in LFPRs.* Modern America has witnessed steadily increasing dispersion in state-level prime male LFPRs since at least 1980. Further, major, enduring, and sometimes even widening gaps in prime male LFPRs are evident between geographically adjoining states (Maine and New Hampshire; West Virginia and Virginia/Maryland, etc.). Economic theory would suggest that the national labor market would move toward equilibrium over time in the face of demand shocks. Just the opposite, however, has been taking place across the United States for most of the period in which the long-term decline in male LFPRs has been underway.

3. *There is America's curiously poor prime male LFPR performance in comparison with other affluent never-Communist democracies.* Between 1965 and 2015, US levels fell faster and sank lower than in any comparator country save for Italy (where official employment figures notoriously neglect "unofficial" work income). Yet America's race to the bottom in prime male LFPRs is not readily explained by lackluster

FIGURE 12.1

NILF RATES FOR MEN 25–54 YEARS OF AGE, UNITED STATES, 1965–2018

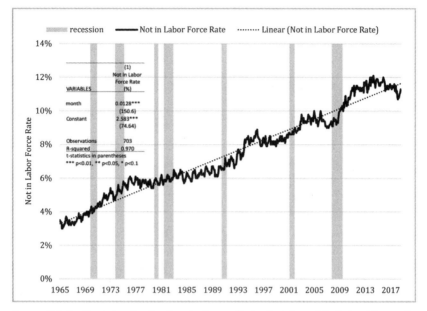

Source: Nicholas Eberstadt, using data from the Bureau of Labor Statistics and the National Bureau of Economic Research

economic growth (also known as inadequate demand). While it is true that the United States apparently grew more slowly than most of these countries over that half century, as would be expected with "economic convergence" and "catch-up growth," US LFPR trends were nonetheless also distinctly worse than those of the countries whose pace of growth lagged behind America's over that half-century—for example, Canada, Denmark, and Sweden, to say nothing of Greece.

4. By no means the least important, *there are dramatic and systematic differences in prime-age male LFPRs within the less-educated segment of that population* (see figure 12.2).[7] LFPRs for both married and unmarried immigrant prime-age men without high school diplomas are over 90 percent—close to the levels for America's prime-age males with college degrees (93 percent). Married, native-born prime-age men *without* high school diplomas have LFPRs comparable to overall rates for prime-age men *with* diplomas (i.e., around 80 percent). LFPRs for

native-born, never-married prime-age male high school dropouts are in an abysmal class all of their own, hovering just over the 50 percent mark: over 25 points below married native-born counterparts, and about 40 points below foreign-born high school dropouts.

FIGURE 12.2

LABOR FORCE PARTICIPATION RATE FOR PRIME-AGE MEN (25–54) WITH LESS THAN A HIGH SCHOOL DIPLOMA: FOREIGN BORN AND NATIVE BORN, MARRIED, AND NEVER MARRIED, UNITED STATES, 1994–2017

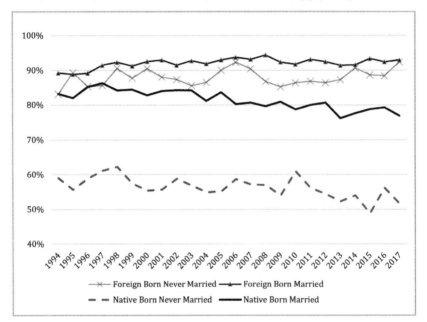

Source: Integrated Public Use Microdata Series

Like the other inconvenient facts enumerated above, the pronounced heterogeneity of labor market outcomes within the overall pool of less skilled men underscores that important forces are at play in America's men-without-work crisis that have nothing to do with demand factors. Recognition of this reality perforce tempers the role we might expect education to play in addressing this crisis, since it is apparent that male worklessness in America today is due to much more than just a dearth of learning and training.

More realistic expectations for education in this crisis may be had if we consider additional causes—what economists would call "supply-side" and "institutional" effects. Three of these are family structure, government benefit dependence, and criminal justice.

Although discussion of family structure and its consequences is considered off-limits in some academic and political circles these days, the strong relationship between family structure and employment status for men is obvious from first glance. Overall, LFPRs in 2015 were over 10 percentage points lower and work rates over 14 points lower for never-married prime-age men than for their currently married counterparts. Even after controlling for age, ethnicity, and education, married men are decidedly more likely to be in the workforce than men who never married. This marriage effect is so powerful that married prime-age male high school dropouts generate LFPRs essentially indistinguishable from their never-married, college-grad peers; further, LFPRs are consistently higher for married black prime-age men than their white never-married counterparts. Unfortunately, US family structure has been transformed over the past several generations and in ways that generated severe downward pressure on prime male LFPRs. In 1965, for example, 85 percent of prime-age men were married; by 2015, that share had dropped by almost 30 percentage points.[8]

Consider next dependence on government benefit programs, specifically disability programs, intended to provide income, goods, and services to working-age men and women who are prevented from working or seeking work due to physical or mental impairment. The federal government provides a multiplicity of such programs. Though intended as social insurance platforms, evidence suggests that such programs in practice are increasingly used as income-support mechanisms for men on a work-free life track. (At this juncture, most NILF men appear to be long-termers, dropouts from the workforce for at least one year and perhaps longer.) No single source of data shows exactly how many prime-age men are obtaining one or more disability benefits from government (federal, state, and local). Even so, as of 2013 a clear majority of prime NILF men lived in households that received payments from at least one government disability program—a substantially higher fraction than in the 1980s.[9] Disability benefits are never lavish, but, taken together with additional benefit eligibility unlocked by disability enrollment, and with resources from family and friends, they evidently make viable a nonworkforce existence for many millions of prime-working-age men today. Apart from the very small fraction (just over a tenth) of prime-age male NILFs who are adult students, the remainder report spending much of their waking hours watching (and playing on) screens—over two thousand hours per year on average.[10] And almost half of these NILF men report consuming pain medication every day.[11] Taken together, these varied strands form a mesh of supply-side constraints that may keep many out of the labor force even if their educational qualifications or test scores might in theory allow them to function in it.

Then there are institutional effects that constitute barriers to workforce entry, beginning with mass felonization. Readers will be generally aware of the notorious scale of incarceration nowadays—with about 2.5 million people behind bars in America, and a higher imprisonment ratio than virtually any other country on earth. But the vast scale of felonization is little known to the public, mainly (and scandalously) because the US government simply does not collect data on this demographic component of the population. One study attempting to reconstruct the size and flow of the US felon population, however, estimated that as of 2010 nearly 20 million adults in America had been convicted of at least one felony.[12] A little arithmetic suggests that the current US felon and ex-felon population is now on the order of 24 million—meaning that well over 20 million of them are not presently behind bars. Since sentenced criminals are disproportionately male, one can estimate that more than one in eight adult men in the civilian noninstitutional population (the pool from which labor force statistics are drawn) has a felony in his background—and the ratio for prime-age men today is likely even higher. Preliminary research suggests that irrespective of age, ethnicity, and educational attainment, men are much more likely to be out of the labor force nowadays if they have been to prison than if they "only" have an arrest record—and correspondingly more likely to be NILF with an arrest in their background than if they have had no trouble with the law. (Among the reasons: legislation that restricts ex-felons from entering certain occupations, and employer concerns about hiring ex-cons.) Mass felonization thus looks to be an important, albeit commonly overlooked, component of the men-without-work crisis in America today.

—————

If the men-without-work crisis were basically a demand-side problem, the task for the US education system (broadly construing that system) would be fairly straightforward and in a sense comparatively easy. In that case, the education system would "only" have to provide the needed but missing training and skills to rising generations of youth and existing generations of working adults, so as to abet their rescue from occupations, fields, industries, and sectors that are dying due to lack of demand.

But as our post–Great Recession economic expansion moves into its tenth year, the dissonance between the demand-side narrative and actual conditions in the real America has become increasingly jarring. Today we have, at one and the same time, both an incipient labor shortage and Depression-style work rates for men. The BLS Jobs Openings and Labor Turnover Survey (JOLTS) for November 2018 reported 6.9 million unfilled positions in the US workforce.[13] By way of comparison, at this writing there were roughly 1.7 million prime-age male high school dropouts and 3.6 million prime-age men with just high school diplomas in America who are neither working nor looking for work.

Not all the open job slots are for computer coders or chemical engineers. To the contrary, over nine hundred thousand of these unfilled positions are in "accommodation and food services," eight hundred thousand are in "retail trade," and another quarter million are in construction. Whether one views such work as attractive or not, or sufficiently remunerative, the fact is that most of these positions do not require any higher education, and a great many do not even require high school diplomas. Reportage has put a human face on the paradox of a country awash in low-skill jobs at a time when millions of lower-education men are out of the workforce: in these recountings, positions go unfilled because of disinterest by nonworkers, unreliability of applicants to show up for work regularly, or applicants cannot keep sober or pass drug tests.[14]

This is a devilishly difficult world in which to expect the US education system (again broadly construed) to make an appreciable impact on relieving joblessness. And yet expect we do, because at a time when so many other institutions in civil society are in disarray or retreat, the school system (along with the fire department, perhaps) is not only still standing, but still largely trusted and respected.

As other institutions in civil society fail or fade, educators and trainers are loaded down with ever more responsibilities and assignments previously undertaken by others: teachers must not only be teachers, but surrogate parents, secular confessors and makeshift therapists, boot-camp drill instructors, financial advisers, de facto cops, even truant officers or dress-rehearsal probation officers. Little wonder they cannot accomplish all these missions—much less the more modest but hardly trivial mission of inculcating academic excellence.

In the face of today's often distressing realities, herewith a few general thoughts about how the US education system, broadly construed, could make some difference in the men-without-work problem.

Improving the quality of public K–12 education would be vital—especially in neighborhoods where schooling is mediocre or worse. That, of course, should be a top priority of all educators, as it has been for champions of educational reform for many decades, and there are many paths and strategies for effecting such improvements.

The virtues of career and technical education (once known as vocational training) have gone underappreciated—by policymakers, educators, and parents as well—for at least half a century, while the male worklessness problem has gradually worsened. A narrow focus by guidance counselors on college does not serve all students well. College is not for everyone—but everyone should graduate with a skill. High schools should be capable of equipping students with some of these skills, and CTE should be treated as the important opportunity that it is.

Improving training for the working (and nonworking) adult population must also be a high-priority objective, but this is easier said than done. "Lifelong learning" has been little more than a slogan for the past generation. Serious consideration must be given to the many different possible avenues and methods for advancing this goal. Our federal system would seem well suited to offer a laboratory for local experimentation in this realm.

Reaching workers is one thing, however, and reaching nonworkers is something else again. Among nonworkers, the unemployed may generally be easier to reach and train than the NILFs, precisely because the former by definition desire to be in the labor force. Reaching NILFs may require major and systematic changes in the way we deal with other public policy issues—such as disability programs, sentencing, and reentry. We may want to consider, for example, whether our disability programs could be entirely overhauled under a work-first precept, with an emphasis on training and skills for those who can indeed function in the workforce. And we may want to think about the potential of skills and training under different auspices and modalities for ex-offenders as they address the arduous prospect of "employment reputation repair."

In these and other ways, the US education system might make inroads against the men-without-work crisis. But we would do well not to overpromise. The men-without-work crisis in America today is in large measure a consequence of long-term historical changes and profound transformations in society. More schooling will not repair the family, or other institutions that long formed the foundation for male work in America. For that we may need to await the next Great American Awakening—a matter far beyond the scope of this essay.

NOTES

1. For data for December 2018, see US Department of Labor, Bureau of Labor Statistics, *Labor Force Statistics from the Current Population Survey*, table A-13. For data for 1940, see Amitabh Chandra, "Labor-Market Dropouts and the Racial Wage Gap: 1940–1990," *American Economic Review* 90, no. 2 (2000): 333–338; US Census Bureau, "1940 Census of Population: The Labor Force (Sample Statistics)," table 1, accessed August 16, 2019, https://www.census.gov/library/publications/1943/dec/population-labor-force-sample.html; US Census Bureau, "Divisions and States," table 1, accessed August 16, 2019, https://www2.census.gov/library/publications/decennial/1940/population-institutional-population/08520028ch2.pdf; "Selected Manpower Statistics," Assistant Secretary of Defense Manpower, Personnel and Reserve, Department of Defense, January 24, 1956, https://apps.dtic.mil/dtic/tr/fulltext/u2/a954007.pdf. For data for 1930, see Linda Levine, *The Labor Market during the Great Depression and the Current Recession* (Washington, DC: Congressional Research Service, June 19, 2009), https://digital.library.unt.edu/ark:/67531/metadc26169/m1/1/high_res_d/R40655_2009Jun19.pdf. For data from 1930, the percentage is calculated for the total enumerated population, not the civilian noninstitutional population. For the second column showing 1930 data, the percentage refers to men ages twenty-five to forty-four—the corresponding male 25/44 work ratio for 2015 would be 85.3 for civilian noninstitutional population alone. Data accessed March 2, 2016, by the author.

2. US Department of Labor, Bureau of Labor Statistics, *Labor Force Statistics from the Current Population Survey*, table A-13, "Employment Status of the Civilian Non-Institutional Population by Age, Sex and Race," December 2018, https://www.bls.gov/web/empsit/cpseea13.htm.

3. This is true for the past half-century, but also for the past decade: the magnitude of the drop in employment rates was much less severe for prime-age women than prime-age men, and the snap back in work rates was faster for females than males. US Department of Labor, Bureau of Labor Statistics, "Labor Force Statistics from the Current Population Survey: One- Screen Data Search," accessed August 16, 2019, https://data.bls.gov/PDQWeb/ln.

4. Council of Economic Advisers, *The Long-Term Decline in Prime-Age Male Labor Force Participation* (Washington, DC: The White House, 2016), https://obamawhitehouse.archives.gov/sites/default/files/page/files/20160620_cea_primeage_male_lfp.pdf.

5. Ibid., 3–4.

6. For labor force data, see US Department of Labor, Bureau of Labor Statistics, "On- Screen Data Search: Men 25–54 from 1948–2015," accessed August 16, 2019, https://data.bls.gov/PDQWeb/ln. For recession data, see National Bureau of Economic Research, "US Business Cycle Expansions and Contractions," accessed August 16, 2019, https://www.nber.org/cycles.html. The

data used to create this figure are from the "Current Population Survey" (CPS) as downloaded from the Bureau of Labor Statistics. The data used to create the regression table in the upper left corner are also from the "Current Population Survey" but downloaded from IPUMS-CPS for statistical manipulation. Each recession variable indicates recessions that occurred during the following periods: 1969–1970; 1973–1975; 1980–1982; 1990–1991; 2001; and 2007–2009.

7. Sarah Flood, Miriam King, Renae Rodgers, Steven Ruggles, and J. Robert Warren, *Integrated Public Use Microdata Series, Current Population Survey: Version 6.0*, dataset (Minneapolis: IPUMS, 2018), https://doi.org/10.18128/D030.V6.0.

8. To be clear, the relationship between family structure and employment profiles is complex, with causal arrows pointing in both directions. That said, one aspect of that dynamic has been the negative pressure that family breakdown has exerted on male employment profiles.

9. Nicholas Eberstadt, *Men without Work: America's Invisible Crisis* (West Conshohocken, PA: Templeton Press, 2016), 115.

10. Ibid., 134–36.

11. Alan B. Krueger, "Where Have All the Workers Gone? An Inquiry into the Decline of the US Labor Force Participation Rate," *Brookings Papers on Economic Activity,* BPEA Conference Drafts (September 7–8, 2017), https://www.brookings.edu/wp-content/uploads/2017/09/1_krueger.pdf.

12. Sarah K. S. Shannon et al., "The Growth, Scope, and Spatial Distribution of People with Felony Records in the United States, 1948–2010," *Demography* 54, no. 5 (2017): 1795–1818, https://link.springer.com/article/10.1007/s13524-017-0611-1.

13. US Department of Labor, Bureau of Labor Statistics, *Labor Force Statistics from the Current Population Survey*, "Table 1: Job Openings Levels and Rates by Industry and Region, Seasonally Adjusted," August 6, 2019, https://www.bls.gov/news.release/jolts.t01.htm.

14. See Shayndi Raice and Eric Morath, "Iowa's Employment Problem: Too Many Jobs, Not Enough People," *Wall Street Journal*, April 1, 2018, https://www.wsj.com/articles/iowas-employment-problem-too-many-jobs-not-enough-people-1522580400; Nelson D. Schwartz, "Economy Needs Works, but Drug Tests Take a Toll," *New York Times,* July 24, 2017, https://www.nytimes.com/2017/07/24/business/economy/drug-test-labor-hiring.html; Anora M. Gaudiano, "How the Opioid Epidemic Is Exacerbating a US Labor-Market Shortage" *Marketwatch*, June 29, 2018, https://www.marketwatch.com/story/how-the-opioid-epidemic-is-exacerbating-a-us-labor-market-shortage-2018-06-28.

CHAPTER 13

Rethinking the Mission of High School

by Ramesh Ponnuru

IN HIS 2010 State of the Union address, President Barack Obama said that "in this economy, a high school diploma no longer guarantees a good job."[1] He urged Congress to take various steps to make college, including community college, more affordable.

Obama's predecessor, President George W. Bush, had different positions from him on many issues. But the two saw eye to eye on this basic point. Accepting his party's presidential nomination for a second time in 2004, Bush lamented that too few Americans completed even two years of college and pledged to "help more Americans start their career with a college diploma."[2]

Both were speaking from within a decades-long, bipartisan American consensus. That consensus has viewed a college education as a prerequisite for both individual and national success. As the wages of Americans with college degrees have pulled away from those of Americans without them, parents and policymakers have considered it vital for young people to follow high school with college. That way they can capture that wage premium, and the economy can reap the benefits of a skilled—which is to say schooled—workforce.

Colleges have long been respected institutions and they naturally agree with this perspective even apart from their material interest in it. So they tend to reinforce it, and they may do so more actively in coming years as demographic change reduces college enrollment and forces many colleges out of operation.

The consensus that sending more young people to college should be our priority has frayed a little at the edges but remains strong. If you go to the homepage of the website for the Bill and Melinda Gates Foundation, for example, you will see that one of their missions is to "[i]ncrease students' college completion rates." Clicking on that mission takes you to another page that outlines the foundation's goal: "to ensure that all students who seek the opportunity are able to complete a high-quality, affordable postsecondary education that leads to a sustaining career." Scroll down a little further, and the foundation explains that its College-Ready Education program aims "to ensure that all students graduate from high school prepared to succeed in college and in a career."[3]

Our government and, one might say, our culture have made a concerted effort to increase the number of young people who attend college. For a long time, that strategy arguably succeeded. College-degree attainment rates rose for several decades; that rise coincided with a massive increase in the wealth of the nation and especially the part of it with degrees. It made sense that these trends would coincide.

But that strategy may have hit a point of diminishing returns and hit it well short of where we might have hoped. Some of our apparent success in raising enrollment rates has taken the form of putting young people into college who are not ready for it. As of 2009, nearly half of all college students had taken at least one remedial course within six years of entry. The figure for community colleges was also nearly 70 percent.

Dropout rates are also quite high. According to the National Center for Education Statistics, more than one-third of the students who enrolled in four-year colleges in 2003 had failed to receive a degree within the next six years; the same was true of nearly two-thirds of those who enrolled in community colleges. The Bureau of Labor Statistics reports the good news: The wages of people who went to college but did not graduate are higher than those who never went to college at all. Less encouragingly, it reports that their wages are nonetheless closer to those of high-school dropouts than to those of college graduates. And the "some college" group, unlike the high-school dropouts, has student-loan debt.

Even among those who do earn college degrees, many do not take jobs that require those degrees. In a recent paper for the Manhattan Institute, Oren Cass pointed to research showing that more than one-third of employed college graduates work in jobs for which the majority of jobholders did not consider a college degree necessary.[4] He also noted research from Burning Glass Technologies and the Strada Institute, which used a slightly different definition of underemployment but concluded that close to half of those college graduates whose first job does not require a degree are still in jobs ten years later that do not require a degree.

For all the emphasis on the necessity of a college education, moreover, 43 percent of high-school freshmen do not end up enrolling in college in the first place. Taking account of that datum, Cass calculates that only 16 percent of ninth graders will make it through college to a job that requires a college degree—which is to say that only a small minority of them will follow the education-to-career path that our system treats as an ideal.

These disappointing results have caused many people to have second thoughts about whether we should be quite so single-minded about funneling students from high school into college. They *should* have this chastening effect. They should have it even if we put no weight on Bryan Caplan's argument that the wage premium from schooling mostly reflects the signal that diplomas provide about a prospective employee's intelligence, studiousness, and conformity to social norms rather than the skills and knowledge that schools impart.[5] To the extent we accept Caplan's analysis, we have even more reason to think that neither government nor society should be seeking to raise college enrollment.

My own skepticism about college as the main or only route to making a good living has led me to write about questions of public policy that affect people after high school. My point has not been that we should simply stop telling people to go to college, hope that fewer people decide to enroll, and call it a day. What we should try to do, instead, is clear pathways for people who do not go to college to be able to make adequate livelihoods and contribute to their communities.

I have written favorably, for example, about proposals by some members of Congress to change the rules that govern the accreditation of colleges in order to give graduating high-school students more options, the hope being that new options might work better for some students than the traditional ones.[6] Liberalizing occupational licensure rules is another idea that might open pathways to economic success that particularly benefit those without college degrees.[7] I would add that governments at all levels should give serious consideration to relaxing educational requirements for various job categories within the public sector and thus allowing people without college degrees to fill more positions.

Whether we think everyone should go to college also has major implications for how we think about primary and especially secondary education. It affects the very purpose of K–12. Very often, I think, policymakers, educators, and parents primarily conceive of that purpose as making sure that students are ready for college. Worse, they sometimes assume it is making sure that students enroll in college, ready or not.

This assumption has a way of insinuating itself easily into our schools. Third grade follows second, middle school follows elementary school, and at each step a teacher's job is in some sense to help prepare a child for the next step. That next step is predetermined, it is in key ways the same for all children, and it takes place at a school.

The assumption that college enrollment should be the next step is, as a result, not always a conscious one. It was an influence in 2015, when a Republican Congress passed and a Democratic president signed the Every Student Succeeds Act (ESSA). That legislation amended and reauthorized the federal government's major K–12 programs. The act requires that states publish report cards that include, among other things, any information they collect about the percentage of each high school's graduates who enroll at postsecondary institutions. States are not required to include any information about college completion rates or employment rates.

The website for the federal Department of Education has a page about this law that explains how it builds on recent progress, of which it offers three examples. "High school graduation rates are at all-time highs. Dropout rates are at historic lows."[8] (You may notice that these first two examples are more or less the same thing said twice.) The passage continues, "And more students are going to college than ever before. These achievements provide a firm foundation for further work to expand educational opportunity and improve student outcomes under ESSA."

It is safe to say that this language was not designed to be controversial. It was written and approved by people to whom it has almost certainly never occurred that getting more people to go to college is not an accomplishment at all—let alone the only post–high school accomplishment worth noting.

———

Moving away from a college-centric model for K–12 education would require a different conception of its purpose. What follows twelfth grade—the next phase for which each grade has been a preparation— should not necessarily be college; it should be adulthood. Primary and secondary schools should aid parents in getting children ready to make responsible choices about what to do with their lives. Those schools should inculcate in them the knowledge, skills, and dispositions that will help them make wise choices—choices that are informed both about their options and about themselves. This mission is very different, of course, from preparing all children to take one obvious next step.

Under this conception of the purpose of schools, our criteria for success would also have to be different. A good high school would no longer be one in which a high percentage of graduating seniors go to college in the fall. It would be one in which a high percentage of graduating seniors either complete college within a few years or find gainful employment. Using this measure of success, a high school would get credit within a state accountability system or *U.S. News*–type ranking when its graduates were truly ready for college. But it would not get credit when graduates who are not ready, or do not have the aptitude or interest, enroll in college.

This proposed measure is not perfect. A focus on college graduation rates could become a reason for colleges to lower standards; a focus on high school graduation rates has sometimes had this effect. Collecting this information and using it to judge high schools would of course be more administratively difficult than gauging matriculation rates. But that is not an argument for adopting the wrong measure of success. Keeping an eye on how well high schools are preparing students for college or the labor market would also tend to counteract the negative side effect of the focus on high school graduation rates. The incentive would be to make the high school diploma valuable to employers. If high schools were successful in this task, perhaps employers would screen job applicants for college degrees less often.

In a world where success is defined in terms of college completion or employment rather than matriculation rates, administrators seeking to improve their high schools' reputation would have a stronger incentive to devote attention to the non-college-bound portion of their student bodies. They would also have an incentive to steer students toward the path most likely to work for them. Ideally, they would avoid heavy-handed tracking, but that danger does not justify a status quo that is heavy-handed in its own way and that is also failing many young people.

This reorientation of schools also suggests a need for changes in academic standards and curricula. A few years ago, Andrew Kelly, then a colleague of mine at the American Enterprise Institute, noted that the Common Core standards are supposed to promote both college and career readiness. "But instead of defining 'career-ready' separately," he wrote, "the architects have equated the two."[9]

No one can doubt that there is a lot of overlap between what students need to learn for college and what they need to learn for a career that does not involve college. All students should be literate; know basic math, science, and civics; and have some familiarity with art, literature, and history. All students should be supported, too, in forming habits of mind and conduct, including honesty and industry, that will help them become upright citizens. As I noted earlier, they need those things to form them as adults capable of choosing how to spend their adulthood. Yet it would be a surprising coincidence if the things students need to learn for college turned out to be *identical* to what they need to learn for a career that does not involve college.

A similar confusion afflicts even those who have been moving away from the college-for-all model, suggesting both that we are in the early stages of a rethinking and that this model retains a very powerful grip on our minds. Recall that the Gates Foundation has a program designed to ensure that all high-school students are prepared to succeed at college and a career: again, the excluded possibility is that students may be prepared to succeed at a career without being prepared to succeed at college. The foundation also has another program, "whose goal," it explains, "is to dramatically increase the number of young people who obtain a postsecondary degree or certificate with labor-market value." Those final words are a laudable acknowledgment that college degrees are not for everyone.

But there is a tension between the programs' goals. If a significant fraction of high-school students are to go on to earn "a certificate with labor-market value" rather than a college degree, why do all of them need to be ready for success in college?

One way out of this conflict is suggested by a less well-known non-profit organization, now named PeerForward but formerly called College Summit. The group takes partial credit for ESSA's inclusion of the requirement that states report every high school's postsecondary enrollment rate. It says, "We have finally reached consensus as a nation on the postsecondary purpose of the American high school. High school graduation is now a milestone on the way to matriculation; it is no longer the endpoint."[10] But it then explains that it wants us to revise our understanding of college. Instead of picturing "a leafy four-year campus adorned with brick buildings, tweed-clad professors, and strolling students with time to read, reflect, and yes, play," we should have in mind a new definition: "any postsecondary educational experience with value in the marketplace."[11] The group goes on, however, to say that it's important for colleges and universities to award both more four-year degrees and more postsecondary certificates.

I agree that our view of college should not be restricted to tweed and brick. One of the benefits of changing the accreditation rules, as suggested above, would be to enable a greater variety of postsecondary institutions. But I hope that this broader-mindedness would lead further.

If we want to say that college degrees are not for everyone, perhaps we should say *that* instead of trying to change the meaning of the word "college." Perhaps we should consider, too, whether it is right to think that a path to success without a traditional college degree has to involve getting a formal certificate for training efforts begun after high school. Might it be possible for preparation to start during high school? Even after high school, might a young person's actual provision of labor-market value—that is, his working a job—sometimes be at least as valuable a credential as his possession of any piece of paper at all? And while we're thinking through the question of college and career readiness: Might the term "career" itself indicate too narrow a way of thinking about students' futures? A lot of students do not want, and will not have, the kind of employment path that the term can connote.

Skeptics of the college-for-all template for success typically call for an expansion of apprenticeships and of career and technical education (although, given what I have just said, it might be better to go back to the discarded label of "vocational education").

It certainly seems appropriate for governments to redirect some of the money they now spend trying to get young people to get college degrees to those young people who will not. What makes that case especially compelling is that the major beneficiaries of the current spending—the people who actually receive the degrees and then have careers that require them—have much better economic outcomes as a group than those who do not.

I am no expert on how best to design and support such programs. I do think that hands-on experience working for an employer could be valuable for many students, less because it is a form of training for a specific job than because it helps get them used to the world of work. As an aside, my strong sense is that nearly all students could use more instruction than they get in personal finance.

I would again raise the caution that college-for-all assumptions can easily sneak back into our thinking about these programs. There is nothing wrong with a participant's choosing to go on to college. We should not, however, judge these programs by their effect on college enrollment rates or try to structure them so as to boost those rates.

Defenders of college-for-all frequently suggest that the critics are elitists who wish to let only a select few through the doors of universities and reserve their great benefits to that fortunate minority. These defenders observe that many of the skeptics are themselves college graduates and that their children typically follow the college track. David Leonhardt has, for instance, sounded this note in the *New York Times*.[12]

The critics should not be intimidated by this charge. They could even, in a way, fling it back at their accusers. A system oriented toward college enrollment already works mostly for the advantage of a select few. They often lead us to ignore or condescend to those who are uninterested in following that path. My point is not that everyone who believes we should try to get more people to go to college is a snob. But the adherents of that view should reckon with the way in which they have fostered a culture in which people without degrees are sometimes written off as losers.

Our debates over education policy are dominated on all sides by people who have college degrees and who expect their children to earn them as well. People whose degrees come from the most selective colleges have vastly disproportionate influence in those debates and do not always appreciate how few Americans go to such schools. These facts distort our thinking about education even though almost all of these people have good intent. The distortion has become worse as the country's social life has become more stratified on the basis of education. The policymakers, journalists, and think-tankers who talk about education have to stretch to imagine what the world looks like to people who do not share their educational goals and assumptions.

A more pluralistic approach would be compatible with targeted efforts to identify young people who are not bound for college but whom we have good reason to think would benefit from it, and to help them apply, arrange financing, and so forth. We could, for example, make it easier for them to make income-share agreements that would enable them to go to college—or, of course, to follow a noncollege track.

The point is that what is right for some is not right for all. Parents, including upper-middle-class parents who themselves have college degrees, should be open to the possibility that college may not be a good fit for all of their children. As they help their children determine their options, they should be cognizant of our low college-completion rates.

Our goal should be to open, not close, doors to opportunity. Those doors are not found exclusively on college campuses. A K–12 education is not a failure if it leads somewhere else. In all of our thinking about schools and schooling, let us not lose sight of that truth.

NOTES

1. US Congress, *Congressional Record Index*, Senate, 111th Cong., 2nd sess., vol. 156, pt. 1, 756.
2. "Transcript: George W. Bush," *Wall Street Journal*, September 2, 2004, https://www.wsj.com/articles/SB109416902915408839.
3. "Postsecondary Success," Bill and Melinda Gates Foundation, accessed August 15, 2019, https://www.gatesfoundation.org/what-we-do/us-program/postsecondary-success.

4. Oren Cass, *How the Other Half Learns: Reorienting an Education System That Fails Most Students* (New York: Manhattan Institute, 2018).

5. Bryan Caplan, *The Case against Education: Why the Education System Is a Waste of Time and Money* (Princeton, NJ: Princeton University Press, 2018).

6. Ramesh Ponnuru and Yuval Levin, "How Republicans Can Improve Higher Education," *Washington Post*, November 6, 2014, https://www.washington post.com/opinions/how-republicans-can-improve-higher-education-and -help-the-party/2014/11/06/d82aeb02-6532-11e4-836c-83bc4f26eb67_story .html.

7. Ramesh Ponnuru, "Obama Sees the Light on Job Licenses," *Bloomberg Opinion*, July 30, 2015, https://www.bloomberg.com/opinion/articles/2015-07-30 /obama-sees-the-light-on-job-licenses.

8. "Every Student Succeeds Act (ESSA)," US Department of Education, accessed August 15, 2019, https://www.ed.gov/essa.

9. Andrew Kelly, "Preparing Students for the World of Work," in *Reviving Economic Growth: Policy Proposals from 51 Leading Experts*, Brink Lindsey, ed. (Washington, DC: Cato Institute Press, 2015), 149.

10. "The Purpose of the American High School," Peer Forward, accessed August 15, 2019, https://www.peerforward.org/with-the-passing-of-essa-our-nation -reaches-a-consensus-on-the-purpose-of-the-american-high-school/.

11. Ibid.

12. For example, see David Leonhardt, "Is College Worth It? Clearly, New Data Says," *New York Times*, May 27, 2014, https://www.nytimes.com/2014/05/27/ upshot/is-college-worth-it-clearly-new-data-say.html; David Leonhardt, "College for the Masses," *New York Times*, April 24, 2015, https://www. nytimes.com/2015/04/26/upshot/college-for-the-masses.html; David Leonhardt, "A Winning Political Issue Hiding in Plain Sight," *New York Times*, March 19, 2018, https://www.nytimes.com/2018/03/18/opinion /education-campaign-issue.html; David Leonhardt, "A $20 Million Gift for College," *New York Times*, May 18, 2018, https://www.nytimes.com/2018/05/18 /opinion/college-advising-corps.html.

CHAPTER 14

The Cultural Contradictions of American Education

by Kay S. Hymowitz

FOR SEVERAL DECADES now, educators in the United States have focused much of their attention on the disappointing school performance of low-income kids. No one can argue with their concern. As education became more critical to climbing the ladder into the middle class, poor children were being left behind. Growing inequality, intractable racial disparities, and moribund test scores and college graduation rates signaled that America was not fulfilling its central promise of opportunity for all.

So it may seem clueless, even "privileged," to ask us to turn the magnifying glass back to the middle class. Statistically speaking, they're not the ones struggling to read and to pass their algebra exams. They're not the ones flailing in our globalized, knowledge-based, and volatile labor market.

Yet understanding some fundamental facts about the middle-class mind-set is crucial to diagnosing what ails America's education system, not just as it affects the children of two married doctors, but also those of a single-mother bus driver. Let's not forget that schools are designed and administered by college-educated, middle-class professionals. They inevitably bring their own cultural psychology to the task.

I contend that there is something in that middle-class psychology that makes running a classroom and designing its curriculum a paradoxical undertaking, one that has to be negotiated with understanding of the trade-offs involved. Call it "the cultural contradiction of American education."

To explain the contradiction, it's helpful to begin in the nursery. Cultural psychologists—people who study the way culture shapes cognition and emotion—have done some fascinating work comparing the behavior of American mothers and their sisters in young motherhood in other countries, including Western countries that share our commitment to individual liberty and rights. Their research illuminates a little-understood realm of American exceptionalism.

Consider one modest but revealing study of parental attitudes toward sleep by Sara Harkness and Charles Super.[1] Comparing similar groups of Dutch and American mothers of newborns, the authors discovered that the two nationalities had very different theories about what was going on inside those tiny brains. The American mothers saw the yawning or fussy infant as expressing his own internal drives; babies "know" and can tell us when they are tired and how much sleep they need. Dutch mothers look at their babies differently. They believe that parents must provide children "regularity and rest." "Whereas the American parents described their child's sleep patterns as innate and developmentally driven," the authors write, "the Dutch parents hardly mentioned these ideas and instead spoke frequently about the importance of a regular sleep schedule, which they saw as fundamental to healthy growth and development." (Sleep-deprived American parents might be interested to know that, at six months of age, Dutch infants were getting an average of two hours more sleep per day than their self-regulating American counterparts.)

As the sleep study hints, from the time a child is born, American parents—more specifically, middle-class American parents—act on the cultural belief that each child is an individual with a distinct inner nature and unique needs, abilities, and predilections. That inner nature demands their deference. Other foreign cultures, past and present, would find this a little weird. For most of human history, the job of parents and the broader community has been to turn the uncivilized child into a capable citizen of an existing community with its own rules and history. In France, for instance, writes Kim Willisher, a British mother raising her children in Paris, a child is "a small human being ready to be formatted, partly by its parents. . . . It has to be *encadré*, kept within a clearly and often rigidly defined framework that places disciplines such as manners and mathematics above creativity and expression."[2]

American parents, by contrast, put their emphasis on unleashing and supporting their little ones' individuality; customs, rules, and routines are an unfortunate, though admittedly sometimes necessary, burden. I'd wager it's no coincidence that, like their Dutch comrades in diapers, French babies sleep through the night earlier than American babies do.[3]

In order to arouse and stimulate their intrinsic selves, American parents talk to their infants more frequently and energetically than parents in other cultures. They cheer their babbling, smiles, and giggles. They celebrate as significant individual achievements the first time they roll over, crawl, and walk. As time goes on, they decorate their kitchens with their earliest finger paintings. Compare that to Scandinavians, who follow the "law of Jente"[4] and discourage attention-seeking. Kay Xander Mellish, an American mother living in Denmark, describes an incident that perfectly captures the contrast between American thinking versus that of other Europeans, specifically Scandinavian. Seeing a little boy at a day care center take his first steps, she called out excitedly, "Come on! You can do it!" only to be reprimanded by a nearby teacher for giving the child the false impression that he was special.[5]

In other cultures, both East and West, parents prize manners and ritualized courtesies over the child's self-expression. The French teach their two-year-olds to say, "Bonjour, Madame," or "Monsieur" in every encounter, Pamela Druckerman informs us in *Bringing Up Bebe*; not doing so leaves parents ashamed of a *"mal eleve."* Cultural psychologists find that parents all over the world share this interest in manners. Japanese mothers, for instance, expect their children to be courteous—to say thank you and good morning—and compliant—to come when called, by four years of age.[6] Ritualized greetings strike Americans as artificial and a worrying sign of an overly programmed child. As the long-popular *What to Expect: The Toddler Years* warns, "Children who are nagged about their manners or punished for not using a fork . . . won't feel positive about manners and are likely to ignore them completely when out from under the eye of the enforcing parent."[7] I've been noticing a new tendency among adults to "high-five" young children. The gesture gives both adult and child an American-style escape from formality; instead of awkwardly proper—"Good morning, Mr. Smith"—a greeting becomes a moment of egalitarian playfulness.

This is not to say that manners, not to mention sleep, don't matter to American parents. Nor does it imply that American-style individualism is an altogether noxious strain. But it does set the stage for the aforementioned cultural contradiction of American education. There is a noticeable tension between the innateness of the child's interests, talents, and self-expression on the one hand, and the school as a collective enterprise on the other. An American mommy-blogger living in Norway was shocked to find just how alien that thoroughly Western culture is. "There is just one way, more or less: All kids go to bed at 7, all attend the same style of preschool, all wear boots, all eat the same lunch. . . . That's the *Norwegian* way."[8]

American education institutions, led by professionals, many of whom are parents themselves, inescapably reflect these same cultural norms. Take the dogma that classrooms, especially those for younger children, need low teacher-student ratios. For Americans, small classes allowing for individualized teacher-student interaction are a crucial ingredient for a "quality preschool." (In fact, small teacher-student ratios get a gold star from American parents at every grade level, even college.)

That this expert-endorsed, seemingly transparently obvious truth is actually a cultural preference is one takeaway from the deservedly renowned *Preschool in Three Cultures*, an ethnographic study of early childhood programs in China, Japan, and the United States. The researchers compared videotaped classes of four-year-olds in all three countries; more interestingly, they asked American teachers to comment on what they noticed in the Japanese and Chinese classrooms, the Japanese to comment on the Chinese and American classrooms, and so on. As it happens, in Japan it's not unusual to find a class of 30 four-year-olds with only one adult in the room. Unsurprisingly, after seeing the videotapes, American teachers objected that Asian children weren't getting the amount of individual attention they needed. Asian educators watching tapes of American preschools had the opposite reaction. They actually prefer larger groups of kids in their early childhood classes; American children, they worried, were being confined in a "narrow world." "I wonder how you teach a child to be part of a group in a class that small?" one Japanese teacher asked.[9]

The small classroom is crucial for educators trying to manage the cultural contradiction between each child's individuality and the presence of other equally unique children. It also has the benefit of reinforcing American youngsters' understanding of their own individuality. At Japanese preschools, children learn ritualistic traditional greetings, songs, and festivals. They don't celebrate their own birthdays in the classroom on the date of their birth since all the birthdays of a given month are recognized at the same time. (American parents who have found themselves spreading blue icing on twenty-five chocolate cupcakes at 1 a.m. for their child's school birthday celebration are sighing longingly.) The Japanese do give their young'uns plenty of opportunity for "free play," but while American teachers see that time as a chance for self-expression and free choice, the Japanese believe it is a chance to help develop "group feeling." They read books that teach respect for others and cooperation; Americans like "I think I can, I think I can" stories to encourage individual achievement and self-esteem.

American teachers not only give their charges plenty of choices, they talk about those choices repeatedly throughout the day. "What would you like to do?" The classroom is a teeming warehouse of activities—

water and sand tables, blocks, books, dress-up, painting corners—sure to elicit the interest of the most hesitant child. The *Preschool in Three Cultures* researchers theorized that Americans see giving a child plenty of choices as the best way to appeal to his "intrinsic motivation," an American concept itself.

The relevance of this early childhood anthropology for K–12 educators should be easy to discern. American parents and preschool teachers are unknowingly preparing children to thrive in a particular sort of classroom. When a middle-class youngster trembles at the kindergarten door on the first day of school, if she has been raised by American-born parents, she has already been empowered to make choices for herself, to have her talents and interests recognized and prized, and to speak up about her preferences. She is the perfect customer for a child-centered, constructivist classroom dedicated to intrinsic motivation, one who will work well with "a guide on the side," as up-to-date teachers sometimes imagine themselves to be. Low-income children, unversed in the ways of "What's your favorite color?" "Use your words," and "Good job!"—a phrase my grandson must have heard a thousand times before he reached three—are entering a foreign country.

The singularity of middle-class American child rearing and preschool helps explain the stubborn hold of many progressive ideas on the educator's imagination and the frequent failure of those ideas with poor children. "Whole language" reading instruction, for example, is predicated on the same ideas about the child's intrinsic self as those embraced by middle-class American mothers and fathers. According to whole-language theory, children learn to read by using their innate capacities, the same way they do when they start talking; they don't need explicit instruction in phonics or spelling or grammar any more than they need lessons in how to ask for ice cream. Surround them with a variety of books so they can choose something to their liking; they'll discover sound patterns and whole words by deciphering their context within a given story.

"Balanced literacy" is a revised version of whole language that makes some gestures toward reading instruction, or what supporters carefully describe as "teacher support to develop the literacy growth of each individual student."[10] But the individualistic language—kids "grow" their literacy, each individual student has his own trajectory, "student-centered learning"—betrays the method's close relationship to its antecedent.

The educator's zeal for "creative classrooms" also reflects a particularly American way of thinking about teaching and learning. Creativity enthusiasts see themselves as rebelling against the mechanical, industrial-era, "drill-and-kill" thinking that they believe dominates American schools. Ken Robinson's 2006 TED talk titled "Do Schools Kill Creativity"—the most watched video in TED history—answered the question of his title with a clarion "Yes." Our education system is a "death valley," a "system based on standardization and conformity that suppresses individuality, imagination, and creativity," Robinson admonishes.[11] He and his ilk want schools to be full of creative teachers who shun traditional subject matter and assignments like worksheets, tests, and essays in favor of dioramas, videos, acrostic poems, songs, and "projects." A creative teacher—one of the highest compliments that can be paid to our "guides on the side"—is said to make for "joyful" classrooms and students. And, as future-minded pundits have warned repeatedly, creative thinking is essential for twenty-first-century jobs.

Now, Americans have every reason to revere the creative brains in their midst. The nation's legendary ingenuity, innovation, and dynamism have been crucial for improving productivity and standards of living in the United States and worldwide. The birthplace of innumerable world-changing inventions—the airplane, the suspension bridge, the lightbulb, GPS, and more—the country remains the world's leader in the number of Nobel Prize winners. Its citizens have created one-fourth of the 10 million patents worldwide. We want and need more of that.

But the creativity craze pushes us straight into that dead-end cultural contradiction that confounds the work of schools. Creativity doesn't always play well with others, self-expression can be at odds with civility, and order and safety demand that children curb their energies and keep their voices down. If the complaints of American educators are to be believed, today's schoolchildren are C students at best when it comes to self-control, motivation, civility, or what is often called "soft skills." Employer complaints about the Millennial "soft skills gap" have become a recurrent topic in management reports and at HR conferences.[12] Online laments about younger workers who have trouble getting to work on time, collaborating, communicating, and in general, dealing with workplace discipline and authority are eye-rollingly common. If you think about it, this is one predictable consequence of the hyperindividualism of middle-class American parenting and teaching; the guide on the side appeals to the child's unique inner nature but fails to challenge her natural egotism and immaturity.

This contradiction also helps explain our interminable curriculum battles. American hyperindividualism conflicts with any notion of education as a structured transmission of knowledge from one generation to the next. The traditional disciplines that liberals used to—and many conservatives still—prize get reduced from a shared body of knowledge to, at best, a rummage sale for enhancing individual meaning, identity, and creativity. In addition to constituting a culturally meaningful body of knowledge as yet unknown to the child, the disciplines—with their chronological history, separate subdisciplines, and step-by-step mastery of increasingly complex material—demonstrate the value of reason, order, and shared reality. They communicate adults' recognition of children's inescapable ignorance. The teacher knows something the child does not know. He is an authority; the child is, well, a child.

———

Personalized learning is the latest reform to weaken the idea of education as a collective, social activity. Portrayed as the welcome triumph of twenty-first-century know-how over the industrial-age, teacher-centered classroom, personalized learning is better understood as the supreme pedagogical expression of American individualism. Supporters, including powerful tech-funded charities like the Chan-Zuckerberg Initiative, the Bill and Melinda Gates Foundation, and the Susan and Michael Dell Foundation, want to use data and digital technology to more fully customize education to train children to rely on their own "self-reflection" and "self-assessment." (I note without comment that many tech worthies severely restrict their own children's screen time.) Admittedly, the term is sometimes claimed by educators who are more interested in sounding up-to-date than in digitizing their classrooms, but as imagined by enthusiasts, personalized learning bypasses any notion of shared curriculum, shared expectations, shared knowledge, and even the classroom itself. Each student is an island, with their own "personalized learning path" setting "their own academic goals," "enabling student voice and choice in what, how, when, and where they learn."[13]

It's too early in the personalized learning revolution to know exactly how it will unfold, but a 2019 article in the *New York Times* about a Kansas school district foreshadows trouble ahead for Silicon Valley's education plans.[14] The district introduced a computerized, online system developed by Facebook engineers and funded by Chan-Zuckerberg that tested the approach. "Students are becoming self-directed learners and are demonstrating greater ownership of their learning activities," the district superintendent assured the reporters. But parents and students were complaining. One special-needs student had seizures from too much screen time. The program accidentally linked to "adult content" or a tabloid newspaper article. Student-directed learning was supposed to free up teachers to spend at least ten minutes a week with each student, but those meetings often shrank or vanished as teachers struggled to keep up with all the student questions about the program.

Ironically, the individualism of American parents and educators can be at odds with their future employers' needs. For a recent paper, Duke sociologist Jessi Streib interviewed 132 middle-class students up to four times during their "transition to adulthood."[15] She discovered that the 51 percent of the young adults in the group who appeared to be on a "downward trajectory" from the middle-class comfort they had grown up with had one quality in common: they were loath to adapt to more structured environments. Some saw themselves as too smart and talented to have to put up with required coursework. Some dropped out of college or avoided grad school when they found they were unable to "customize" their schooling to fit their preferences. Some quit jobs because they didn't like having bosses tell them what to do. "The very practices that middle-class parents pass down to their children," she writes, "may move them toward class reproduction when they are young and in school and away from it as they become older and enter college and the workforce."[16]

Notice, however, that almost half of Streib's subjects were on their way to "class reproduction." Middle-class parents may cultivate their children's individuality, but they also tend to promote some level of civility—apologizing for pushing someone, saying, "Please" and "Thank you," using their "inside" voices, picking up their dirty socks. They also have predictable routines—sitting at the dinner table, brushing their teeth twice a day, putting away their toys.

For lower-income students, the problem with the hyperindividualist classroom is not that it promotes entitlement, as Streib suggests. It's that family life hasn't prepared them for the assumptions of today's middle-class educators. In all likelihood, their parents haven't organized activities around their interests and strengths; perhaps they haven't even taken note of those interests and strengths. Adults have not prodded these children to "use their words" or express their feelings or asked them a lot of questions about what they thought about a story or what they noticed during a walk to the grocery store. They're lacking the "cultural literacy"—to recall E. D. Hirsch's invaluable term—to thrive in the contemporary classroom.

That helps explain why charter schools with structured curricula, rigorously defined rules, and expectations have sometimes had better success with disadvantaged students. The school forces students to practice order and routine that middle-class children brought with them from home. At the same time, those environments are less dependent on the uniquely American vocabulary and ideals of individualism so familiar to the middle class.

So, can teaching "soft skills"—grit, self-control, attentiveness—compensate for the deficits that Streib and so many employers describe, deficits that I believe can at least be partially attributed to the hyperindividualism of American education itself? A lot of educators are enamored of the possibility, but I have doubts. In most cultures, soft skills are built into routines and shared understandings of proper behavior taught by parents and schools, and reinforced by encounters with neighbors, shopkeepers, family, and friends. American kids may learn to pick up their toys and say, "Thank you," but their opportunities for practicing soft skills are fewer than those for children in more decorous cultures. One of the French mothers quoted in *Bringing Up Bebe* explains that she insists her child say, "Bonjour, Madame," not because she sees her child as a martinet, but because the greeting reminds children "they're not the only ones with feelings and needs." With no soft-skills curriculum in sight, the child is learning habits of empathy, humility, persistence, emotional control, and self-efficacy. If you want to see children learning grit, watch Chinese kids memorizing the characters of their alphabet or Japanese kids studying for a spelling bee.

Besides its impact on learning, we need to consider what role an excessively individualistic pedagogy plays in the coming apart of American society. Growing up in a multiracial, multiethnic environment, American students already share fewer commonalities than those from more homogeneous nations. Instead of recognizing this danger, educators have all but abandoned the mission of creating an *e pluribus unum*, of instilling a sense of common history and culture—outside, that is, of a few video games and a music or sports celebrity or two. Middle-class kids with strong families and social networks are able to counter the fragmentation, disintegrating trust, and loneliness of contemporary American education—and life.

If only their less advantaged peers were so lucky.

NOTES

1. Sarah Harkness et al., "Parental Ethnotheories of Children's Learning," in *The Anthropology of Learning In Childhood*, David F. Lancy, John Bock, and Suzanne Gaskins, eds. (Lanham, MD: AltaMira Press, 2010).
2. Kim Willisher, "The Parenting Gap: Why French Mothers Prefer to Use the Smack of Firm Authority," *The Guardian*, January 1, 2012, https://www.theguardian.com/lifeandstyle/2012/jan/01/parenting-france-britain.
3. Pamela Druckerman, *Bringing Up Bébé: One American Mother Discovers the Wisdom of French Parenting* (East Rutherford, NJ: Penguin, 2014).
4. *Wikipedia*, "The Law of Jante," accessed June 15, 2019, https://en.wikipedia.org/wiki/Law_of_Jante.
5. Kay Xander Mellish, "Raising Kids in Denmark: Social Engineering Begins in Day Care," *How to Live in Denmark* (blog), April 12, 2014, https://www.howtoliveindenmark.com/stories-about-life-in-denmark/raising-kids-in-denmark/.
6. Hidetada Shimizu, "Foundational Models of Self and Cultural Models of Teaching and Learning in Japan and the United States," in *A Companion to Cognitive Anthropology*, David B. Kronenfeld et al., eds. (Malden, MA: Blackwell Publishing, 2011), 436.
7. Heidi Murkoff et al., *What to Expect: The Toddler Years*, 2nd ed. (New York: Workman, 2009), 132.
8. Joanna Goddard, "10 Surprising Things about Parenting in Norway," *A Cup of Jo* (blog), July 15, 2013, https://cupofjo.com/2013/07/10-surprising-things-about-parenting-in-norway/.
9. Joseph J. Tobin, David Y. H. Yu, and Dana H. Davidson, *Preschool in Three Cultures: Japan, China, and the United States* (New Haven, CT: Yale University Press, 1989).
10. Kelli Westmoreland, "New to Balanced Literacy? Here's What You Need to Know," *BookSource Banter Blog*, January 24, 2017, https://www.booksourcebanter.com/2017/01/24/new-balanced-literacy-heres-need-know/.
11. Ken Robinson, *Do Schools Kill Creativity?* video hosted on Ted.com, accessed August 16, 2019, https://www.ted.com/talks/ken_robinson_says_schools_kill_creativity?language=en; Ken Robinson and Lou Aronica, *Creative Schools: The Grassroots Revolution That's Transforming Education* (New York: Viking, 2015).
12. *Bridging the Soft Skills Gap* (Washington, DC: US Chamber of Commerce Foundation, 2017), https://www.uschamberfoundation.org/reports/soft

-skills-gap; Payscale, "2016 Work Skills Preparedness Report," accessed June 15, 2019, https://www.payscale.com/data-packages/job-skills.

13. Scott Johns and Mike Wolking, *The Core Four of Personalized Learning: The Elements You Need to Succeed* (San Carlos, CA: Education Elements, 2018), https://www.edelements.com/hubfs/Core_Four/Education_Elements _Core_Four_White_Paper.pdf; Nellie Bowles, "Silicon Valley Came to Kansas Schools. That Started a Revolution," *New York Times*, April 21, 2019, https://www.nytimes.com/2019/04/21/technology/silicon-valley-kansas -schools.html.

14. Bowles, "Silicon Valley Came to Kansas Schools."

15. Jessi Streib, "Class, Culture, and Downward Mobility," *Poetics* 70 (2018): 18–27, https://osf.io/preprints/socarxiv/ws9gj/.

16. Ibid.

CHAPTER 15

You Can't Argue with Success—Or Can You?

by Mona Charen

S HE IS sixteen years old, very pretty, but modest. Her glasses and short hairstyle don't detract from her beauty, but lend her a scholarly mien. She has been to funerals, but never to a wedding. Her mother, who has done a great job raising her but who has had a rough go, is not married. Her friends' parents are not married either. Her neighborhood is downscale and can be dangerous. She attends a charter school. Her teachers, noting her intelligence, have encouraged her and kindled hope for a better life.[1]

What are the most important things she should know?

There is broad agreement that American students need a good grounding in core academic subjects—reading, math, history, science, civics, and a foreign language. Some would say that an arts curriculum is also indispensable to a fully rounded curriculum, along with economics, geography, and physical education.

But what about life advice? What about the great obstacles to success that arise not just from impoverished neighborhoods and weak academics but from poor choices? That is where consensus, such as it is, dissolves. That is where tangled questions of morality, paternalism, and, in the words of one critic, "cultural beefs" come into play. Schools are supposed to prepare students for successful lives, yet questions of marriage and family, so central to life success, have long been thought too personal or radioactive to broach. Considering the demonstrated differences in life outcomes for those who hew to what can be called "bourgeois virtues" compared with those who don't, failing to at least mention them can seem like malpractice.

It isn't as if schools shy away from life lessons altogether. Our sixteen-year-old student, so full of promise, will almost certainly be advised in any school in America to limit her screen time, to avoid drugs, to forswear driving under the influence, to get enough sleep, to get plenty of exercise, and to resist cigarettes. She will commonly be taught to practice "safe sex," both for health and pregnancy avoidance.

But only in a few experimental programs will she be told that by following three simple steps, she is nearly certain to avoid poverty and very likely to enjoy a middle-class income.

The three steps, first outlined by Brookings scholars Isabelle Sawhill and Ron Haskins in 2003 and updated a number of times since, are as follows:

1. Finish high school.
2. Get a full-time job.
3. Wait until age twenty-one to marry and have children.

They've labeled it "the success sequence," as that's also the order in which one should take those steps. Relying upon Census Bureau data, Haskins and Sawhill calculated that those who followed all three norms had only a 2 percent chance of living in poverty and a 75 percent chance of joining the middle class with a salary of fifty-five thousand dollars or more.[2] As Haskins summarized it in a Brookings paper:

> Policy aimed at promoting economic opportunity for poor children must be framed within three stark realities. First, many poor children come from families that do not give them the kind of support that middle-class children get from their families. Second, as a result, these children enter kindergarten far behind their more advantaged peers and, on average, never catch up and even fall further behind. Third, in addition to the education deficit, poor children are more likely to make bad decisions that lead them to drop out of school, become teen parents, join gangs, and break the law.[3]

Sawhill, whose research has focused on lifting people out of poverty, estimated that if rates of unwed pregnancy had remained at the 1970 rate, the current childhood poverty rate would be cut by one-fifth.

That is the stark fact that so many shrink from confronting: Unwed childbearing increases poverty. It ought to be a simple thing to counsel kids to avoid. In fact, when it came to *teenage* pregnancy, the nation did achieve something like consensus to do just that. And it worked.

But when it comes to advising the same kids against unwed pregnancy after turning eighteen, cultural leaders fall silent.

———

In past decades, the topic of family breakdown carried a racial charge. In the mid- to late twentieth century, rates of unwed parenting were dramatically higher in the African American community than among whites or others. In 1965, when Daniel Patrick Moynihan issued his famous report on the "Negro family," the illegitimacy rate among African Americans was 23 percent, compared with 3 percent for whites.

In the intervening decades, the stark contrast between black families and others faded, but not for good reasons. The rate of unwed childbearing rose for all groups, so that by 2013, the illegitimacy rate among blacks was 71 percent, among Hispanics 53 percent, and among whites 36 percent. In 1965, Moynihan was alarmed that fewer than half of African American children were spending their whole childhood with two parents. That is now true of American children from all backgrounds.

It was misguided to imagine that drawing attention to illegitimacy was racist in 1965—and Moynihan was subjected to unconscionable slander—but surely by now, when single parenting has clearly become more linked with education and class than with race, it's time to retire our reticence about addressing it honestly.

Further, family structure is a key variable affecting upward mobility. Shouldn't that commend the topic to those, especially on the left, who seem preoccupied with inequality?

Income gaps have been increasing over the past fifty years. The rich have, as always, gotten richer, but they've also gotten richer faster than the middle and lower classes (which, despite conventional wisdom, have also experienced gains). Left-leaning analysts regard the income gap as potentially catastrophic for social cohesion. Economists Emmanuel Saez of the University of California at Berkeley and Thomas Piketty of the Paris School of Economics became stars—and not just in academia—for arguing that the rich were enjoying a disproportionate share of national wealth. *New York Times* columnist Paul Krugman asserted that "describing our current era as a new Gilded Age or Belle Époque isn't hyperbole; it's the simple truth."[4] President Barack Obama called income inequality a "fundamental threat to our way of life." The names of Bernie Sanders and Elizabeth Warren are practically synonymous with calls to ameliorate inequality.

Yet for all the pained concern among progressives about the rich getting richer, they have turned their faces away from one of the chief causes of intergenerational poverty: the decline of marriage. The past few decades have offered prodigious evidence that family structure is key to life success. College-educated Americans, who tend to occupy the upper third of the income scale, faithfully follow the success sequence. At the other end of the spectrum, less-educated Americans have more disordered and chaotic homes. In fact, as Andrew Cherlin has observed, America holds the dubious distinction of leading the developed world in unstable adult relationships.[5]

We cannot say for certain that adhering to bourgeois virtues causes success. As every social scientist knows, correlation is not causation. But the correlation between the success sequence and avoiding poverty is striking.[6] The numbers are virtually written in neon.

Following up on the Haskins/Sawhill work, Wendy Wang and W. Bradford Wilcox of the Institute for Family Studies evaluated how the oldest of the Millennial generation—i.e., those born between 1980 and 1984—were faring based on the criteria that Haskins and Sawhill had identified. They found that nearly 97 percent of Millennials who followed all three steps are in the middle class or above by the time they reach the prime years of young adulthood (twenty-eight to thirty-four years old).[7]

Among Millennials who reached that age bracket and had not followed any of the success sequence steps, a majority (53 percent) were poor. But among those who followed all three steps, the poverty rate was just 3 percent.[8] The results were quite similar to the Haskins/Sawhill work.

Wang and Wilcox further found that the success sequence is not merely a restatement of class distinctions. The encouraging news is that those Millennials who grew up in poor homes were also able to reach the middle class or above by following the three steps. "[Eighty] percent of those with lower-income backgrounds," Wang wrote, "made it into middle- or upper-income brackets when they followed all three steps, versus only 44 percent for those who missed one or more steps."[9]

Cultural patterns vary widely, of course. Unwed parenting and divorce are now quite uncommon among college graduates. Sixty-seven percent of children whose parents are college graduates grow up with both of their parents, and another 18 percent live with remarried parents. Only 12 percent live with one parent, and just 2 percent live with cohabiting parents.[10]

By contrast, among high school graduates, only 33 percent of children live with their married parents. Twelve percent live with remarried parents, 13 percent with cohabiting parents, and 41 percent with single parents.[11] Among high school dropouts, the numbers are even more dramatic: 67 percent of Millennials without a high school diploma had a baby before marriage.[12]

The sequence pays off. African Americans who married before having children were almost twice as likely to be in the middle- or upper-income category (76 percent) as those who had children first (39 percent). For African Americans who followed all three steps, 84 percent were in the middle- or upper-income brackets by young adulthood.[13]

Sadly, many young people are unaware of their own capacity to shape their destinies. A young woman who was featured at an American Enterprise Institute panel on the success sequence reported that no one in her world talked about the importance of following the three steps. Another offered her impression that marriage was something you did if you were very much in love, but it was unrelated to childbirth or a life plan.

Perceiving that many young people from less-advantaged backgrounds are simply not exposed to the data, New York City launched a public information campaign targeting young people during the Bloomberg administration. It ran ads on buses and subways, offering statistics on poverty and teenage childbearing, promoting the importance of responsible fatherhood, and more. Some ads explicitly itemized the success sequence: "If you finish high school, get a job, and get married before having children, you have a 98 percent chance of not being in poverty."

The backlash was immediate. State Senator Liz Krueger objected, "This campaign seems laser focused on shaming already struggling teen parents, or ludicrously, convincing teens not to get pregnant because really bad things will happen."[14] Planned Parenthood objected that the campaign "creates stigma, hostility, and negative public opinions about teen pregnancy and parenthood."[15] Well, yes, that was the goal. Is it better to leave teenagers ignorant of the consequences of such choices?

Ian Rowe, who founded the single-sex Public Prep group of charter schools and whose excellent essay also appears in this book (see chapter 16), speaks of the uphill battle he is waging to get educators to take on this responsibility. Public Prep schools are located in the South Bronx and lower Manhattan. The students are from extremely disadvantaged backgrounds; in the South Bronx, the illegitimacy rate is 85 percent.

Rowe doesn't dispute that racism and other social ills place obstacles in the paths of students. But students, he advises, cannot rid society of racism or sexism all by themselves. What they do have direct control over are the choices they make. And the data are overwhelming that—even in a world afflicted with racism and other ills—those decisions matter.

Some teachers are concerned that mentioning norms like work and marriage unfairly stigmatizes the already marginalized. These educators further fear that including these norms in classroom curricula may hurt the feelings of students' parents, many of whom will not have followed the success sequence themselves. Some of the teachers, for that matter, will not themselves have abided by all three norms.

Yet such delicacy carries costs. In the name of not hurting the parents' (or teachers') feelings, the children may be deprived of essential facts that might well influence them and shape their future lives. That seems an awfully steep price to exact. Nor is it necessarily one that the parents themselves would endorse. As Isabelle Sawhill pointed out when I asked her about this problem, "Parents usually want what's best for their children, whether or not it's something they themselves did. Would a parent who only graduated from high school not want her child to attend college?" One could also argue that choosing to forgo a high school diploma is not something that educators should weigh in on, and those decisions, too, are to some degree culturally determined. High school dropout parents might feel some sense of stigma. Yet no teacher would stay mum on dropping out—and encouraging students to educate themselves doesn't make waves.

The difference, granted, is that dropping out of high school, while long considered unfortunate or unwise, is not usually thought to be immoral. Unwed parenting, by contrast, once carried a severe stigma. Fine. But fear of stigma is blinding many to the whopping price being paid by the poor and their children.

Though most of the resistance to teaching the success sequence comes in the form of vague discomfort, there are some more pointed critiques as well. Richard Reeves—also at Brookings—focuses on gaps:

Even when African Americans follow all the success sequence steps, he observes, their outcomes still lag behind whites and others:

> About 73 percent of whites who follow all three norms find themselves with income above 300 percent of the federal poverty line for their family size, while only 59 percent of blacks who adhere to all three norms fare equally well.[16]

This is true but, as noted above, blacks who follow the sequence still do nearly twice as well as those who fail to follow it. The gap with white achievement is regrettable, but hardly, as Reeves suggests, discrediting.

The CATO Institute's Michael Tanner argues that racism, sexism, and "economic dislocation" are responsible for many poor people choosing to have children outside marriage.[17] This is hard to square with the fact that in 1965—when racism and sexism were more pervasive, and living standards lower than today—three-quarters of black children were born to married parents.

The Progressive Policy Institute's Matt Bruenig thinks the success sequence is a sham because "work does all the work." Even if a worker is making the minimum wage, he advises, his annual income will exceed the poverty level if he works full-time. Therefore, the other steps are mere "superfluous cultural preferences."[18]

But this overlooks parenthood. Most women will become mothers at some point and will find it difficult if not impossible to work full-time. At that stage of life, having a husband to share expenses and contribute his salary to the family's income is the best antipoverty program possible.

Also looming over the success sequence debate is the shadow of the culture wars about teaching birth control versus abstinence. The latest skirmish came with the Trump administration's decision to cut $200 million in funding for teen pregnancy prevention programs.

Teaching the success sequence cannot become mired in that swamp.

As the Child Trends Foundation acknowledges, evidence shows that some abstinence programs succeed, as do some comprehensive sex education curricula.[19]

The key challenge is to decide, as a society and as educators, that promoting the success sequence is worthwhile. Schools already teach most of the behaviors that lead to good decisionmaking. We are awash in "teen pregnancy avoidance" programs. The Office of Adolescent Health at the Department of Health and Human Services maintains lists of hundreds of successful programs,[20] as does the National Conference of State Legislatures.[21] The Affordable Care Act included funding for lessons on healthy relationships, communication skills, conflict avoidance, and so on.

These programs have been part of a culture-wide push to discourage teenage pregnancy. It's impossible to say for certain how much any one program contributed—but something worked. The National Campaign to Prevent Teen Pregnancy, the HBO show *16 and Pregnant*, the hundreds of local, state, and federal education programs, and celebrity public-service announcements have had noticeable effects. Between 1991 and 2014, the teen pregnancy rate declined by 52 percent.[22]

The effort to discourage teen pregnancy had one huge advantage—cultural consensus. With rare exceptions, left and right agree that delaying childbearing until adulthood is a worthy aim. There is every reason to extend that same consensus to the success sequence. Debates about poverty, disadvantage, racism, and social ills will continue. But is there any doubt that individuals, even those from less than ideal homes, have some power to shape their own futures?

Is it even arguable that getting educated, working, and waiting until marriage to have children leads to better outcomes for men, for women, and particularly for children?

Think about that sixteen-year-old young lady growing up in a community where education, work, and marriage are all ailing. She faces many obstacles, but she may also be unaware of the ladders up and pathways out. Students from poor backgrounds often overestimate the obstacles to their success. Many imagine, for example, that the best colleges are out of reach due to cost. Ian Rowe makes it a point to inform his students that full scholarships are available at even the most selective schools, including the Ivy League, to those whose family incomes fall below certain thresholds.

Just as poor students should know that the best colleges are available to them if they are academically prepared, shouldn't they know that certain personal choices are likely to result in a middle-class life?

The tools to teach the success sequence are readily available. The Dibble Institute has created a widely imitated curriculum called "Relationship Smarts" that mentions the success sequence as part of a package about healthy sexuality, relationships, conflict resolution, goal-setting, and other lessons.[23]

The Public Prep schools employ *The Seven Habits of Highly Effective Teens* by Sean Covey as the core text for counseling students about following the three success sequence steps. The schools have found, along with others who teach risk prevention,[24] that near-peer counselors are extremely helpful.

A wealth of data is available about techniques that work. Let a thousand curricular flowers bloom. Teach it as part of career readiness programs, or health, or sex ed. Consult the Dibble Institute, the Catholic school approach to lessons on self-control,[25] character education curricula, or any of the myriad efforts undertaken by the Campaign to Prevent Teen Pregnancy.

We educate our children for life success, not just for academic achievement. We warn against smoking, illegal drugs, and other hazards. Can we, in good conscience, withhold the facts about the centrality of education, work, and family? They are the indispensable building blocks not just of financial success but of health and happiness. Young people from homes and neighborhoods that don't convey this reality deserve to hear it from someone.

NOTES

1. A graduate of Girls Prep, Kesi Wilson, spoke at an American Enterprise Institute conference on the success sequence on June 14, 2017. This portrait is a composite based partly on her and partly on others.

2. Ron Haskins, "Three Simple Rules Poor Teens Should Follow to Join the Middle Class," *Brookings*, March 13, 2013, https://www.brookings.edu/opinions/three-simple-rules-poor-teens-should-follow-to-join-the-middle-class/.

3. Ibid.

4. Quoted in Michael D. Tanner, "Five Myths about Economic Inequality in America," CATO Institute, September 7, 2016, https://www.cato.org/publications/policy-analysis/five-myths-about-economic-inequality-america#full.

5. Andrew J. Cherlin, *The Marriage-Go-Round: The State of Marriage and the Family in America Today* (New York: Vintage Books, 2009), 206.

6. Isabel V. Sawhill, "Why Does the Success Sequence Work?" *CATO Unbound*, May 11, 2018, https://www.cato-unbound.org/2018/05/11/isabel-v-sawhill/why-does-success-sequence-work.

7. Wendy Wang and W. Bradford Wilcox, *The Millennial Success Sequence: Marriage, Kids, and the "Success Sequence" among Young Adults* (Washington, DC: American Enterprise Institute and the Institute for Family Studies, 2018), 4, https://www.myrelationshipcenter.org/getmedia/f983b85a-b750-4f2f-9879-ad951f711f21/IFS-MillennialSuccessSequence-Final-(1).pdf.aspx.

8. Wang and Wilcox called the third step marrying before having children, not necessarily waiting until the age of twenty-one.

9. Wendy Wang, "'The Sequence' Is the Secret to Success," *Wall Street Journal*, March 27, 2018, https://www.wsj.com/articles/the-sequence-is-the-secret-to-success-1522189894.

10. Pew Research Center, "The American Family Today," December 17, 2015, http://www.pewsocialtrends.org/2015/12/17/1-the-american-family-today/.

11. Ibid.

12. Wang and Wilcox, *Millennial Success Sequence*, 9.

13. Ibid., 21.

14. Liz Krueger, "Statement: City's Teen Pregnancy Ad Campaign 'Pathologically Mean-Spirited,'" *New York State Senate* (blog), March 8, 2013, https://www.nysenate.gov/newsroom/press-releases/liz-krueger/statement-citys-teen-pregnancy-ad-campaign-pathologically-mean.

15. Chris Boyette, "NYC Teen Pregnancy Prevention Campaign Comes under Fire," *CNN*, March 7, 2013, https://www.cnn.com/2013/03/07/health/new-york-planned-parenthood/index.html.

16. Richard V. Reeves, Edward Rodrigue, and Alex Gold, "Following the Success Sequence? Success Is More Likely If You're White," *Brookings*, August 6, 2015, https://www.brookings.edu/research/following-the-success-sequence-success-is-more-likely-if-youre-white/.

17. CATO Institute, *#CatoConnects: Building an Inclusive Economy*, video, December 13, 2018, https://www.cato.org/multimedia/events/catoconnects -building-inclusive-economy

18. Matt Bruenig, "The Success Sequence Is about Cultural Beefs Not Poverty," *MattBruenig.com*, July 31, 2019, http://mattbruenig.com/2017/07/31 /the-success-sequence-is-about-cultural-beefs-not-poverty/.

19. Jennifer Manlove, Heather Wasik, and Jenita Parekh, "Preventing Teen Pregnancy: Good News for Communities," *Child Trends* (blog), January 27, 2017, https://www.childtrends.org/preventing-teen-preg nancy-good-news-communities.

20. "Evidence-Based Teen Pregnancy Prevention Programs," Centers for Disease Control and Prevention, accessed August 15, 2019, https://www.cdc .gov/teenpregnancy/practitioner-tools-resources/evidence-based-programs.html.

21. , "Teen Pregnancy Prevention," National Conference of State Legislatures accessed August 15, 2019, http://www.ncsl.org/research/health/teen -pregnancy-prevention.aspx#4%5C.

22. Melissa S. Kearney and Phillip B. Levine, *Teen Births Are Falling: What's Going On?* (Washington, DC: Brookings Policy Brief, March 2014), https: //www.brookings.edu/wp-content/uploads/2016/06/teen_births_falling _whats_going_on_kearney_levine.pdf.

23. Marline E. Pearson, *Relationship Smarts PLUS 4.0* (Berkeley, CA: Dibble Institute, 2018), https://www.dibbleinstitute.org/NEWDOCS/sample_lessons /RQ+4-Sample-Lesson-9-11-18.pdf.

24. Interview with Michelle Toews in Stephanie Cassanova, "K-State Gets Grant for Sexual Risk Avoidance Program," *The Mercury*, July 20, 2017, http: //themercury.com/k-state-gets-grant-for-sexual-risk-avoidance-program /article_38ed85bf-42ac-5112-9314-975815c0ceed.html.

25. Michael Gottfried and Jacob Kirksey, *Self-Discipline and Catholic Schools: Evidence from Two National Cohorts* (Washington, DC: Thomas B. Fordham Institute, 2018), https://fordhaminstitute.org/national/research /self-discipline-and-catholic-schools-evidence-two-national-cohorts.

CHAPTER 16

Measure What Matters
FAMILY STRUCTURE AND STUDENT OUTCOMES
by Ian Rowe

I F WE ARE honest with ourselves, there comes a turning point moment in the life of every education reformer when we must confront the limitations of education reform. Such an experience happened to me around 4 p.m. on July 11, 2016, near Third Avenue and 149th Street in the heart of the South Bronx.

Earlier that year I had read the 2015 Citizens' Committee for Children's (CCC) annual ranking of New York City's fifty-nine Community Districts, based on eighteen different measures of child well-being. In education, the three categories are the share of three- and four-year-olds enrolled in early education programs, passing rates on the state's elementary and middle school reading and math tests, and high school graduation rates.

In 2015, among the fifty-nine districts, the five showing the highest overall risk to child well-being were all located in the South Bronx. Table 16.1 illustrates the disparity between the highest-risk district, Hunts Point, and—less than two miles away—the lowest-risk district on Manhattan's Upper East Side.[1]

Around the same time, another study showed that at ninety New York City schools, *not a single black or Hispanic student had passed the 2014 state tests*.[2] Zero. Many of these schools were also located in the South Bronx. Indeed, by virtually every measure, educational opportunity in the South Bronx was in free fall, and had been for generations.

Meanwhile, as CEO of Public Prep, a network of all-boys and all-girls public charter schools, I was in the midst of strategic discussions

TABLE 16.1

SELECTED EDUCATION OUTCOMES COMPARED IN THE HIGHEST- AND LOWEST-RISK COMMUNITY DISTRICTS IN NEW YORK CITY, 2015

2015 HIGHEST-RISK COMMUNITY DISTRICT Hunts Point (Bronx 02)			
Early education enrollment	ELA state test pass rate	Math state test pass rate	High school graduation rate
53%	10.5%	12.1%	37.2%
2015 LOWEST-RISK COMMUNITY DISTRICT Upper East Side (Manhattan 08)			
Early education enrollment	ELA state test pass rate	Math state test pass rate	High school graduation rate
81.9%	64.5%	71.1%	81.1%

Source: Citizens' Committee for Children

regarding where to locate our future schools. Given the glaring need for more high-quality education options in the Bronx, as well as overwhelming demand for our Boys Prep and Girls Prep schools, we decided to concentrate our growth in the South Bronx.

Thus, at the end of the 2015–16 school year, Public Prep moved its headquarters from tony Tribeca to the battered South Bronx. We leased an office location that abuts an outreach center that provides a syringe exchange and mental health counseling to local drug addicts. This is exactly where we needed to be to better understand the community we serve and the challenges facing the kids we educate.

On that hot July afternoon, my team took a walking tour of the neighborhood to find a convenient bank, office supply store, bodega, and where to score the best chili relleno. Along the way, we encountered a twenty-seven-foot-long, baby-blue Winnebago truck, that—judging by the cheery reaction of the people standing nearby—was a familiar and welcome fixture in the neighborhood.

That was my turning point.

On the side of the truck, vividly inscribed in graffiti lettering, was the phrase "Who's Your Daddy?" The truck turned out to be a mobile DNA testing center that charges $350 to $500 to answer questions such as "Is she my sister?" or "Are you my father?"[3] Demand had been so robust that the owner added a second truck so he could offer Who's Your Daddy? services in other boroughs and neighboring cities.

I was surprised that such a truck and its on-demand services even existed. But what astonished me more was the absolute normalcy and acceptance of its existence. The Who's Your Daddy? truck was clearly providing a needed function to the community. The owner describes why people used his service: "I realized that many of [my clients] were carrying around a huge burden—sometimes for decades. They live daily without the assurances that most people take for granted, such as: Who is my mother? Who is my brother? Am I really who I think I am?"[4]

Why were so many people pondering such profound questions? I looked back at the CCC data to explore some additional categories related to children and youth. Table 16.2 displays some of what I found (again comparing Hunts Point with the Upper East Side).[5]

TABLE 16.2

SELECTED DATA RELATED TO CHILDREN AND YOUTH COMPARED IN THE HIGHEST- AND LOWEST-RISK COMMUNITY DISTRICTS IN NEW YORK CITY, 2015

2015 HIGHEST-RISK COMMUNITY DISTRICT Hunts Point (Bronx 02)			
Children in single-parent families	Teen birth rate	Teen idleness (16 to 19 years old)	Adults without a high school degree
60.0%	28.0%	19.0%	42.5%
2015 LOWEST-RISK COMMUNITY DISTRICT Upper East Side (Manhattan 08)			
Children in single-parent families	Teen birth rate	Teen idleness (16 to 19 years old)	Adults without a high school degree
13.9%	3.8%	1.5%	1.9%

Source: Citizens' Committee for Children

Could it be that the educational disparities between these two districts were not just due to geography, economics, and race? Could it be, perhaps, that differences in family structure, as evidenced by the yawning gap in the percentage of children being raised in single-parent families, were a major explanatory factor for why education outcomes in the South Bronx have been so poor for so long?

Asking these questions led me down a path of no return.

———

I decided to study state health data related to all births[6] and nonmarital births[7] in the Bronx. In 2016, the nonmarital birth rate was 63 percent for all women, and nearly 80 percent for women under twenty-five. (Nonmarital birth data are not collected for men.) The latter represented 4,133 newborns in the Bronx who were likely going to be raised in single-parent households with unstable family structures, and very likely to suffer the same consequences represented in the CCC child well-being rankings.

Continuing with my research, I discovered that what was happening in the Bronx was a microcosm of the United States. As shown in figure 16.1, there has been a five-decade explosion in nonmarital birth rates among women of all races.[8] And as we see in figure 16.2, over the past quarter century the rate of increase has been greatest among white and Hispanic women, although it remains very high among African American women too.[9]

I began to wonder how these staggeringly high nonmarital birth rates, particularly among young women, and the ensuing large numbers of children being raised in single-parent families correlated to student achievement outcomes—not just in the Bronx but across New York and the nation.

I turned to the New York State Education Department's (NYSED) easy-to-use data site, which allows users to filter state test and graduation data by many factors, including school, gender, race/ethnicity, migrant status, geographic district, English language learner status, economic status, and disability status. Yet it provides no way to disaggregate achievement data by family structure. No other states seemed to do so either.

FIGURE 16.1

PERCENTAGE OF ALL BIRTHS TO UNMARRIED WOMEN, BY RACE AND HISPANIC ORIGIN, SELECTED YEARS, UNITED STATES, 1960–2014

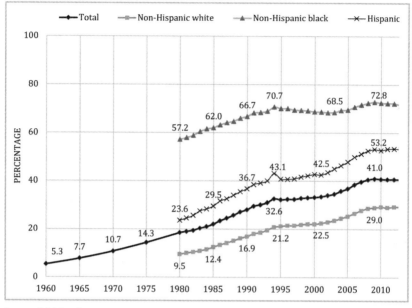

Source: Child Trends

FIGURE 16.2

PERCENTAGE OF BIRTHS TO UNMARRIED WOMEN AGES 18 OR ABOVE, BY SELECTED RACE/ETHNICITY, UNITED STATES, 1990 AND 2016

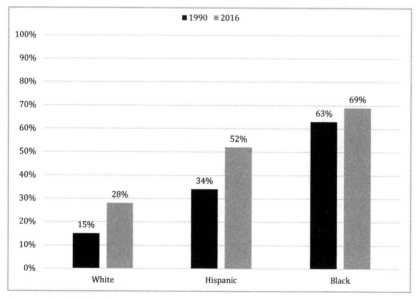

Source: National Vital Statistics Reports

So I turned to the National Assessment of Educational Progress (NAEP) and its useful Data Explorer, which allows users to "create statistical tables, charts, maps . . ." by grade, subject, and jurisdiction "to help . . . explore decades of assessment results, as well as information about factors that may be related to student learning."[10] Per Section 303 of the NAEP law, NAEP must "include information on special groups, including, whenever feasible, information collected, cross tabulated, compared, and reported by race, ethnicity, socioeconomic status, gender, disability and limited English proficiency."[11] And yet here, once again, as in New York and the other forty-nine states, I found no way by which to review results by family structure, despite the fact it is clearly a "factor that may be related to student learning."

Finally, I accessed the Data Quality Campaign (DQC), the nation's foremost organization advocating for effective education data policy and use. DQC's underlying premise is that "When students, parents, educators, and policymakers have the right information to make decisions, students excel," and as part of its work, the organization reviews state assessment systems. Take this excerpt from its 2017 *Show Me the Data* report:

> [Eighteen] states do not disaggregate student performance by at least one legally required subgroup (including race, ethnicity, gender, English language learners, students with disabilities). In nine states, performance data is not disaggregated by any subgroup, which can hide achievement gaps and the students who need more support. It also keeps schools that are doing well with traditionally underserved students from being celebrated and emulated.[12]

This is powerful feedback for states to improve the lenses through which student achievement data are reported. Yet—once again—there's no mention, much less criticism, of the fact that no state disaggregates such data by family structure.

It should not be this way.

Major social changes, particularly in the family structures in which children are raised, have occurred over the last several generations. Yet gauges and categories used to evaluate progress in student achievement have stubbornly focused on race, class, gender, and geography. By disregarding family structure, the data obscure how this massive demographic shift might be an explanatory factor that rivals and perhaps overpowers other well-documented achievement gaps.

Perhaps the reason for this omission is that family structure is not a static concept. Families change. Maybe it's impossible to create measures around a moving target, right?

Wrong.

In its 2010 report *Family Structure and Children's Health in the United States*, the National Center for Health Statistics declared, "In view of the changing family structure distribution, new categories of families such as unmarried families or unmarried stepfamilies need to be studied so that the health characteristics of children in non-traditional families can be identified."[13]

The report defined seven distinct and mutually exclusive family structures: "nuclear," "single-parent," "blended," "unmarried biological or adoptive families," "cohabiting," "extended," and "other," the last being defined as a family consisting of one or more children living with related or unrelated adults who are not biological or adoptive parents (e.g., grandparents).

The report observed that children found to have the most consistently positive health outcomes were raised in nuclear families, that is, "living with two parents who are married to one another and are each biological or adoptive parents to all children in the family."

Four years later, the same federal agency conducted another study to assess, by family structure type, the likelihood of "adverse family experiences," defined as potentially traumatic events or circumstances that children may have experienced that can have lasting negative consequences into adulthood. We see the results in figure 16.3.[14]

FIGURE 16.3

PERCENTAGE OF CHILDREN AGES 0–17 YEARS WITH SELECTED TYPES OF ADVERSE FAMILY EXPERIENCES, BY NUMBER OF BIOLOGICAL PARENTS LIVING IN THE HOUSEHOLD, UNITED STATES, 2011–2012

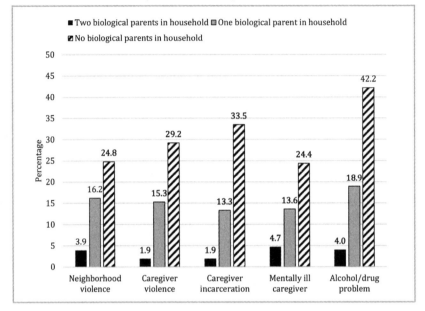

Source: Centers for Disease Control and Prevention, cited in National Health Statistics Reports

As we see, and as the Center's report states, "Children living with one biological parent were between three and eight times as likely as children living with two biological parents to have experienced neighborhood violence, caregiver violence, or caregiver incarceration or to have lived with a caregiver with mental illness, or an alcohol or drug problem."

We also see that "in view of the changing family structure distribution," healthcare leaders and analysts have begun to study causal and correlational links between family structure and a range of child outcomes. Most importantly, these analyses are yielding new explanations for seemingly entrenched problems and ushering in a new wave of family-focused prescriptions in the health arena.

In education, on the other hand, even among ardent reformers and careful analysts doing their best to understand and do something about student achievement gaps, family structure is virtually never considered as a possible, even critical, factor in explaining those gaps. In 2017, I had the temerity to call out Bill Gates[15] for literally omitting the words *parent* and *family* from a three-thousand-word essay in which he lamented that, even after seventeen years of investing billions of dollars in education reform, "by and large, schools are still falling short on the key metrics of a quality education."[16]

Months later, Bill and Melinda Gates released their 2018 annual letter,[17] this one focused on the ten "toughest questions" that they get asked. Question two is, "What do you have to show for the billions you've spent on US education?" To which they replied, "Unfortunately, although there's been some progress over the past decade, America's public schools are still falling short on important metrics, especially college completion. And the statistics are even worse for disadvantaged students." Once again, however, there was no mention of the potential impact of family structure on why America's public schools are still falling short.

Yet more than half a century ago, the Coleman report,[18] still widely considered the most important education study of the twentieth century, established the primacy of family structure and stability in driving educational outcomes for children.[19] Today, we have a mountain of irrefutable evidence that children raised in stable, married, two-parent households (regardless of gender) have, on average, far superior life outcomes, not only in education but also in virtually every other category of healthy human development. What's weird about the deafening silence on the impact of family structure is that the education reform community and the charter-school sector have already signaled in several ways that they understand the criticality of family stability to educational outcomes.

Consider, for example, the fact that many top charter schools do not "backfill" or enroll transfer students after third grade. Why? One reason is that the risk is so great that a *single* eight-year-old could be from an unstable family and thus so disruptive to the classroom environment that it is better to deprive *any* eight-year-old of the opportunity for a seat.

The omission of family structure and stability as a measure crucial to child development is no benign oversight. It has consequences, the least of which is that diagnoses based on narrow data snapshots that ignore family structure as *causal* of poor outcomes tend to lead to narrow prescriptions that fail to leverage the transformative power of family structure to *improve* outcomes.

Take, for example, the Office for Civil Rights 2014 Data Collection on Early Childhood Education, which reported that "racial disparities in discipline begin in the earliest years of schooling. Black students represent 18 percent of preschool enrollment, but 42 percent of preschool students suspended once, and 48 percent of students suspended more than once."[20]

What could be causing such huge disparities by race when it comes to discipline? Consider (see figure 16.4) a 2017 Pew Research Center study showing that more than half (58 percent) of black children live with an unmarried parent, alongside 36 percent of Hispanic children and 24 percent of white children.[21] Can anyone seriously doubt that the absence of a second parent (most often the father) leads to behaviors that include acting out in school?

This is apt to get even worse. For 2017, the National Center for Health Statistics reports that the nonmarital birth rate to women under twenty-five was 71 percent (see table 16.3).[22]

Every racial group is impacted, but the issue is most acute in the black community, where nine out of ten babies born to women under twenty-five in 2017 were outside of marriage. And in a depressing example of how the racial achievement gap is being closed, 61 percent of babies born to white women under twenty-five were also outside of marriage. Worse still, more than 41 percent of unmarried women

TABLE 16.3

NUMBERS OF BIRTHS TO WOMEN AGES 24 AND UNDER, BY RACE/ETHNICITY, UNITED STATES, 2017

	WHITE (NON-HISPANIC)	BLACK	HISPANIC	ASIAN	OTHER	TOTAL
BIRTHS TO WOMEN: AGES 10−24	415,207	188,720	289,334	18,369	49,444	961,074
NONMARITAL BIRTHS TO WOMEN: AGES 10−24	252,264	170,327	210,205	6,733	38,677	678,206
PERCENTAGE OF BIRTHS TO UNMARRIED WOMEN: AGES 10−24	60.76%	90.25%	72.65%	36.65%	78.22%	70.57%

Source: National Health Statistics Reports

FIGURE 16.4

PERCENTAGE OF CHILDREN YOUNGER THAN 18 LIVING WITH MARRIED, SOLO, AND COHABITING PARENTS, BY SELECTED RACE/ETHNICITY, UNITED STATES, 2017

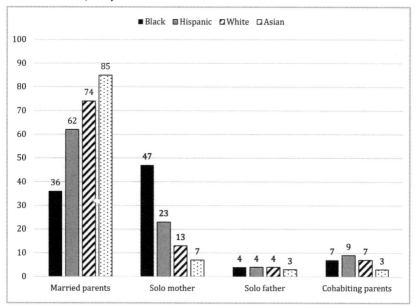

Source: Pew Research Center analysis of 2017 Current Population Survey March Supplement (Integrated Public Use Microdata Series)

under twenty-five who gave birth in 2017 were bearing their *second to eighth child*.

In my rough estimate, unmarried young women who gave birth during the single year of 2017 were raising some 1.1 million children, creating enormous stress for these young mothers valiantly trying to hold it together. Nationwide, huge numbers of young single mothers are raising very young children, in many cases multiple children, from different fathers who often abandon their responsibilities. As a result, these children are growing up in environments where they are much more likely to experience the kinds of toxic stress that have lifelong, adverse consequences on their development, which can likely lead to a generational treadmill of poverty, and that foster antisocial behavior in school.

Is it not possible that these differences in family structure by race are a large factor in explaining the racial differences in disciplinary outcomes? We will never know unless we have the courage to ask and then answer the question.

Absent such data, a common explanation for this huge racial disparity in student discipline is that teachers are either explicitly or implicitly biased against black students. This assumes that some of the most talented, "woke" people in the country—teachers—who have committed their lives to social justice and improving the lives of disadvantaged children, are in fact discriminating on a racial basis, whether intentionally or not, against the very students they have sworn to educate.

Because of this assumption, there has been an explosion in antibias training, indeed the formation of a whole cottage industry. In New York City alone, Schools Chancellor Richard Carranza has committed $23 million to speed up antibias training for about 125,000 educators and employees, calling it a "cornerstone" of his plan to improve schools.[23] Organizations like Teaching Tolerance and Border Crossers (renamed the Center for Racial Justice in Education) "train educators to #DISRUPTRACISM" and provide participants with opportunities to "identify instances where they themselves may have witnessed or committed racial microaggressions, and gain strategies to interrupt them."

Similarly, Teaching Tolerance offers free resources to help "educators grow their racial competence" and programs that "emphasize social justice and anti-bias."

This one-size-fits-all explanation and set of interventions is wrong. We must break the perception that every disparity that exists between groups (e.g., race) is due to a negative association with that grouping (e.g., racism), as opposed to a factor that transcends that grouping (e.g., family structure).

It is not clear whether the lack of recognition of the role and potential impact of family structure is willful or just plain ignorance. But the dearth of student outcome data parsed by family structure makes it much easier to come to erroneous, race-focused conclusions. It also masks opportunities to implement *different* types of interventions that could improve life outcomes for the next generation. For example, understanding the role of family structure could lead more schools to teach middle and high school students the success sequence, that is, the series of life decisions—education, work, marriage, then children—that has led 97 percent of individuals who follow this progression to achieve economic success and often a break in the intergenerational cycle of poverty.[24] (See Mona Charen's excellent discussion of the success sequence in chapter 15.)

In my own research into the role that family structure plays in determining educational outcomes, I discovered Chester Finn's simple analysis of the *limited leverage of schools*: "Formal education occupies a surprisingly slender portion of our children's lives. The youngster who faithfully attends class six hours a day, 180 days a year, from kindergarten through twelfth grade, will, at the age of eighteen, have spent just 9 percent of his hours on earth under the school roof. The other 91 percent is spent elsewhere."[25] The quality of the "elsewhere" environment is heavily determined by the structure and stability of that child's family.

If we truly want to improve outcomes for children, we must have the moral courage to measure student achievement outcomes by family structure groupings as routinely as we already do by race, class, and gender. We have to create a more complete picture to understand the primary forces impacting student achievement. The present dearth of data analyzing student outcomes by family structure is no victimless crime, for the void has been filled by causal explanations and interventions primarily by race and class, factors that do not tell the whole story.

More importantly, we must expand the universe of solutions and interventions we deploy to assist young people to find pathways to success, especially in historically disempowered communities. They must be helped to understand that they have power in their individual choices, and that those decisions can shape their destiny despite structural barriers associated with race, class, and poverty. We in education need to explicitly communicate to children of all races and genders the importance of, and likely rewards that come from, sequentially completing an education, getting a job, and forging a strong and stable family life (which usually entails marriage before the baby carriage).

Once I encountered the Who's Your Daddy? truck in the Bronx three years ago, I was forced to confront my own beliefs about the factors that drive the progress we have made (or not) in educational outcomes. Why have some groups of children consistently succeeded while others remain stagnant or grow worse? In answering that question, I have found that convenient categories of race, class, and gender generally do not hold, and that a deeper analysis is always necessary to get to the truth.

Based on decades of powerful research, there are factors more fundamental to human development that transcend those familiar categories, with (in my view) the most prominent being the structure and stability of the family within which a child is raised.

What we measure does matter.

On behalf of the kids whose lives we are seeking to improve, I hope that we education reformers can face up to our own identity shackles and the self-limiting beliefs that they may be placing on us.

I hope.

NOTES

1. Citizens' Committee for Children, *CCC Community Risk Ranking: Child Well-Being in New York City's 59 Community Districts*, February 2015, https://www .cccnewyork.org/wp-content/uploads/2015/01/CCCRiskRankingNYC.pdf.

2. Stephen Rex Brown and Ben Chapman, "Exclusive: 90 City Schools Failed to Pass a Single Black or Hispanic Student on State Tests, Study Shows," *New York Daily News*, September 2, 2014, https://www.nydailynews.com /new-york/education/exclusive-achievement-gap-worsens-black-hispanic -students-article-1.1924366.

3. , "Who's Your Daddy Truck—Blog Posts," Health Street accessed August 16, 2019, https://www.health-street.net/tag/whos-your-daddy-truck/.

4. Jared Rosenthal, "New Docu-Reality TV Series—Who's Your Daddy Truck," *Health Street* (blog), February 6, 2014, https://www.health-street.net /vh1-swab-stories/new-docu-reality-tv-series-whos-your-daddy-truck/.

5. Citizens' Committee for Children, *CCC Community Risk Ranking*.

6. New York State Department of Health, "Table 7: Live Births by Mother's Age and Resident County New York State–2016," accessed August 15, 2019, https://www.health.ny.gov/statistics/vital_statistics/2016/table07.htm.

7. New York State Department of Health, "Table 10: Out-of-Wedlock Live Births by Mother's Age and Resident County New York State–2016," accessed August 15, 2019, https://www.health.ny.gov/statistics/vital_statistics/2016 /table10.htm.

8. *Births to Unmarried Women: Indicators on Children and Youth* (Washington, DC: Child Trends, 2015), 3, https://www.childtrends.org/wp-content /uploads/2015/03/75_Births_to_Unmarried_Women.pdf.

9. Elizabeth Wildsmith, Jennifer Manlove, and Elizabeth Cook, "Dramatic Increase in the Proportion of Births Outside of Marriage in the United States from 1990 to 2016," *Child Trends* (blog), August 8, 2018, https://www .childtrends.org/publications/dramatic-increase-in-percentage-of-births -outside-marriage-among-whites-hispanics-and-women-with-higher-edu cation-levels.

10. "The Nations Report Card," accessed August 15, 2019, https://www.nations reportcard.gov/.

11. "The NAEP Law," National Assessment Governing Board, accessed August 16, 2019, https://www.nagb.gov/about-naep/the-naep-law.html.

12. *Show Me the Data: 2017* (Washington, DC: Data Quality Campaign, 2017),

https://2pido73em6703eytaq1cp8au-wpengine.netdna-ssl.com/wp-content/uploads/2018/01/DQC-Show-Me-the-Data_final.pdf.

13. D. L. Blackwell, *Family Structure and Children's Health in the United States: Findings from the National Health Interview Survey, 2001–2007*, Vital and Health Statistics 10, no. 246 (Hyattsville, MD: National Center for Health Statistics, Centers for Disease Control and Prevention, US Department of Health and Human Services, 2010), https://www.cdc.gov/nchs/data/series/sr_10/sr10_246.pdf.

14. Matthew D. Bramlett and Laura F. Radel, "Adverse Family Experiences among Children in Nonparental Care, 2011–2012," *National Health Statistics Reports*, no. 74 (May 7, 2014), https://www.cdc.gov/nchs/data/nhsr/nhsr074.pdf.

15. Ian Rowe, "Speaking Truth to Power: Another Missed Opportunity to Address the Role Schools Must Play to Break the Cycle of Poverty," *Flypaper,* Thomas B. Fordham Institute (blog), October 26, 2017, https://fordhaminstitute.org/national/commentary/speaking-truth-power-another-missed-opportunity-address-role-schools-must-play.

16. Bill Gates, "Our Education Efforts Are Evolving," *Gates Notes* (blog), October 19, 2017, https://www.gatesnotes.com/Education/Council-of-Great-City-Schools.

17. Bill Gates and Melinda Gates, "Our 2018 Annual Letter," *Gates Notes* (blog), February 13, 2018, https://www.gatesnotes.com/2018-Annual-Letter.

18. "Re-Visiting the Coleman Report," *Education Next*, January 5, 2016, http://educationnext.org/revisiting-the-coleman-report/.

19. Barbara J. Kiviat, "The Social Side of Schooling," *Johns Hopkins Magazine*, April 2000, http://pages.jh.edu/jhumag/0400web/18.html.

20. US Department of Education, Office for Civil Rights, *Data Snapshot: Early Childhood*, Issue Brief, no. 2, March 2014, https://www2.ed.gov/about/offices/list/ocr/docs/crdc-early-learning-snapshot.pdf.

21. In figure 16.4, children who are not living with any parents are not shown. See the Pew Research Center analysis of 2017 Current Population Survey March Supplement (IPUMS): Pew Research Center, "Nearly Half of Black Children Live with a Solo Mom," accessed August 30, 2019, https://www.pewresearch.org/fact-tank/2018/04/27/about-one-third-of-u-s-children-are-living-with-an-unmarried-parent/ft_18-04-11_unmarriedparents_race/.

22. Joyce A. Martin et al., *National Vital Statistics Reports: Births: Final Data for 2017* (Hyattsville, MD: National Vital Statistics System, 2018), https://www.cdc.gov/nchs/data/nvsr/nvsr67/nvsr67_08-508.pdf.

23. Christina Veiga, "Carranza Aims to Speed Up Anti-Bias Training for Educators," *Chalkbeat*, August 15, 2018, https://www.chalkbeat.org/posts/ny/2018/08/15/carranza-aims-to-speed-up-anti-bias-training-for-educators-calling-it-a-cornerstone-to-school-improvement/.

24. Wendy Wang and W. Bradford Wilcox, *The Millennial Success Sequence: Marriage, Kids, and the "Success Sequence" among Young Adults* (Washington, DC: American Enterprise Institute and the Institute for Family Studies, 2018), http://www.aei.org/publication/millennials-and-the-success -sequence-how-do-education-work-and-marriage-affect-poverty-and-finan cial-success-among-millennials/.

25. Mitch Pearlstein, "What to Do about the Schools," *Center of the American Experiment*, April 4, 2011, https://www.americanexperiment.org/article /what-to-do-about-the-schools/.

PART 4

Renewing the Conservative Education Agenda

CHAPTER 17

Back to Basics for Conservative Education Reform

by Yuval Levin

PUBLIC POLICY DEBATES about primary and secondary education are oddly disoriented in our time. At almost any point in the 1990s or 2000s, it would not have been hard to say what these debates were about and what reformers were eager to achieve. Higher scores on standardized tests of math and reading skills were at the center of it all—whether they were understood as means of imposing accountability on schools, teachers, and administrators; as ways to measure racial gaps in educational achievement; or as a strategy to help America produce students and workers on par with its foreign competitors.

If scores turned out to be too low, in relative or absolute terms, an argument would emerge between the left and right flanks of the reform coalition about whether more competition might help or more money for public schooling could address deficiencies. There was much talk of "accountability." But that debate happened within the framework of a broadly bipartisan coalition focused on quantifiable achievement scores. That coalition had opponents to its left and to its right, but it involved leading education experts in both political camps, and leading politicians of both parties were willing to play ball.

That era of the reform coalition did achieve some worthy, if modest, improvements in American education. Test scores increased some, especially early in that period. The charter-school movement is stronger, the idea of accountability for schools and educators is more widely accepted, and there is now a more equitable distribution of public-education funding within states—so that differences in local property-tax revenue are not as decisive as they once were. There is a fair bit for both the left and the right to appreciate in these accomplishments.

But the era of the reform coalition also exacted some real costs. Above all, it made American education policy awfully clinical and technocratic, at times blinding some of those involved in education debates to the deepest human questions at stake—social, moral, cultural, and political questions that cannot be separated from how we think about teaching and learning. This has meant less of a focus on public schooling as a source of solidarity in American life, which was once a powerful theme on the left in particular. And it has meant less of an emphasis on character formation and civic education, which were once fundamental to the right's way of thinking about schooling.

Whatever its costs and its benefits, however, the era of the education reform coalition seems now to be behind us. The coalition broke down from both directions. The fight over Common Core drained it of energy from the right, as the case for accountability—which began as the predicate for school choice—came to be identified instead (rightly or wrongly) with an effort to consolidate and homogenize American education. Meanwhile, the resurgence of the teachers' unions as a force to reckon with in Democratic Party politics undermined the reform coalition from the left. And the intense polarization of our political culture has increasingly made bipartisanship of the sort that characterized the reform coalition impossible to sustain. The reform era that lasted from the early 1990s through the beginning of the 2010s is therefore effectively over.

What will follow it as a political matter will probably at first be a period of gridlock and dysfunction. Much the same can be said about the politics of many other policy arenas. Our national politics, and even state-level politics in too many places, just isn't focused on public policy for the time being. But what will follow the reform era as an intellectual matter—in the work of education reformers, and as preparation for the next constructive phase of education policy, whenever it might come—is a more interesting question.

Frustrated by the collapse of the reform coalition but also liberated from its constraints, the right and left will probably take somewhat different directions in education-policy thinking in the coming years. For that reason, it remains useful to consider education policy and politics in terms of left and right. In fact, it may be that the deepest differences between the most intellectually coherent forms of the American left and right actually emerge most clearly around questions of education, and not by coincidence. And for each camp, the concerns that were put aside for the sake of working together in the reform coalition seem likely to be those that now come to the fore.

Some reformers on the right would argue that full-bore school choice itself was put aside to make some bipartisanship possible. But that perspective may itself be a function of the intellectual inhibitions engendered by the reform coalition—it is effectively a way of seeing education policy as a set of questions about modes of accountability. Certainly, more could have been done to advance the choice agenda in recent decades. Especially at the national level, accountability was separated from choice, and the latter was often sacrificed for the former. Margaret Spellings was famously willing (even eager) to leave private-school choice behind in her negotiations with Democrats early in the George W. Bush years. But in the states and at the local level, the movement for parental control saw real progress. Both charter schooling and private-school choice remained—and remain—near the center of the conservative education agenda.

To see what conservative educational priorities were truly put aside in the era of the reform coalition, we would have to really put ourselves outside the accountability and achievement framework and remind ourselves that the emphasis on accountability was itself a concession of sorts. What really couldn't be talked about in these decades was the role of schooling in the molding of the souls of rising citizens—rather than just the minds of future workers. Both civic education and character education were sometimes pushed to the side for the sake of more technocratic notions of the purpose of schooling, notions more in line with the economic logic of our meritocracy but less in line with the civic ideals underlying our republic.

If we are really to look beyond the framework of the achievement-scores agenda, and if we want to consider what conservatives can bring to the table now that has for too long been forgotten, we would need to look not just to the conservative wing of the technocratic reform coalition but to the core of conservative thought itself, and the essential role it ascribes to culture, to moral formation, and therefore to education more fully understood.

To see what this might mean, we should ask a couple of questions that seem almost as foreign to this moment in our politics as the idea of earnest policy innovation. They are questions that could hardly be more important to the right in the age of Trump, but that don't come naturally: What really is conservatism? And what does it have to offer?

There are, of course, a near infinity of ways we might go about answering these questions, and distinguishing the left from the right. But there is one particular approach that can help highlight the implications of these differences *for education*. The left and right both have something to teach. Each wants to make sure our society doesn't take something for granted, and so each tries to remind the rising generation of something it might otherwise neglect. But each has something distinct in mind.

The left wants to be sure we do not take injustices in our society for granted—that we see the ways in which the strong oppress the weak, that we take them seriously, that we never walk by them and pretend they don't exist. A huge amount of progressivism's cultural and intellectual energies is directed to this fundamentally educational cause.

The right, on the other hand, wants to be sure we do not take social order for granted—that we see the ways in which our civilization protects us, enriches us, and elevates us, that we never imagine that this is all easy or natural, and never forget that, if we fail to sustain this achievement, we will all suffer for it. A huge amount of conservatism's cultural and intellectual energies is directed to this fundamentally educational cause.

These two different sets of concerns suggest that left and right begin from different assumptions about the human person and society—different anthropologies and sociologies. Briefly (and so no doubt crudely) summarizing these could help us think more clearly about the role of education.

American conservatism has always consisted of a variety of schools of social, political, and economic thought. But they are nearly all united, in a general sense, by a cluster of anthropological assumptions that sets them apart from most American progressives and liberals. Conservatives tend to see the human person as a fallen and imperfect being, prone to excess and to sin, and ever in need of self-restraint and moral formation.[1] This fundamentally gloomy conception of humanity sets conservatives apart from libertarians and progressives alike, and sits at the core of most conservative thinking about society and politics.

It leads, to begin with, to low expectations of human affairs and away from utopianism. Conservatives expect the most profound and basic human problems to recur in every generation because they are intrinsic to the human condition—a function of our permanent limitations that must be acknowledged, counterbalanced, mitigated, or accommodated but that can never really go away.

The fact that these limits are inherent in humanity also leaves most conservatives persuaded that the experiences of different generations will not be fundamentally different—or, as some have put it, that human nature has no history. This leaves conservatives not only resistant to the lure of utopias but also far more concerned about the prospect of social and cultural degradation than they are confident about the prospects for enduring progress.

Regardless of how much intellectual and material progress a society may make, every new child entering that society will still join it with essentially the same native intellectual and biological equipment as any other child born in any other society at any other time in the history of the human race. Raising such children to the level of their societies is a prerequisite for any form of progress. But a failure to initiate the next generation of children into the ways of our civilization would not only delay or derail innovation, it would put into question the very continuity of that civilization. This is a crucial reason why conservatives care so deeply about culture.

And this same assumption, rooted in low expectations, also often leaves conservatives impressed by, and protective of, enduring, successful social institutions. The fallen character of man means that, left to itself, the default condition of the human race is more likely to be miserable than happy, and that failure in society is more likely than success. Conservatives are therefore often far more thankful for success in society than we are outraged by failure. Progressives tend to feel differently because their expectations are much higher: they assume social order is the easy part—and that any deviation from equality and justice is therefore an intentional result of acts of malice by those who are strong in our society and who choose to use their power to oppress the weak.

This difference of expectations is at the center of a lot of our most divisive political debates. It shapes how conservatives and progressives understand the nature and sources of the problems that American society confronts. If you assume that dangerous chaos is our default condition while social order is a hard-earned achievement, you will tend to see society's problems as resulting from a failure to form fallen people into civilized men and women. You will assume, as has been well said, that "man is born to trouble, as the sparks fly upward," and will see politics as a struggle to sustain institutions that might make us capable of some balance of freedom and order in a hard world. If you assume that equality and order are the human default, however, then you will see social iniquities and dysfunctions as resulting from intentional misbehavior by people in power. You will assume, as has also been well said, that "man is born free but is everywhere in chains," and will look at politics as a struggle to liberate individuals from structures of oppression.

As the economist Arnold Kling has noted in his important book *The Three Languages of Politics*, this means conservatives tend to view political controversies as involving a tension between civilization and barbarism while progressives view such controversies as involving a tension between oppressor and oppressed. Think about how people on the right and the left talk about immigration, for instance, or urban policing, or almost any of the most intensely debated cultural and political controversies we face, and you'll get a sense of what Kling's framework can show us.

The implications of all this for education are enormous, of course. It means that conservatives place heavy emphasis on sustaining the institutions necessary for moral formation and social peace while progressives tend to emphasize liberating individuals from the oppressive burdens of a social order steeped in injustice. As a result, progressive education wants to liberate the student to be himself or herself while conservative education wants to form the student to be better suited to the responsibilities of citizenship.

This points not so much toward different curricular choices in character and civic education as toward a far greater emphasis on both of those disciplines on the right and an inclination to discount or avoid them on the left—or to replace them with an ideal of education as liberation from injustice.

An emphasis on the quantifiable in education, which has been the organizing principle of the reform coalition for more than two decades, tends to downplay both of these ways of thinking about curricular content and emphasis. That is not to say, of course, that this has been a period devoid of struggles about curriculum. Nor is it to suggest that character education has been altogether absent from the national debate: an emphasis on character has been important to the success of some of the most prominent choice experiments and charter programs serving disadvantaged students, for example.

But in putting accountability, achievement gaps, and international competitiveness at the forefront, the reform coalition has deemphasized the formation of students as human beings and citizens. This has succeeded, in part, in shielding the politics of primary and secondary education from the very worst ravages of our increasingly intense culture war—at least until recently. But it has also kept out of bounds some essential tools and ideas that could play important roles in strengthening American education, including in closing achievement gaps and helping students learn the basics.

Any idea of education that is not connected to an idea of formation—of habituation in virtue, inculcation in tradition, veneration of the high and noble—is unavoidably impoverished. And in the wake of the collapse of the education reform coalition, conservatives are well positioned to help it become less impoverished.

That doesn't mean that all conservatives could agree on a precise curriculum in these areas, or that they need to use state power to impose it. But it does mean that it is now incumbent on us to make education-policy debates less technocratic, and thus more suited to the particular kinds of challenges that America confronts today.

The last few years of our politics have shown us that our country is living through a serious social crisis. Many Americans are alienated from our core institutions and distrustful of them, and we seem to have less and less recourse to any foundation of mutual commitments. At the same time, an epidemic of isolation and estrangement is breaking down the lives of millions, leaving them disconnected from sources of belonging and meaning. And we are witnessing the loss of a common civic vocabulary, which is leaving us less capable of defining our Americanness in positive, rather than just negative terms. These are obviously connected problems, and they relate as well to the tendency of all of our major institutions to shirk the task of moral formation in favor of moralistic performance and virtue signaling.

It should be obvious that there is a crucial role for schools in addressing these problems, even if it is not obvious exactly what it would mean to play that role effectively and responsibly. The question should be how, not whether, to place a greater emphasis on character and on civics in American education.

This is so partly because education is inherently formative, so that to keep character and civics out of the equation is implicitly to tell students that they do not matter. If we organize our schools around the premise that math and reading scores are what education is about, we effectively tell our children that math and reading are the essence of what the civilization they are inheriting has to offer them. And we can't really believe that's true.

But there is another, less obvious reason, why a formative idea of education would have to be at the center of a broader social renewal. Key to the reason why our mediating institutions—institutions of family, community, religion, and civic life—have lost some of their ability to bring us together and shape our character for flourishing is that they have lost some of their practical purposes in our lives.

The logic of the welfare state and the logic of the market economy (which are far from the enemies or opposites they are sometimes thought to be) have both expanded their reach in the past half century so that between them they now penetrate into every crevice of our common life. For good and for ill, this has meant that many Americans are less dependent on sources of help (in the family and community) that might demand something of us in return, or might offer us a place and a connection. And it has meant that local civic and charitable groups, religious institutions, and fraternal organizations simply have less to do, and therefore fewer ways to attract people out of isolation and into community. The character of modern markets and the character of modern governments have both enervated our traditional mediating institutions.

Yet these kinds of institutions and the connections they offer are still essential to our building relationships and attachments. They are vital to our psychic and social well-being. But we cannot expect them to remain strong if that is all they do for us. As Robert Nisbet put it more than half a century ago:

> Family, local community, church, and the whole network of informal interpersonal relationships have ceased to play a determining role in our institutional systems of mutual aid, welfare, education, recreation, and economic production and distribution. Yet despite the loss of these manifest institutional functions, we continue to expect them to perform adequately the implicit psychological or symbolic functions in the life of the individual.[2]

This tendency has only grown more acute since then, so that one crucial way to understand the social crisis many Americans confront is that the institutions that have provided us with moral formation and social connection as their secondary purposes have been robbed of their primary purposes, and so are struggling to function.

But schools are an exception to this pattern. They remain essentially local institutions, and we still need them to perform an absolutely necessary function—educating the young. That means they can still successfully play a further formative function, and to a degree that few other mediating institutions can. We must therefore demand that they take that formative role seriously, and so we must put it at the center of how we think about education.

―――――

Needless to say, all of this adds up to a controversial understanding of the purpose of primary and secondary education, and one that will tend to fan the flames of our culture wars. Whether we like it or not, the next phase of conservative education-policy thinking will need to be willing to do that—not to the exclusion of emphases on core math and reading competencies, on school choice, and on accountability, but alongside them.

Over the last few decades, our approach to education became highly technocratic for reasons both substantive and political. But in the coming years, conservatives will need to find appealing, responsible ways to return to our roots and remind ourselves and the country of just what children need from schooling, and what an ideal of education more thoroughly rooted in an ideal of human flourishing could have to offer.

Character formation, civics, and the inculcation of the best of our traditions are inseparable from any meaningful idea of education. Conservatives will now have to press that case—and to help our fellow citizens see its promise.

NOTES

1. Russell Kirk, "Ten Conservative Principles," The Russell Kirk Center for Cultural Renewal, accessed October 17, 2019, https://kirkcenter.org/conservatism/ten-conservative-principles/.
2. Robert Nisbet, "The Problem of Community," in *Communitarianism: A New Public Ethics*, Markate Daly, ed. (Belmont, CA: Wadsworth Publishing, 1993), 143–144.

CHAPTER 18

Rebuilding a Conservative Consensus
THE NEED FOR A GREAT RELEARNING

by William J. Bennett

I CONCLUDE these eighteen essays by returning to the beginning: the questions our editors posed to be explored. They challenged us to bring "fresh answers" to questions that go to the heart of education policy, such as "Where is the country heading?" "How is education helping—or not—to get there?" and "Is college and career readiness a sufficient mission for our education system?"

In thinking about those questions, I turned to the most important of them all: What is the purpose of school? This led me to the statement by a former Harvard education school dean, Patricia Albjerg Graham, that the purpose of our schools should be "to nurture and enhance the wit and character" of our children.[1] The question is how to get there? I endeavor to answer that question here.

The editors began this quest with the assertion that in recent years the pendulum of activity and thought leadership in education has become dangerously dominated by those who now label themselves "progressives." True enough. But this wasn't always the case. Over the course of a few decades, conservatives developed a robust body of thought and work on education issues, which was then directly transferred by an impressive group of political leaders—liberal and conservative alike—with the courage and the vision to challenge the status quo into a sustained wave of policymaking.

Yet taking honest stock of the outcomes of that wave of policymaking, one must conclude that the results are mixed and, in some cases, disappointing, at least when viewed through the lens of standardized test results (although we should avoid overreliance on that or any other single indicator).

Decades ago, I coined the phrase "The Three Cs" that I hoped captured a fairly broad consensus—not of my making—in conservative education thought, ideas powerful enough that many liberals also came to support some versions of them in the hope of improving schools.

The Cs were content, character, and choice. Just a few words on each, going backward from their original presentation:

- Choice is an important value, and its spreading adoption in its many forms has opened new avenues for millions of families. But it is also a means to an end. Choice is a tool to drive the other two. As with any tool, it has limitations.
- Paraphrasing the philosopher Martin Buber, all education is the education of character, or can be. Character is developed by rule, precept, and most importantly, example. The ethos of our schools matters.
- Content is my present focus.[2] As Saint Paul might say, content is the greatest of the three. I applaud the call for better civics and history education in several of the essays that precede this one, yet I submit that it is only one piece of the more fundamental problem of content that we must address.

In tackling this assignment, I assume three roles that I have regularly exchanged throughout my career. First, as a provocateur, challenging and instigating—maybe even irritating—around why we conservatives find ourselves in the diminished position that the editors aptly describe. Second, as a philosopher. Philosophers are supposed to get to the essence of the matter, and I will try. Third, as a policy proponent. We must translate our ideas into real-world policies if we are to help lawmakers enact real change. As we put it at Conservative Leaders for Education (CL4E), a group of state education policy leaders that I chair, after any robust yet abstract discussion, "Now what is it you think the Senate education chair in Kentucky or Wisconsin should do?" In my view, a discussion of education is incomplete if it doesn't reach that question, or some variation of it, for federal, state, or local leaders.

———

I begin with provocation.

First, to conservatives. Two fundamental ideas have dominated conservative education thought for decades: choice and accountability. The power of these ideas and the intellectual and political capital behind them were such that even many centrists and liberals joined with conservatives to advance them.

Broad support for the concept of choice remains in various forms,[3] but choice is mostly a means to an end. It has limitations. Choice only works when students have an engaged adult to direct, encourage, or approve—all too often not the case. And in many parts of rural America, the idea of multiple school options is just not reality. In those settings, the local, district-operated public school is often viewed as the key unifying social institution in the community—and one that "choice" might threaten. Further, when measured by academic outcomes, the results of some choice programs, at least in some places, have been disappointing. Moreover, our broader policy hope that the introduction of choice into a community would raise the performance of all schools in that community remains elusive even where "choice" schools are showing impressive results.

I do not want to be misunderstood. Choice is an important value. Be it charter schools, Education Savings Accounts, open enrollment, homeschooling, course choice, vouchers, or something else, choice has resulted in many individual student and school success stories, a fact in which conservatives and other choice proponents should rightly take pride. In no way do I suggest that conservatives abandon choice. But it would be intellectually dishonest to not recognize the limitations of choice, given that more than four in five students continue to attend traditional public schools and the effective exercise of choice requires parents who participate and teachers and schools that teach well.

A conservative consensus also formed around accountability in the later 1980s and 1990s. In basic terms, that consensus sought to create high standards, measure performance against those standards, and take meaningful action when performance failed to measure up. What ended up as the Common Core began as part of this sound, fundamental effort to set universal high standards that could be compared across jurisdictions. Yet this effort went awry, partly due to a backlash against too much testing (we need fewer and better tests), but mostly because Common Core was wrongfully appropriated, distorted, and effectively turned into a federal quasi-mandate.

In somewhat similar fashion, the solid conservative concept that the key to accountability is measuring performance and judging schools on the basis of their results turned into overreliance on summative state tests. This caused a backlash with parents and teachers alike.

As with choice, I do not want to be misunderstood on accountability and assessments. The fact that there are problems with current tests and testing regimes does not mean conservatives should abandon accountability. Just the opposite is true. We have the ingenuity and technology to figure out better ways and to better link these tests to content and individual student achievement. In fact, important conservative-led initiatives seeking better assessment approaches are currently under way in Georgia and Louisiana.

Those two concepts, choice and accountability, yielded something of a conservative-defined policymaking consensus that touched every state and school in the nation over the past several decades. But the consensus is no more. Today there is no agreed-upon vision among conservatives.

Having provoked the right, I now turn to the left. The liberals whom conservatives could engage on education are, for the most part, long gone. The new liberals—and old liberals who do not want to be run out of their party—have a vision that they are coalescing around, and it is not a good vision for our nation.

That newly ascendant liberal vision answers the question "What is the purpose of school?" in this way: school is for advancing social engineering projects and notions of social justice. Borrowing a headline from the American Enterprise Institute's Rick Hess, "Education is so far left, it can't really see right." He went on to say:

> I honestly don't think most people in education have any clue just how ideologically loaded are their day-to-day assumptions and discussions. For instance, the word "equity" has become the organizing principle of K–12 school improvement. . . . And, of course, equity is a good and important value. It's why many on the left get out of bed each morning. But it also turns out that there are other virtues—like liberty, personal responsibility, and community—that not infrequently come into conflict with equity.[4]

Achievement, excellence, and the successful transfer of knowledge should all be added to Hess's list, particularly in the school setting. "Equity" is hardly a lofty goal if its actual result is, to borrow from Winston Churchill, "the equal sharing of misery."

Take one recent example. A major study released in early 2019 examined the application of a "restorative justice" initiative in the schools of Pittsburgh in an attempt to reduce suspensions.[5] It found that, while the technique did reduce suspensions, academic performance also declined, particularly among minorities. A former official at the US Department of Education said of the study, "I'm very much heartened by the finding that suggests that *we could actually use this to address gaps*, which has just been a challenge" (emphasis added).[6] The "gaps" she refers to, however, are in discipline data. The fact that the practice might actually widen academic gaps was apparently not worthy of note. The goal of "restorative justice" had clearly become primary, subordinating other education goals to it.

The reality of the left's new priorities was well summed up in a recent observation by Connor Williams, a fellow at the Century Foundation, who said, "If you are a progressive right now, the likelihood that your primary concern with the United States is education is really, really low. There are other issues, like wealth inequality and economic opportunity, where the left agrees with these unions more."[7]

Yes, equity is an important value, and serious attention should be paid to any forms of discrimination in discipline and other aspects of schooling. Yet "solutions" advanced by the left that might have a short-term impact on disciplinary statistics while not addressing—and possibly worsening—academic gaps will damage equity in the long term. The emerging vision of the left is a very serious threat that demands attention and, ultimately, a reinvigorated conservative response.

Unlike conservatives, however, the left does have a vision, and given its power and the assistance it receives from the unions and the rest of the education establishment, there is currently a big imbalance in that direction.

The conservative response should still incorporate choice and accountability. But I believe that it must reach deeper to an even more fundamental principle: content.

———

I now doff my provocateur hat and don my philosopher's hat.

Knowledge matters. It is the critical building block for successful instruction.

Many of the fads of the last decade have centered on the ill-guided, unproven, and psychologically erroneous notion that skills can be divorced from knowledge. Even if it were possible to learn skills without knowledge, skills would not suffice. It is simply not enough to learn *how* to do something; a student must acquire real, hard knowledge, such as vocabulary and history and science facts. It is fine to "learn how to learn," but you must start by learning something, beginning in the elementary grades that today are often content-barren.

One of the foremost champions of content and the critical place it must play in a comprehensive vision of education policy has long been E. D. Hirsch Jr.[8] Today, a contingent of education thinkers are trying to build on Hirsch's seminal work. To quote an important content ambassador and distinguished cognitive psychologist, the University of Virginia's Daniel Willingham:

> When I hear that science, history, geography, and other core subjects are being squeezed out in frantic preparation for reading tests, I am concerned. It may help with reading tests (which are really decoding tests) in first grade, but this practice will come back to haunt school systems when these kids get to fourth or fifth grade—their lack of world knowledge will hurt them on reading comprehension tests.[9]

Learning begins with knowledge. Consider vocabulary, a fundamental building block of knowledge. As Hirsch first demonstrated and as others have confirmed, vocabulary is a direct predictor of SAT scores, which are well correlated with success in college and beyond.[10] When replacing knowledge—in this instance, vocabulary—with so-called skills, schools directly undermine the first link in that chain of success. As Hirsch has written:

> Reading, writing, and all communication depend on taken-for-granted background knowledge that is not directly expressed in what is written. Therefore, in order to teach children how to understand what is written, we must teach them that taken-for-granted background knowledge. . . . Higher-order thinking is knowledge-based: The almost universal feature of reliable higher-order thinking about any subject or problem is the possession of a broad, well-integrated base of background knowledge relevant to the subject.[11]

When schools attempt to divorce skills from knowledge, those most harmed are students who have the least exposure to knowledge outside school. As Willingham wrote, "Disadvantaged students are disproportionately dependent on schools to provide the background information that will make them effective readers because wealthy students have greater opportunity to gain this knowledge at home."[12]

A study released in April 2019 found that children would have heard the following numbers of words by the time they were five years old based solely on how often they were read to:

- Never: 4,662 words
- 1–2 times per week: 63,570 words
- 3–5 times per week: 169,520 words
- Daily: 296,660 words

Note that these figures are solely for words read and do not include the differences associated with conversation and other kinds of learning.[13]

A robust set of shared knowledge is vital both to an individual's ability to succeed and to a society's ability to thrive. One might call it a common set of core knowledge. At the risk of offending the fainthearted, it could even be shortened to "common core."

Recall that the basic concept of Common Core took shape at a meeting dominated by the nation's governors. At that meeting, an idea was adopted that had long been under development by conservative thought leaders, myself among them. The concept was that establishing universal high standards grounded in a shared set of knowledge that all citizens should possess was critical to addressing many of the problems that *A Nation at Risk* had illuminated.

It was a sound concept then, founded in fundamental conservative philosophy and principles. It remains a sound, conservative concept today.

What was effectively launched at that "education summit" convened by President George H. W. Bush in Charlottesville in 1989 mutated over two decades into something it never should have become. This is the result of politics and a failure of leadership, not flaws in the idea itself. To be clear, I am not suggesting relitigating what became known as Common Core. But a common basis of knowledge is required to unite a nation's people, to build the *unum* that accompanies the *pluribus*. Whatever the background, race, or ethnicity any individual student brings to school, success and contentment depend upon knowing things.

Choice and accountability are about processes—very important processes with deep moral implications and complex practical dimensions, all in need of serious and reinvigorated conservative attention. But content is the substance of it. Content, however, has had the least effort expended by conservatives to develop a durable and robust consensus to inform and drive policymaking. As stated well by Robert Pondiscio, "There is a story, and it's about curriculum—perhaps the last, best, and almost entirely un-pulled education-reform lever."[14]

Now to my third hat, that of a policy proponent.

If we are to build consensus around content, we must do the hard work of developing concrete solutions for policymakers, which must begin by reviewing a half-dozen exhausted alternatives of what *not* to do:

- Do not think skills can be taught independent of knowledge.
- Do not back away from the demand for robust, comprehensive standards in all critical subjects, not only math and English.
- Do not allow any of the new "skill-based" fads to distract from the focus on content.
- Do not allow the unintended consequence of testing reading and math—obviously critical—to crowd out other critical content.
- Do not seek federal mandates for what states and schools should do on content (and perhaps avoid future use of the word "common" in the same paragraph as "core").

- Do not think that content isn't central to every educational endeavor, including the current enthusiasm for career and technical education.

But a list of "do nots" is not enough for shaping and changing policy. So I offer some concrete thoughts, focused at the state level, with the hope of building a conservative consensus on content, drawing on an outstanding summary of research and discussion of state policies and options compiled in 2017, and a new paper, released in April 2019, by Chiefs for Change in collaboration with David Steiner and Ashley Berner at the Johns Hopkins Institute for Education Policy.[15] They found that improvements in content and curriculum are potentially far more effective—and certainly more cost-effective—than other fashionable reforms, such as class-size reduction.

It's also important to reflect on the experience of Massachusetts in aggressively pursuing the standards-and-curriculum path. Beginning in 1997, the Commonwealth mandated excellent content, created at least some public school choices, developed and mandated a challenging high school graduation test, and created a content-based test that new teachers had to pass.

Perhaps most important is that these important steps had both Democrats and Republicans among their proponents. Although the reforms may be regarded as mostly conservative—indeed, sprung directly from the "conservative consensus" referenced above—they were adopted and implemented in one of the most liberal states in the country. This was a collaborative effort involving, among the principals, a libertarian Republican governor, Bill Weld; a conservative Democrat whom Weld defeated but later appointed to chair the State Board of Education, John Silber; a very liberal state senator, Tom Birmingham; and a longtime Democrat, Thomas Finneran, who would become Speaker of the Massachusetts House. They and others combined to play a critical role, offering a rare but exemplary display of sustained bipartisan commitment.

We are all familiar with the results: if Massachusetts were a country, its Program for International Student Assessment (PISA) scores would have made it tenth in the world. Its National Assessment of Educational Progress (NAEP) scores rose impressively—and led the country. And its results improved for students at all socioeconomic levels.

That path requires a sustained commitment across many different policy dimensions. For example, while standards, assessments, and the development of challenging curriculum frameworks were the focus of the first phases, shortly thereafter the effort moved to standards for educators in preservice and professional development. In 1998, "expanding educators' knowledge of subject matter" was listed as the highest priority in the state's plan for professional development. It's no coincidence that Massachusetts has regularly scored among the highest-achieving states in the nation.

Another state of interest is Louisiana. Almost a decade ago, the Bayou State made significant policy moves focused on content and curriculum. Louisiana created processes to identify content-rich, high-performing curricula and created systems to encourage (but not mandate) the use of such curricula. Louisiana has attempted with apparent success to incorporate teachers into this process and thus created the kind of bottom-up buy-in that is so important to sustain the implementation of any reform.

Louisiana was also among the first states to be approved in the Innovative Assessment Pilot program under the Every Student Succeeds Act (ESSA). That is relevant because the thrust of the state's new pilot builds upon its decade-long effort toward a more knowledge-based approach to curriculum.

Florida is another state worth noting. It adopted a comprehensive reform strategy twenty years ago and has stuck with and built upon those reforms. Former CL4E member and House education chair Mike Bileca and current CL4E member and House education chair Jennifer Sullivan have both been instrumental in this sustained course of reforms.[16] The basics of the strategy were—and remain—strong accountability, creation of choice and options, and driving evidence-based practices throughout the state's schools. Coeditor Michael J.

Petrilli recently summed up the results of those twenty years of work as follows:

> The most compelling numbers come from the National Assessment of Educational Progress, a.k.a. The Nation's Report Card. From the late 1990s until 2017, the reading performance of black fourth graders in Florida skyrocketed 26 points—equivalent to more than two grade levels worth of progress. For Hispanic students, the gain was 27 points, and for low-income kids it was an astonishing 29 points. The numbers for eighth-grade math were almost as impressive: rises of 27 points for black, 19 for Hispanic, and 21 for low-income students.[17]

All of this was achieved while per-pupil spending in Florida remained flat at about $9,750 per child in 2016 dollars.

With that background, and drawing from the work of Steiner and Berner as well as experiences and discussions with CL4E members, here are at least the beginnings of concrete ideas for state policy leaders[18] to consider:

- Create processes and deadlines for the creation of rigorous state standards in all core subjects where such standards do not yet exist; institute regular processes and deadlines for ongoing tough and honest review and improvement of those standards.
- Develop a mechanism to examine and rate curricula widely offered in the state on critical measures such as alignment with standards and richness of content.
- Review teacher education, licensing, and professional development programs and expenditures with a focus on developing requirements and/or incentives to improve the subject-matter knowledge of the state's teaching force—approaches that CL4E member and Senate Education Committee Chair Amy Sinclair is working on in Iowa.

- Create data and information to advance the content discussion, bringing transparency to what curricula are in use. Engage in research on student impacts of curriculum and content choices.
- Develop better accountability systems that encourage strong content-based learning, and explore innovative approaches that link a content/knowledge-rich approach to the state's assessment system. As former CL4E member and Pennsylvania Senate education chair John Eichelberger pointed out to me, policymakers need practical ways to see how well what they are doing on content is actually working.

It would be naïve to conclude without attention to the real-world politics in which states operate. The number-one issue, as once identified to me by Wisconsin's Luther Olsen, the longest-serving state education chairman in CL4E, is "stick-to-it-ness." In state education policy, initiatives and reforms are too often sold as silver bullets. Then those who promoted them move on or are replaced, and last year's grand strategy gets swamped by a rush to the next shiny object.

Real change of the kind suggested here requires sustained commitment. It requires buy-in up and down the system, which takes time and skillful leadership to achieve. In most states, sustaining a strategy over the long term requires at least some sort of bipartisan involvement.

The lack of conservative consensus on content has real and negative consequences. It leaves reform advocates and policymakers without practical ammunition to move forward. And the vacuum cedes the field to the other side, which knows very well what it intends to do.

So is a good school, a great school, a great set of schools, even a great state of schools possible in America? Yes. It is possible because once it was actual. And we see real possibilities of sound educational actuality developing in states today. I believe the areas of content and curriculum reform are ripest and most urgently in need of development among conservative education leaders. I do not call these ideas new, but they are certainly "fresh," given the many decades of drift and neglect on questions of content in our schools. To borrow from author Tom Wolfe, what we need most to do is "engage in a great relearning." Content must be at the center of any new conservative consensus on education.

Notes

1. William Raspberry, "Good Old Nostalgia High," *Washington Post*, June 21, 1989, https://www.washingtonpost.com/archive/opinions/1989/06/21/good-old-nostalgia-high/45cf60a8-1032-4591-86e6-f7d29f6a74ff/.

2. For purposes of this chapter, the terms "content" and "curriculum" are essentially interchangeable, in that both are intended to encompass not just the materials utilized in instruction but also the full range of pedagogy employed both in instruction and measuring outcomes.

3. Political observers will note that while the intellectual "consensus" on the theory of choice remains solid, the political support for choice is fraying in two critical ways: (1) Democrats previously supportive of choice are fleeing from even school choice measures limited to public schools such as charters; and (2) Republican support for choice, particularly in more rural areas, is softening under severe and sustained pressure from local school districts. Observe recent charter school or ESA attempts in Kentucky, West Virginia, and Tennessee, where the only programs that could gain support were limited to a few urban centers.

4. Rick Hess, "Education Is So Far Left, It Can't Really See the Right," *Education Week*, November 17, 2016, https://blogs.edweek.org/edweek/rick_hess_straight_up/2016/11/education_is_so_far_left_it_cant_really_see_the_right.html.

5. While a strong proponent of a well-disciplined school culture and the right of students not to have their own education disrupted by others, I am not a proponent of out-of-school suspensions, which often result in students being sent into a completely unsupervised environment, leading to more harm. Alternative schools, in-school suspensions, and supervised detention rooms are generally preferable.

6. Matt Barnum, "Major New Study Finds Restorative Justice Led to Safer Schools, but Hurt Black Students' Test Scores," *Chalkbeat*, January 4, 2019, https://chalkbeat.org/posts/us/2019/01/04/the-first-gold-standard-study-of-restorative-justice-is-out-heres-what-it-tells-us/.

7. Michelle Hackman and Nour Malas, "Democrats Line Up behind Striking Teachers," *The Star*, January 18, 2019, https://www.thestar.com/wsj/world/2019/01/18/democrats-line-up-behind-striking-teachers.html.

8. "E. D. Hirsch Jr." Core Knowledge Foundation, accessed August 15, 2019, https://www.coreknowledge.org/about-us/e-d-hirsch-jr/.

9. "Q&A with Dr. Daniel Willingham," Reading Rockets, accessed August 15, 2019, https://www.readingrockets.org/article/qa-dr-daniel-willingham.

10. E. D. Hirsch Jr., "A Wealth of Words," *City Journal*, Winter 2013, https://www.city-journal.org/html/wealth-words-13523.html.

11. Joe Kirby, "What We Can Learn from Core Knowledge and E. D. Hirsch?" *Pragmatic Reform* (blog), January 19, 2013, https://pragmaticreform.wordpress.com/2013/01/19/hirsch/.

12. Daniel Willingham, "A Brief Appreciation of E. D. Hirsch," *Daniel Willingham: Science and Education* (blog), March 26, 2018, http://www.danielwillingham.com/daniel-willingham-science-and-education-blog/a-brief-appreciation-of-e-d-hirsch.

13. Jessica Logan et al., "When Children Are Not Read To at Home: The Million-Word Gap," *Journal of Developmental and Behavioral Pediatrics* 40, no. 5 (2019): 383–86, https://journals.lww.com/jrnldbp/Abstract/2019/06000/When_Children_Are_Not_Read_to_at_Home__The_Million.9.aspx.

14. Robert Pondiscio, "Louisiana Threads the Needle on Ed Reform," *Education Next* 17, no. 4 (2017), https://www.educationnext.org/louisiana-threads-the-needle-ed-reform-launching-coherent-curriculum-local-control/.

15. *Choosing Wisely: How States Can Help Districts Adopt High-Quality Instructional Materials* (Washington, DC: Chiefs for Change, 2019), http://chiefsforchange.org/policy-paper/7092/.

16. While this chapter draws on the specific experiences of several current and previous members of CL4E, I wish to acknowledge all CL4E members. The conversations with them across the entire range of education policy issues over the past several years have been of immense assistance to my thinking, and have greatly informed this essay.

17. Michael J. Petrilli, "The Results of Florida's Education Reforms Are Impressive. Their Return on Investment Is Totally off the Charts," *Education Next*, May 28, 2019, https://www.educationnext.org/results-floridas-education-reforms-impressive-return-investment-totally-off-charts/.

18. This chapter focuses on the role of state policy leaders of the type I am currently working with at CL4E. But district and school leaders will also need to be critical players in the design and implementation of any fresh conservative consensus around content-driven education reform.

Conclusion
How to Educate an American
by Michael J. Petrilli and Chester E. Finn, Jr.

Twenty-five years ago, conservative ideas had considerable traction in K–12 education, as in such other domestic-policy realms as welfare reform and policing. Burgeoning charter schools were celebrated as a new form of public education. Choice among schools—as among churches, colleges, entertainments—was emerging as a fundamental right of families in a free society. Vouchers were finally being tried—and generally found effective. Public education's creaky, rule-bound governance structures were in some places yielding to more flexible arrangements, less dominated by adult interests and more amenable to changes that benefit students. Teach For America supplied a route into classrooms for talented college graduates seeking to sidestep the unhelpful courses, wrongheaded thinking, and widespread indoctrination of ed schools. Academic standards were rising and results-based accountability for taxpayer dollars invested in education became the watchword in reform circles, even on the center-left—a sharp break from the never-ending call for simply spending more money. "Character education" was being taken seriously, even if widely misconstrued. And much more.

Yet no victory is ever final. The education establishment's pushback against all of those reforms has been relentless. The system's tendency to act like a giant rubber band, resuming its previous shape as soon as outside tension eases, is remarkable. Furthermore, in recent decades many of the aforementioned reforms, even if given conceptual life by conservatives, have been recast and transformed by progressives.

Now most of the reform crowd is obsessed with social justice, racial disparities, the school-to-prison pipeline, and other shibboleths of the contemporary left.

Meanwhile, much education discourse and policy energy on the right has been reduced to a single talking point: more school choice is what America needs, with or without academic quality, with or without evidence of student achievement, and with or without the results-based accountability for schools and educators that enables the "choice marketplace" to fulfill its public-interest as well as its private-interest role.

Let us be clear: we have long embraced school choice and still do. It's faithful to America's commitments to freedom and to markets. It's compatible with a society that has long taken for granted that parents will and should select just about everything else for their children, from food and clothing to friends and activities to worship and residence. It enables those—including many conservatives—who crave robust character education and civic education for their children to seek out schools that provide it. For these and many other reasons, choice is essential to a vibrant education system that meets the variegated needs of an increasingly diverse society—and it's made impressive gains. Choice must remain at the top of the policy agenda.

Yet it's no cure-all. As Naomi Schaefer Riley demonstrates, for example, choice alone cannot successfully address the needs of the toughest-case youngsters, such as those in foster care or otherwise without functional families. As William Bennett explains, choice does not guarantee the kind of content-rich curriculum that makes for true knowledge and builds the foundation for further learning. Choice does not assure that children will acquire the citizenship, self-discipline, and historical understanding that make them good parents, astute voters, and considerate neighbors. Schools of choice are not always good schools—and not all parents are skillful at distinguishing those that are.

A single-minded focus on choice also tends to neglect the huge fraction of American children who remain in traditional, district-operated schools, including many who live in small towns and rural communities where those schools have functions that go well beyond teaching the young. It's true that many traditional schools are academically mediocre, that they neglect key elements of a great education, and that they've largely had their policies, practices, pedagogies, and curricula driven from the left. But they're the schools that most young Americans attend, and it's fruitless—bloodless, too—to assume these schools will just evaporate.

Careful readers will note parallels with the larger debate now underway within conservative circles—a debate that includes the extent to which market-based reforms, whether in education or other policy realms, are up to the challenges America faces today, especially in the parts of the nation that feel left behind. Much soul searching can already be glimpsed regarding the future of conservatism, what it stands for, and what it wants for others. Glimpses of that debate are visible in the volume you now hold.

We surely see a major continuing role for market-based reforms within K–12 education. It seems to us self-evident that Americans who care about kids and about education should continue to push for plenty more girls and boys to be given "exit permits" from bad schools and for many more of the schools they opt into to deliver the quality education they deserve. Robust school choice is, we believe, necessary for a well-functioning education system. Indeed, there's some evidence that competition from choice also puts healthy pressure on the traditional parts of that system to improve. But it's simply not sufficient. What's needed is both more quality choice and a renewed and sophisticated effort to improve the outcomes for youngsters who remain in those traditional settings. Which means that conservatives shouldn't shy away from—or despair at the prospects for—debates on how to effect such improvements.

To the contrary. We and the other authors of this volume believe that conservatives must reengage with earnest efforts at education renewal. They should engage personally when possible—in legislative committees, on state boards of education, on local school boards, and more. And they should speak up, as do we, for a trifecta of essential education emphases in the years to come.

First, *let us refocus on preparing young people for informed citizenship.* Not just civic activism, not just protest, not just the odd community-service project, but the totality of informed citizenship for a democratic republic that values its *pluribus* but also requires a lot of *unum*. We need to stop viewing education reform in purely utilitarian terms—giving people stronger skills so that they are better prepared to earn a living and make the country prosperous—or just to get them through the college door. Nobody is saying those things aren't important (though the college-going part gets carried too far, as several authors note). As with academic standards, choice, and accountability, they're necessary but insufficient to ensure either the well-being and success-ful functioning of citizens in our republic or the well-being and suc-cessful functioning of the republic itself.

The fine chapters in this book by Eliot Cohen, Robby George, and Jonah Goldberg underscore the ways in which better education for American citizenship—including a solid, appreciative understanding of the country's warts-and-all history as well as the workings of its governance—benefits both the individual and the society. Bill Bennett emphasizes the knowledge base on which this—and just about every-thing else—must rest. And Adam Meyerson and Adam Kissel explain how nonprofit organizations and the institutions of civil society can augment the work of public policy and formal schooling.

Second, *let us restore character, virtue, and morality to the head of the education table where they belong.* No human attribute matters more than good character, and nothing is more important for schools to do than to foster such character. As the founder of Phillips Exeter Acad-emy wrote more than two centuries ago (cited in Peter Wehner's chap-ter), "Above all, it is expected that the attention of instructors to the disposition of the minds and morals of the youth under their charge will exceed every other care; well considering that though goodness without knowledge is weak and feeble, yet knowledge without goodness is dangerous, and that both united form the noblest character, and lay the surest foundation of usefulness to mankind."

We are in no way ignoring the knowledge part. See Bennett's essay for an eloquent, well-reasoned, and solidly grounded explanation of how it undergirds all further learning. John Phillips was correct in noting that "goodness without knowledge is weak and feeble." In recent decades, however, American education has paid even less attention to goodness than to knowledge.

Today, sadly, we are reaping the harvest. We can see—around the planet, not just at home—the harm done by political leaders who lack character, by business leaders who lack virtue, by celebrity figures who lack morality—and by a citizenry that too often doesn't seem to care all that much, or perhaps can't tell the difference.

While we can also see hopeful signs of renewed attention to character (and, often, religious faith) in pursuit of usefulness to mankind as well as basic integrity and decency, that renewal hasn't reached very far into our institutions of formal education.

As Yuval Levin argues, some of the fault can be laid at our feet and that of fellow reformers. We've been so focused on raising test scores and improving other measurable outcomes that too often we either forgot what a great education is really about or muzzled ourselves in order to make common cause with liberals. Great education is not just about college matriculation, not just jobs or economic opportunity, not even just social mobility—important though all of those are—but also about forming good men and women, and a country where true human flourishing is commonplace.

Fortunately, we can find outstanding examples of schools that embrace this fuller understanding of education's mission. As Wehner noted, the excellent book edited by James Davison Hunter and Ryan S. Olson, *The Content of Their Character: Inquiries in the Varieties of Moral Formation*, profiles ten exemplary—but very different—schools, that succeed with character development and moral foundation in their students.

In the book you're holding, we call particular attention to the excellent chapters by Wehner, William Damon, Heather Mac Donald, and Rod Paige. Wehner shows how American schools once placed character education at the center of their mission and explains the importance of regaining such an emphasis. Damon connects both the development of character and the emergence of a reasoned allegiance to America itself as dividends that accumulate for young people who have purpose in their lives—purpose that schools can assist them to find. Paige extends that reasoning to education reform itself and says the fatal flaw in previous reform efforts has been their failure to engender more student effort.

A core attribute of sound character is self-discipline—and a core problem facing educators and reformers alike is indiscipline in the schools. How to address this has emerged as a key distinction between contemporary liberals and conservatives. The former tend to focus on whether disciplinary actions taken by schools are discriminatory, that is, they concentrate on the interests of the perpetrators—while the latter tend to focus on the interests of well-behaved learners whose education is being disrupted. Mac Donald's fine essay explains how overwrought concern with issues such as the race of those being disciplined ends up harming them as well as their schoolmates.

———

Third and finally, *let us build an education system that confers dignity, respect, and opportunity upon every youngster*, including those who don't go to college as well as those capable of zipping through it. Committed as we are to a solid, shared core in everyone's curriculum, we mustn't suppose that everyone is headed to the same destination or moving at the same speed. This is compatible with choice, too—a choice of pathways into adulthood as well as the velocity at which one will arrive there. While educational personalization ought not lead to Babel or the forfeiting of a shared body of common knowledge, young people truly differ. Some grasp skills and knowledge faster than others—and some grasp one or two subjects faster than other parts of the curriculum. Michael Barone's chapter describes how American education once did far better than it's been doing lately at educating gifted learners and urges renewed attention to the cultivation of that valuable human resource.

While students should be encouraged as early as middle school to consider an array of career options, certainly by the midpoint of high school it's important to open multiple pathways for them—and to make clear that these have equal merit. At least one such path should, of course, point toward traditional four-year colleges and universities. At least one should point toward community colleges and other sources of technical learning. And several should point toward true career readiness, perhaps through skilled apprenticeships, perhaps incorporating some form of postsecondary education. As both Ramesh Ponnuru and Arthur Brooks argue, America has overemphasized college-for-all at the expense of high-quality career education and other honorable alternatives, thereby (Brooks and coauthor Nathan Thompson note) robbing many people of the dignity, respect, and "neededness" that make for a healthy society.

More than cognition is entailed in forging a life of dignity, one deserving of respect and capable of seizing opportunity. Character, responsibility, and self-discipline reappear here too. Young people who adhere to the success sequence in their personal lives are far likelier to succeed in career terms too. Therefore, as Mona Charen and Ian Rowe explain in their chapters, it's incumbent on educators—as well as parents, policymakers, and the institutions of civil society—to do everything in their power to foster and encourage such adherence, even as they construct the several pathways into adulthood that lead to careers worth having.

———

We're not naïve. We don't expect all who view themselves as conservative to agree in full with our recommendations. Even were they all to do so, that mighty conservative army must still expect to lose many debates and policy battles at the local, state, and national levels. Leftist, Howard Zinn–style curricula will often continue to prevail over proper respect for America's history in all its wondrous complexity. Social-emotional learning and "action civics" will often swamp purposeful efforts at true character education and civic education. College-for-all and hostility to gifted-and-talented education will often win out over plural pathways and timely acceleration. Cries for social justice will often drown out calls for thoughtful patriotism.

But defeat is not inevitable—nor are conservatives weaponless in the education wars. Those who vigorously engage will win some debates and reasonable compromises will be forged in the heat of other debates. Many times, states, districts, and schools will find a way forward that takes the best ideas from left and right, rather than from the left alone. That's essentially what happened during the previous era of school reform, back when compromise was a way of getting important things done and bipartisanship wasn't a curse word.

Even now, in these fractured, fractious times, it can happen, occasionally even in Washington. The distinguished senior senator from Tennessee, author of this book's preface, himself a proud conservative and lifelong Republican, teamed up with Washington's Democratic Senator Patty Murray to pass both the Every Child Succeeds Act and, more recently, the latest iteration of the Perkins Act.

Yes, agreement and compromise remain possible today, even on Capitol Hill. But primary-secondary education has always been—and, as Lamar Alexander reminds us, will continue to be—chiefly the responsibility of states, districts, and individual schools, as well as teachers and parents. That's where most of the action happens, a fact that creates many different opportunities for reform and renewal. As we write, twenty-seven states have Republican governors, and sixty-one of ninety-nine state legislative chambers have GOP majorities. Conservatives with well-founded and persuasive ideas should often be able to prevail. But only if they engage—and if they're convincing when they explain how their proposals will benefit everyone's children.

As we do this, however, we ought to resist overpromising on what formal education alone can accomplish. As Nick Eberstadt explains in his chapter, for example, many adult men, long after exiting from school, are neither working nor seeking jobs, not primarily because they're poorly educated (though many are) but because of other worrisome forces in their lives and the life of the nation. Better K–12 education alone won't vanquish that problem, although higher standards, better career and technical education (including re-entry options for adults), and earlier attention to character and citizenship will help. So—as Meyerson and Kissel remind us—can private philanthropy and nongovernmental institutions.

Now and forever, parents are also key. Naomi Schaefer Riley points to the challenges children face when they have no functional parents—and the obligations this creates for others, including extraordinary schools. And Kay Hymowitz notes how the tendency of American parents (and many educators) to focus on children's individuality, self-expression, and creativity, while praiseworthy in some respects, contributes to a dearth of self-control, civility, and collaboration—the very traits that today's employers value at least as highly as literacy and numeracy.

That formal schooling can't do everything is a lesson that Americans across the political spectrum would do well to learn. We have too often laid on our children's schools the woes that plague adults, and have asked overburdened teachers to take care of them—drugs, AIDS, obesity, smoking, violence, racism, you name it—along with English, math, science, and history. We have too often sloughed onto classrooms the challenges that society otherwise has difficulty meeting. Conservatives need to be mindful of that, too, for it's truly tempting, yet utterly unrealistic and foolhardy, to suppose that "the schools will fix it"—and relieve others of the responsibility.

No, schools can't do it all by themselves. They need effective allies. Yet recognizing the limits of formal education also helps us focus on the essential obligations and distinctive capabilities of schooling itself. Supplying knowledge. Forging citizens. Forming strong character. Bestowing dignity. Placing those obligations front and center is what we have sought to accomplish in this volume—and what we need to accomplish for the sake of our children and the society they will inhabit.

That's how to educate an American.

About the Contributors

The Honorable Lamar Alexander is the senior US senator (R) from Tennessee. A former chair of the Senate Republican Conference, he now chairs the Health, Education, Labor, and Pensions Committee, and the Energy and Water Development Appropriations Subcommittee. A seventh-generation Tennessean, he was twice elected governor of Tennessee and has served as president of the University of Tennessee as well as US secretary of education under President George H. W. Bush. In 2016, he was the first recipient of the James Madison Award from the nation's governors in recognition of his efforts to fix the No Child Left Behind Act. The Every Student Succeeds Act (ESSA), the successor law that Alexander worked to pass, was signed by President Obama in 2015. Senator Alexander is also the author of five books.

Michael Barone is a senior political analyst at the *Washington Examiner* and a resident fellow at the American Enterprise Institute. The principal coauthor of *The Almanac of American Politics,* he has written for such publications as *The Economist,* the *New York Times,* and *National Review,* as well as serving many years as a member of the editorial-page staff of the *Washington Post* and senior writer at *US News.* Barone has authored a number of books, including *Our Country: The Shaping of America from Roosevelt to Reagan* (1990), *The New Americans: How the Melting Pot Can Work Again* (2001), *Hard America, Soft America: Competition vs. Coddling and the Competition for the Nation's Future* (2004), and most recently, *How America's Political Parties Change (and How They Don't)* (2019).

The Honorable William J. Bennett was chairman of the National Endowment for the Humanities and US secretary of education under President Ronald Reagan, then the nation's first drug czar, under President George H. W. Bush. An award-winning professor, he has taught at Boston University, the University of Texas, and Harvard. The recipient of more than thirty honorary degrees, he was formerly host of *Morning in America* and now hosts the podcast *The Bill Bennett Show.* He has written or coauthored more than two dozen books, including *The Book of Virtues: A Treasury of Great Moral Stories* (1993) and *Tried by Fire: The Story of Christianity's First Thousand Years* (2016), as well as *America: The Last Best Hope*, first published in 2012 and newly out in a one-volume edition.

Arthur C. Brooks is professor of the practice of public leadership at Harvard's Kennedy School of Government and senior fellow at the Harvard Business School. He recently concluded ten years as president of the American Enterprise Institute. Brooks is the author of eleven books, including the national bestsellers *Love Your Enemies* (2019), *The Conservative Heart* (2015), and *The Road to Freedom* (2012). He is a columnist for the *Washington Post*, host of the podcast *The Arthur Brooks Show*, and subject of the 2019 documentary film *The Pursuit.* A classical French hornist and former professor at Syracuse University, Brooks is a prolific commentator and speaker who also serves on the board of the Legatum Institute, a London-based think tank.

Mona Charen is a senior fellow at the Ethics and Public Policy Center and a nationally syndicated columnist and political analyst. She served in the White House as Nancy Reagan's speechwriter, associate director of the Office of Public Liaison, and later in the Public Affairs office, helping to craft President Ronald Reagan's communications strategy. She spent six years as a regular commentator on CNN's *Capital Gang* and *Capital Gang Sunday,* and has served as a Pulitzer Prizes judge. A previous fellow at the Hudson Institute and the Jewish Policy

Center, in 2010 she received the Eric Breindel Award for Excellence in Opinion Journalism. Her most recent book is *Sex Matters: How Modern Feminism Lost Touch with Science, Love, and Common Sense* (2018).

Eliot A. Cohen is dean and Robert E. Osgood Professor of Strategic Studies at the Johns Hopkins University School of Advanced International Studies. He has served as a military intelligence officer in the US Army Reserve and as a member of the Defense Policy Advisory Board and the National Security Advisory Panel of the National Intelligence Council, as well as the Council of the International Institute for Strategic Studies and the Committee on Studies of the Council on Foreign Relations. He was counselor of the Department of State during the George W. Bush administration. He is adjunct senior fellow at the Center for a New American Security and has served as adjunct professor at the US Army War College. His latest book is *The Big Stick: The Limits of Soft Power and the Necessity of Military Force* (2017). His articles have appeared in numerous scholarly and popular publications, including the *Washington Post*, *Wall Street Journal*, and *New York Times*, and he is a contributing editor at *The Atlantic*.

William Damon is professor of education at Stanford University, where he directs the Center on Adolescence. A senior fellow at the Hoover Institution, he is also an elected fellow of the American Academy of Arts and Sciences, the National Academy of Education, and the American Educational Research Association. He has received awards and grants from the Carnegie Corporation of New York, the Andrew Mellon Foundation, the John Templeton Foundation, the William and Flora Hewlett Foundation, the John D. and Catherine T. MacArthur Foundation, the Spencer Foundation, and the Pew Charitable Trusts. Damon's current work focuses on vocational, civic, and entrepreneurial purpose among the young and on purpose in families and schools. His most recent books are *The Power of Ideals* (2016) and *Failing Liberty 101* (2011).

Nicholas Eberstadt holds the Henry Wendt Chair in Political Economy at the American Enterprise Institute, where he writes extensively on demographics and economic development as well as international security in the Korean Peninsula and Asia. Domestically, he focuses on poverty and social well-being. A recipient of the 2012 Bradley Prize, Eberstadt is also a senior adviser to the National Bureau of Asian Research. His most recent book is *Men Without Work: America's Invisible Crisis* (2016). Previous works include *Poverty in China* (1979), *The Tyranny of Numbers* (1995), *The End of North Korea* (1999), *The Poverty of the Poverty Rate* (2008), and *Russia's Peacetime Demographic Crisis* (2010). Eberstadt is a frequent commentator on demographic and economic issues and has on multiple occasions testified before Congress and advised government agencies.

Chester E. Finn, Jr. is a distinguished senior fellow and president emeritus at the Thomas B. Fordham Institute, and senior fellow at Stanford's Hoover Institution. Finn served as Fordham's president from 1997 to 2014, after many earlier roles in education, academe, and government, including assistant secretary for research and improvement and counselor to the secretary at the US Department of Education. Finn has served on numerous boards, including the National Assessment Governing Board (which he chaired), the Maryland State Board of Education, and that state's Commission on Innovation and Excellence in Education. He's currently a board member of the National Council on Teacher Quality and Core Knowledge Foundation. Author of hundreds of articles and over twenty books, Finn's most recent (as coauthor) is *Learning in the Fast Lane: The Past, Present, and Future of Advanced Placement* (2019).

Robert P. George is McCormick Professor of Jurisprudence and director of the James Madison Program in American Ideals and Institutions at Princeton University and a frequent visiting professor at Harvard Law School. He has served as chair of the US Commission on International Religious Freedom and the President's Council on Bioethics. He serves on the boards of the John M. Templeton Foundation Religion Trust, the Lynde and Harry Bradley Foundation, the Ethics and Public Policy Center, the Becket Fund for Religious Liberty, the National Center on Sexual Exploitation, and the Center for Individual Rights. He is a past member of the US Commission on Civil Rights and UNESCO's World Commission on the Ethics of Science and Technology. A former judicial fellow at the Supreme Court of the United States, George has authored and edited numerous articles and books. His most recent book (as coauthor) is *Mind, Heart, and Soul: Intellectuals and the Path to Rome* (2018).

Jonah Goldberg is the Asness Chair in Applied Liberty at the American Enterprise Institute and a fellow at the National Review Institute. A longtime editor of *National Review*, he has been a weekly columnist for the *Los Angeles Times* since 2005 and nationally syndicated since 2000. He hosts the podcast *The Remnant with Jonah Goldberg*. His most recent book, *Suicide of the West: How the Rebirth of Tribalism, Populism, Nationalism, and Identity Politics Is Destroying American Democracy* (2018), was a *New York Times* bestseller. Previous books include *Liberal Fascism* (2008) and *The Tyranny of Clichés* (2012).

Kay S. Hymowitz is the William E. Simon Fellow at the Manhattan Institute and a contributing editor of *City Journal*. She writes extensively on childhood, family issues, poverty, and cultural change in America. Her books include *The New Brooklyn: What It Takes to Bring a City Back* (2017), *Manning Up: How the Rise of Women Has Turned Men into Boys* (2011), *Marriage and Caste in America: Separate and Unequal Families in a Post-Marital Age* (2006), and *Liberation's Children: Parents and Kids in a Postmodern Age* (2004). A member of the publication committee of *National Affairs*, she has also written for the *New York Times, Washington Post, Wall Street Journal, New Republic, New York Newsday,* the *Public Interest,* the *Wilson Quarterly,* and *Commentary.*

Adam Kissel is director of civic and higher education programs at the Philanthropy Roundtable and a visiting scholar at American University. His work in higher education has included teaching, writing, research, philanthropy, government service, and defense of academic freedom and individual rights for professors and students. He previously served as deputy assistant secretary for higher education programs at the US Department of Education.

Yuval Levin is a resident scholar and director of social, cultural, and constitutional studies at the American Enterprise Institute and the founding editor of *National Affairs*. He is also a senior editor of the *New Atlantis* and a contributing editor to *National Review*. Levin studies the foundations of self-government and the future of law, regulation, and constitutionalism, as well as American social, political, and civic life, while focusing on the preconditions necessary for family, community, and country to flourish. He served as a member of the White House domestic policy staff under President George W. Bush and is the author of several books on political theory and public policy, most recently *The Fractured Republic: Renewing America's Social Contract in the Age of Individualism* (2016). Forthcoming is *A Time to Build: From Family and Community to Congress and the Campus, How Recommitting to Our Institutions Can Revive the American Dream.*

Heather Mac Donald is the Thomas W. Smith Fellow at the Manhattan Institute, a contributing editor of *City Journal*, and a *New York Times* bestselling author. Her writing has also appeared in the *Wall Street Journal, Washington Post, New York Times, Los Angeles Times, New Republic,* and *New Criterion.* A 2005 recipient of the Bradley Prize, her work has covered a range of topics, including higher education, immigration, policing, homelessness and homeless advocacy, criminal-justice reform, and race relations. Mac Donald's most recent book is *The Diversity Delusion: How Race and Gender Pandering Corrupt the University and Undermine Our Culture* (2018). Previous works include *The War on Cops* (2016) and *The Burden of Bad Ideas* (2001).

Adam Meyerson has been president of the Philanthropy Roundtable since 2001. The Roundtable is America's largest association of foundations and charitable givers committed to the protection of donor intent, the preservation of philanthropic freedom, and the advancement of liberty, opportunity, and personal responsibility through philanthropic giving. Previous positions include vice president for educational affairs at the Heritage Foundation, where he also served as editor-in-chief of *Policy Review*. He has also been an editorial writer at the *Wall Street Journal*. Meyerson chairs the board of the Donors Capital Fund and serves on the board of the State Policy Network.

The Honorable Rod Paige is a lifelong educator and former US secretary of education (2001–2005) under President George W. Bush. As secretary, Dr. Paige was an unstinting advocate of raising student achievement, employing "best of breed" solutions to achieve results toward the department's goal of raising national expectations of educational excellence. He has also served as a trustee and then as superintendent of the Houston Independent School District. Dr. Paige is an active member of several boards, including the Thomas B. Fordham Institute, and has served as a public policy fellow at the Woodrow Wilson International Center for Scholars. He holds two honorary degrees and previously served as interim president of Jackson State University, his alma mater.

Michael J. Petrilli is president of the Thomas B. Fordham Institute, research fellow at Stanford University's Hoover Institution, executive editor of *Education Next*, and a Distinguished Senior Fellow at the Education Commission of the States. An award-winning writer, he is the author of *The Diverse Schools Dilemma* (2014) and editor of *Education for Upward Mobility* (2015). He has published opinion pieces in the *New York Times*, *Washington Post*, *Wall Street Journal*, *Bloomberg View*, and *Slate*. Petrilli helped to create the US Department of Education's Office of Innovation and Improvement and the Policy Innovators in Education Network. He serves on the advisory boards of the Association of

American Educators, MDRC, and the National Association of Charter School Authorizers.

Ramesh Ponnuru is a columnist and senior editor for *National Review*, a visiting fellow at the American Enterprise Institute, a columnist for *Bloomberg View*, and a contributing editor to *National Affairs*. He has written on a range of political and policy topics for many publications and appeared on numerous public affairs and news programs, including *Meet the Press, Face the Nation*, and the *PBS News Hour*. A widely respected voice on conservative policy, his books include *The Party of Death: The Democrats, the Media, the Courts, and the Disregard for Human Life* (2006) and (with Yuval Levin) *Room to Grow: Conservative Reforms for a Limited Government and a Thriving Middle Class* (2014).

Naomi Schaefer Riley is a resident fellow at the American Enterprise Institute focusing on issues regarding child welfare as well as a senior fellow at the Independent Women's Forum. She also writes about parenting, higher education, religion, philanthropy, and culture. A former columnist for the *New York Post* and former *Wall Street Journal* editor and writer, she's the author of six books, including *Be the Parent: Stop Banning Seesaws and Start Banning Snapchat* (2018) and *Til Faith Do Us Part: How Interfaith Marriage is Transforming America* (2013). Her writing has also appeared in such publications as the *New York Times, Boston Globe, Los Angeles Times*, and *Washington Post*. Riley appears regularly on Fox News, Fox Business, and CNBC.

Ian Rowe is CEO of Public Prep, a network of single-sex charter schools in New York City. A proud product of that city's public school system, Rowe is a social entrepreneur and leader who has worked for more than twenty years in the public, private, and nonprofit sectors to effect positive change in the lives of young people worldwide. Prior to Public Prep, he served as deputy director of postsecondary success at the Bill and Melinda Gates Foundation, and senior vice president of strategic partnerships and public affairs at MTV, where he helped develop global and domestic media campaigns aimed at young people.

Nathan Thompson is a former research assistant at the American Enterprise Institute, where he studied institutional and leadership applications of behavioral social science research. He holds a BA in economics and political science from Furman University, as well as an MSc in international relations from the London School of Economics and Political Science.

Peter Wehner is a contributing opinion writer for the *New York Times* and vice president and senior fellow at the Ethics and Public Policy Center. Also a contributing editor for *The Atlantic,* he served in the Ronald Reagan and George H. W. Bush administrations prior to becoming deputy director of speechwriting for President George W. Bush. His most recent book is *The Death of Politics: How to Heal Our Frayed Republic after Trump* (2019). Wehner has also written for many other publications—including *Time*, the *Wall Street Journal*, *Washington Post*, *Financial Times*, and *Weekly Standard*, and he appears frequently as a commentator on MSNBC, CNN, Fox News, CBS, PBS, and C-SPAN.

Index